A WORLD OF INSECURITY

KA

Cor
Anthro
EDITED B
AND CRIS

Culture and
Anthropolog
Freedom and
EDITED BY ALBER

Anthropology, Culture and Society

Series Editors:
Professor Vered Amit, Concordia University
and
Dr Jon P. Mitchell, University of Sussex

Published titles include:

A WORLD OF INSECURITY

Anthropological Perspectives on Human Security

Edited by
Thomas Hylland Eriksen, Ellen Bal and Oscar Salemink

PlutoPress
www.plutobooks.com

First published 2010 by Pluto Press
345 Archway Road, London N6 5AA and
175 Fifth Avenue, New York, NY 10010

www.plutobooks.com

Distributed in the United States of America exclusively by
Palgrave Macmillan, a division of St. Martin's Press LLC,
175 Fifth Avenue, New York, NY 10010

British Library Cataloguing in Publication Data
A catalogue record for this book is available from the British Library

ISBN   978 0 7453 2985 7   Hardback
ISBN   978 0 7453 2984 0   Paperback

Library of Congress Cataloging in Publication Data applied for

10   9   8   7   6   5   4   3   2   1

Designed and produced for Pluto Press by
Chase Publishing Services Ltd, 33 Livonia Road, Sidmouth, EX10 9JB England
Typeset from disk by Stanford DTP Services, Northampton, England
Printed and bound in the European Union by
CPI Antony Rowe, Chippenham and Eastbourne

Contents

PART III: STATES OF (IN)SECURITY

Series Preface

Anthropology is a discipline based upon in-depth ethnographic works that deal with wider theoretical issues in the context of particular, local conditions – to paraphrase an important volume from the series: *large issues* explored in *small places*. The series has a particular mission: to publish work that moves away from old-style descriptive ethnography – that is strongly area-studies oriented – and offer genuine theoretical arguments that are of interest to a much wider readership but which are nevertheless located and grounded in solid ethnographic research. If anthropology is to argue itself a place in the contemporary intellectual world then it must surely be through such research.

We start from the question: 'What can this ethnographic material tell us about the bigger theoretical issues that concern the social sciences', rather than 'What can these theoretical ideas tell us about the ethnographic context'. Put this way round, such work becomes *about* large issues, *set in* a (relatively) small place, rather than detailed description of a small place for its own sake. As Clifford Geertz once said: 'Anthropologists don't study villages; they study *in* villages.'

By place we mean not only geographical locale, but also other types of 'place' – within political, economic, religious or other social systems. We therefore publish work based on ethnography within political and religious movements, occupational or class groups, youth, development agencies, nationalists; but also work that is more thematically based – on kinship, landscape, the state, violence, corruption, the self. The series publishes four kinds of volume – ethnographic monographs; comparative texts; edited collections; and shorter, polemic essays.

We publish work from all traditions of anthropology, and all parts of the world, which combines theoretical debate with empirical evidence to demonstrate anthropology's unique position in contemporary scholarship and the contemporary world.

Professor Vered Amit
Dr Jon P. Mitchell

1
Human Security and Social Anthropology

Thomas Hylland Eriksen

Theoretical concepts go in and out of fashion so discreetly as to be almost unnoticed in the social sciences. For a hundred years, Herbert Spencer's conceptual pair, structure and function, was *de rigueur*, even if the definition shifted somewhat, although not as much as the term 'race'. Spencer's pair of concepts can now finally be proclaimed dead as a dodo, half a century after the fruition of Talcott Parsons' ambitious structural-functionalist theory of society – at the time familiar to every sociologist and many other social scientists, today ignored by everyone except the historians of the discipline. The 1960s and 1970s saw the phenomenal resuscitation of the entire menu of century-old Marxist terms – surplus value, infrastructure, contradiction, Asian mode of production and so on – but apart from a handful of Marxist words which have deservedly entered the everyday language (such as ideology and exploitation), this jargon has become virtually obsolete again. 'Culture', used in the anthropological sense, has been with us for over 130 years now, since Tylor, but many shift uneasily in their seats whenever it is used without a ritual invocation of inverted commas.

THE CONCEPT OF HUMAN SECURITY

The key concept in this book, 'security', is not a technical term and can therefore, being part of everyday language, be expected to outlive most more specialised terms. Even with the rather vacuous qualifier 'human' ahead, the term is almost impossibly vague and wide-ranging. Introduced as an applied social science term by the United Nations Development Programme (UNDP) in one of its annual Human Development Reports (UNDP 1994), the term 'human security' is meant to humanise strategic studies, to anchor development research in locally experienced realities, and to offer a tool to gauge the ways societies function seen from the perspective of their inhabitants.

Attempts to clarify the meaning of the concept, to operationalise it for use in empirical research, have been met with hostility and scepticism among some scholars, while others defend its place in the analytical vocabulary of the social sciences (see Alkire 2002, and the debate in *Security Dialogue* 2004). Some deem it hopelessly fuzzy and impossible to use in actual research; others have claimed that it adds little to extant terminology. It could nonetheless be argued, and in this book we do argue, that the term 'human security' has an important job to do in reorienting social theory and building bridges between the different social sciences. In social anthropology, it may in fact turn out to be a concept which has been needed for some time, a concept that can enable anthropologists to update and rephrase some of the classic problems of the subject without bringing in the excess baggage from functionalist thinking, notably the problems to do with social cohesion and integration, stability and collective identity. The eclectic methodology of contemporary social anthropology moreover makes it eminently suited to grapple with a multi-stranded concept like the one of human security. Anthropologists collect their data in both systematic and unsystematic ways, and may regard a passing anecdote or a chance event as being just as valuable as the results of structured interviews. We relate to media, statistics and history writing; we collect life stories and sit in at public meetings and rituals; and we do our best, within the bounds of ethical guidelines and common decency, to peek over our informants' shoulders to see what they are up to when they think nobody is watching. Unlike many other scientists, anthropologists impose rigour on their material largely during analysis, not during data collection. As the late Eric Wolf famously said, anthropology is 'the most scientific of the humanities, the most humanist of the sciences' (1964: 11).

What anthropologists look for when they sift and sort their diverse materials, are indications of patterns and regularities which can enable them to weave their strands into a tapestry. Asking for the ways in which people under different circumstances strive for security, and conversely identifying the factors that render them insecure, may offer a promising framework for future anthropological research. Using human security as a unifying concept for a variety of research projects, which we have endeavoured to do in this book, can help to counter internal fragmentation and to redirect theory in necessary directions. Donna Winslow notes that: 'the human security approach parallels the shift in economic development and international law from instrumental objectives (such as growth, or state rights) to human development and human rights' (2003: 5). From the viewpoint of the anthropologist, this reads like a shift from the harder sciences of economics to the kind of qualitative approaches we represent.

Although the concept of human security, as it is currently used in the worlds of development studies and peace and conflict research, was introduced as late as the mid 1990s, it can be used to address questions which are as old as the social sciences themselves. The modern social sciences grew out of the frictions and tensions arising from the Industrial Revolution in Europe and North America in the nineteenth century, and questions to do with insecurity were at the core of the early grand theories. Marx famously spoke of alienation under capitalism, and Ferdinand Tönnies introduced the dichotomy between the tight moral community – the *Gemeinschaft* – and the loose, anonymous society – the *Gesellschaft*. Almost every leading theorist had his own foundational dichotomy between traditional or collectivist societies on the one hand, and modern or individualist societies on the other. The human security theorist *par excellence* was nevertheless Émile Durkheim, whose entire *oeuvre* gravitates around a deeply seated anxiety that modernity may entail a loss of societal cohesion because of its pluralism, individualism and fast pace of change.

The first generations of social scientists, especially those lacking first-hand knowledge, portrayed traditional societies in a somewhat romanticising, stylised way owing much to Rousseau, assuming that life in closely knit, kinship-based societies was predictable and stable, unburdened with existential doubt and disruptive challenges to tradition and authority. However, already the first generation of fieldworking anthropologists, who began to publish just after the First World War, described societies which did not seem to fit this view. Life in the Melanesian societies studied by the likes of Bronislaw Malinowski and Reo Fortune seemed profoundly insecure; people appeared to live in perennial fear of either witchcraft attacks or witchcraft accusations, and there were status anxieties associated with political power, gifting obligations towards relatives and economic uncertainties. Anthropologists describing the lives of small, tightly knit groups in Africa, Melanesia and South America show, sometimes inadvertently, that they live in a state of almost continuous anxiety. Anything from warring neighbouring tribes to poisonous snakes or crop failure could put their lives in jeopardy any day of the year.

If we move to more hierarchical, complex societies of the kind customarily studied by anthropologists, they also seem to offer little more in the way of security for their members. It is sometimes said of Egyptians that they tend to die of anxiety in middle age, usually connected with money problems, more specifically an almost chronic inability to look after their relatives economically. Ethnographies from India show that many Indian women live in constant fear of male violence, men worry deeply about dowry payments for their daughters and a thousand lesser expenses, and that everybody fears downward mobility, whether individual or collective.

Security naturally refers to much more than this – and this could be said to be the strength and the weakness of the concept. Most individuals are, presumably, secure in some respects and insecure in others. In official documents from the UN Commission for Human Security, 'freedom from want and freedom from fear' are stressed as common denominators of the concept (UNDP 1994, cf. Alkire 2002). However, if we are to take this delineation in a literal sense, it must in all fairness be pointed out that every society – even the most stable and well-organised one – has its own wants and fears.

Every society, group and individual on earth has its way of dealing with questions of human security. Nobody is immune. Non-believers often assume that religious people have a greater existential security than they do themselves, but such a generalisation is unwarranted. If one belongs to a religion with a notion of hell, or divine intervention, or both, then one had better mind one's step.

Moreover, it is often assumed that insecurity is more pronounced in the global era than it was formerly, given the fundamental vulnerability, the proliferation of risks, the environmental crisis, AIDS, the alienating individualism of neoliberalism, fears of terrorist attacks or outbreaks of war, or the loss of faith in canonical tradition, including religious salvation and protection from supernatural entities, that are assumed to accompany this era. A cursory look at the historical and ethnographic records does not support this view. The risk of being the victim of a terrorist attack for a citizen of Amsterdam in the early twenty-first century can safely be assumed to be much less than the risk of being bitten by a poisonous snake for an Azande in the 1920s. The threats of starvation, disease and war in the poorer countries, horrible as they are, were unlikely to be much less in pre-modern times than is the case today, although their impact was for obvious reasons different.

THIS BOOK

This volume engages with two distinct bodies of literature, one of which is limited in volume and recent in history, while the other is huge and has a long, distinguished past. The first is, of course, the restricted, but growing literature on human security. Most writings on human security tend to be narrowly policy-oriented and strongly focused on insecurities rather than security itself. Moreover, in spite of programmatic statements about placing people first, analyses of human security – often written by political scientists and macro-sociologists – tend to focus on the national and international levels. This book, by contrast, directly addresses questions concerning how people create a situation of (relative) security, and how various dimensions of human security – economic, political, existential, environmental – interact.

The anthropology of human security, as it is developed in this book, aims to combine the classic concerns of anthropology with cohesion, agency and power, with an appreciation of the transnational dimension in contemporary lives. The contributors thereby move beyond both the nostalgia implicit in some of the globalisation literature, as well as the old-style cultural relativism which tacitly assumes that wholly traditional lives are preferable to partly modernised ones.

Creating secure lives in a complex, turbulent world entails hard work. Security-building activities are confronted with risks, some of them transnational; with insecurities associated with war, environmental problems, crime, etc.; and also with individualisation and ideological tendencies favouring individual freedom at the expense of sacrificing security (see Bauman 2001). However, unlike comments on the 'postmodern condition', which argue that contemporary lives are bound to be fragmented and 'liquid', this book shows how much people are willing to invest in security.

The contributors to this book also indicate a wide range of factors militating against security and, accordingly, the many ways in which people living under different circumstances make efforts to strengthen their sense of security.

For convenience, this book has been divided into three parts, although themes necessarily interact and overlap. The first four chapters, following this introduction, concentrate on the political economy of human security, indicating a framework where state politics, popular resistance, market forces and the material struggle for survival interact. The next four chapters focus on the existential dimensions of human security, often summarised under the general heading of identity, looking largely but not exclusively at majority/minority relationships. The final section, comprising three chapters, emphasises the varying role of state power and social planning in creating conditions for (in)security.

In the opening chapter of Part 1, Ton Salman, writing about popular protests in Bolivia, describes a common dilemma: although public protest was risky in Bolivia before the election of Evo Morales in 2006, it was nonetheless perceived as a 'lesser evil' when compared to the government's policies, which placed much of the population in an extremely precarious economic situation. Salman thus shows that people are not necessarily obsessed with security in the sense of safety, but may expose themselves to considerable dangers in order to enhance their long-term security.

Writing from Morocco, Bernhard Venema analyses the economics of ethnicity and state power. The development of a capitalist market for land and produce in the Middle Atlas has made the local Berbers' economic situation precarious and unstable. Venema shows how appeals to religion and tradition have strengthened the local communities, often in ways inimical to the state's aims, and rarely with clear economic benefits, but giving the tribal members a sense of continuity and belonging.

Concluding Part 1 on the political economy of human security, Marjo de Theije and Ellen Bal argue, in their chapter about Brazilian goldminers in Suriname, that while taking apparently extreme physical risks, the goldminers nonetheless make short-term investments in trust and, in the longer term, believe in material security as a compensation for the risks taken.

The second part on security, identity and belonging opens with Ellen Bal and Kathinka Sinha-Kerkhoff's chapter about the reflexive identity work engaged in by Hindustanis (local term for people of Indian descent) in Suriname and in the Netherlands. The Dutch-Hindustanis are doubly removed from their ancestral land, having undertaken two intercontinental migrations in historical memory. The chapter is about existential security, threatened by alienation and a sense of insecurity.

Edien Bartels and her co-authors, also writing from the Netherlands, continue the discussion of cultural identity as a dimension of security, showing how minority identities may enhance the internal sense of security in the group, but may lead to anxieties and (subjectively experienced) insecurity in greater society. Both majorities and minorities are inclined to feel insecure about their belonging and sense of identification in contemporary Western European societies.

Lenie Brouwer's field is a working-class and minority-dense area in Amsterdam, where local authorities have set up Internet and other computer facilities for the citizens in an effort to empower them and facilitate their participation in the wider society. By discussing how the clients at a digital centre use ICT to enhance their integration in Dutch society, Brouwer shows how security and freedom (in the sense of autonomy) can be two sides of the same coin, even if in other contexts they may be mutually opposed.

With André Droogers' chapter on Pomeranian Lutheran migrants in Brazil, the focus moves away from Western Europe, but the issues of identity and existential security remain salient. Working with historical as well as contemporary materials, Droogers demonstrates the crucial role of the German Lutheran Church in creating a sense of cultural continuity for the 'Teuto-Brazilians' historically, and how the group has tried to find new sources of collective identity when the German identity became politically problematic during the twentieth century. Like several of the other contributors, Droogers emphasises belonging and collective organisation as conditions for security.

Opening the third part on states of (in)security, Marion den Uyl analyses policy and ethnicity in Bijlmermeer, an Amsterdam neighbourhood built in the 1970s as a 'model suburb' but today largely inhabited by minorities and seen by the city authorities as a problem area. Drawing on the concepts of trust and social capital, den Uyl suggests that security is unevenly distributed in Bijlmermeer, and that the character of the social networks inside and outside of the area, not the built environment itself, account for the high levels of insecurity. Demolition and rebuilding is, in a word, unlikely to help.

Sandra Evers, writing about the precariousness of everyday life in the Seychelles, is concerned with the ways in which the Seychellois state has used an official security discourse as a pretext for limiting people's personal freedom, and how the result has in fact been an extremely insecure situation for most Seychellois. The government, she writes, has even tried to monopolise Seychellois memory and history. Evers' analysis shows how limitations on individual freedom may threaten security, and is complementary to Salman's perspective in illuminating ways.

Dick Kooiman's chapter about the precarious situation of princely states in India on the eve of Independence (1947) shows, as a useful contrast to Evers' analysis of an omnipresent political power, how former rulers deprived of political power may concentrate their efforts on the ritual and ceremonial aspects of their powerless office, thereby creating a sense of continuity and security among themselves and their followers. It would arguably not be too far-fetched to note the similarities with the ceremonial monarchies of Western Europe, which symbolise continuity in a world otherwise marked with change and lack of predictability.

Finally, also starting with a focus on the symbolic and ritual dimension of security, in his wide-ranging analysis of spiritual healing in Vietnam, Oscar Salemink moves towards a demonstration of the interrelationship between existential security, physical (health) security and economic security. Where the state and market are unable to deliver credible solutions to such anxieties, spirit mediums seem better equipped to deal with the totality of Vietnamese's insecurities.

SECURITY AND BELONGING

Security and belonging in the whirlwind of the contemporary world are common themes in all the chapters of this book, in spite of their empirical diversity and differing emphases. Although people in a traditional past may have been no more secure in their lives than we are – in many cases they were far less secure – at least they tended to belong to a community by default. Nobody challenged their group membership, they knew who to turn to in times of need and scarcity, and they had relatively clear notions of the nature of the moral universe in which they lived. When contemporary social theorists speak of our era as somehow more insecure than the past, this is roughly what they tend to have in mind. Zygmunt Bauman's *liquid modernity* (2000) concerns the floating, shifting qualities of values and social structure in our era; Ulrich Beck's *risk society* (1992 [1986]) emphasises the growth of man-made risks, which have become incalculable in their consequences; and Anthony Giddens' term *post-traditional society* (1991) describes a society where a tradition can no longer be taken for granted, but must actively be defended vis-à-vis its alternatives, which had now become visible. These concepts, and the analyses underpinning them, suggest that the research questions raised by Durkheim and his collaborators a century ago, concerning the conditions of social integration and the human consequences of social disintegration, remain more relevant than ever before. The chapters in this book, briefly summarised above, speak for themselves. Allow me to add some personal thoughts.

Henrik Ibsen's plays from the latter third of the nineteenth century are widely respected for their psychological depth and their accurate depiction of profound contradictions in the bourgeois family of pre-First World War Europe. However, in some important ways his earlier plays *Brand* and *Peer Gynt* (Ibsen 1972 [1867–68]) speak more directly to the sensibilities of the early twenty-first century than the dramas dealing with late nineteenth-century bourgeois society. *Brand*, arguably Ibsen's first masterpiece, was a play about a Protestant fundamentalist despairing at the moral decay and confusion he saw all around him, and his attempts to bracket off his own existence and that of his flock of faithful, from the surrounding turmoil. His attempt to escape from modernity can be described as an attempt to create a controlled space where all questions could be answered, a community which was predictable and morally consistent. Brand is a puritan in the literal sense of the term; he seeks purity and simplicity. By contrast, the protagonist of Ibsen's next play, *Peer Gynt*, is an entrepreneur and an adventurer who lies and cheats his way across the world, who makes a small fortune in the, by then illicit, slave trade, who poses as a prophet in North Africa and as a cosmopolitan gentleman on the Mediterranean coast, before returning to his native mountain valley only to discover that his personality lacks a core. The struggles involving collective identification in the contemporary era, with which much of my research for nearly twenty years has incidentally been concerned, revolve around the questions raised by Ibsen in the 1860s. 'Be who you are/fully and wholly/not piecemeal and divided,' proclaims Brand, a prophet not only of evangelical Christianity but also of the integrity of the person. Peer Gynt, for his part, boasts of having received impulses from all over the world, introducing himself in the fourth act as a 'Norwegian by birth, but citizen of the world in spirit'. Whereas Brand can be said to inhabit a closed universe, Peer Gynt's universe lacks boundaries. The two characters cover, between them, the span between fundamentalism and collectivism on the one hand, and voluntarism and individualism on the other. Brand stands for security, while Peer stands for freedom and insecurity. The contrast between the two, and attempts to stake out third ways, are part and parcel of the experience of the children of immigrants in Western Europe, to mention just one contemporary parallel. Notwithstanding the chapters in this book, which show that freedom presupposes security and vice versa, in this kind of context it is easy to see that the two need not always be complementary, but can be opposing in an either-or way.

In order to begin to understand security in the sense of social belonging, we first have to consider *personhood*. I first realised this, belatedly, when some years ago I was writing a book about identity politics (Eriksen 2004), realising one day that I had passed far too lightly over the groundwork of studying the foundations of any kind of identity, that is the person.

The Latin term *persona* originally meant mask, which indicates that personal identity is shifting and can be treacherous (cf. Mauss 1960). Life is a stage (Shakespeare), and personality is like an onion – layer upon layer, but with no core (Ibsen). When all the layers of make-up and make-believe are peeled away, do we then encounter the real person – or do we instead meet a faceless monster? The answer from social science is: neither. Even 'real persons' have to play out their realness through an identity which is recognisable to others. He or she must possess a linguistic identity, for example. The phantasmagoric point zero, where the 'real person' coalesces with the faceless one, is tantamount to autism. There is no 'other person' behind the social person (see Morris 1994 for a full treatment).

Personal identity is shaped through social experiences. Some of them are easily forgotten, some can be interpreted to fit a present state one wants to belong to (it is never too late to obtain a tragic history or a happy childhood if one really needs one), some may be more or less fictional, and yet others cannot be modified at all. In this sense, personal biographies are reminiscent of national historiography and religious myths of origin. Personal experiences are as malleable as national histories, neither more nor less. They can attach us to a great number of different communities based on gender, class, place, political persuasion, literary taste, sexual orientation, national identity, religion and so on. Yet they cannot be bent indefinitely; certain facts about ourselves are unchangeable. One can deny them, but they keep returning – as the ageing Peer Gynt discovers in the final act. As Bob Marley once put it: 'You can't run away from yourself.'

Peer tries to do just this, and he sacrifices existential security on the altar of unfettered freedom; Brand does the opposite. A parallel to the contrast between Peer Gynt and Brand is found in a metaphor used among some West African peoples. In describing what a person is they compare it with a tortoise. It may stick its head out, making itself visible and vulnerable, but it then retracts its head into the shell, rendering itself hidden and invincible. This metaphor seems to travel well into the world of mass media and reality TV, that infamous Dutch invention. Some of our contemporary tortoises prefer to stay inside their shells most of the time, while others live almost continuously with their heads stuck out for all to see.

SECURE AND INSECURE SOCIALITY

What the tortoise metaphor does *not* claim, is that there exists an insulated, pure self in the inner recesses of the individual, a self which is independent of its surroundings. Such a creature is, besides, difficult to envision. For example, we depend on thinking through linguistic categories, and if we should usually keep our thoughts to ourselves, at least we share them with a few confidantes. The metaphor of the tortoise, transposed to contemporary modern societies, is best understood as stating that human beings switch between being socially extroverted and directed towards the open, uncertain external world, and being socially introverted, limited to that which is secure and familiar. It deals not so much with the internal life of the individual as with two forms of sociality; the secure and the insecure, the closed and the open.

Secure sociality moves in a sphere of undisputed we-feeling. In this realm one may be *backstage*; one can speak one's dialect, laugh at in-jokes, savour the smells of one's childhood and know that one has an intuitive, embodied cultural competence which one succeeds in performing without even trying. In a field of secure sociality, everyone is predictable to each other, and if they are not, there are ways of demarcating displeasure which are immediately understood by others. A relaxed intimacy engulfs secure sociality. It is related to Tönnies' concept of *Wesenswille*, which in his view characterised life in the *Gemeinschaft*, that traditional community where everybody knew each other and had a limited horizon of opportunities. The *Wesenswille* recommends itself, it makes us behave along certain lines without asking critical questions.

Insecure sociality is, to a much greater extent, characterised by improvisation and negotiations over situational definitions. People who encounter one another in this kind of field are much less secure as to whom they are dealing with and, as a result, they are less sure as to who they are looking at in the mirror. The opportunities are more varied and more open to a person in a state of insecure sociality than to someone who rests contented in a condition of predictable routines of secure sociality, but the risks are also much greater.

Insecure sociality appears, typically, in cosmopolitan cities, along trade routes and – especially after the Industrial Revolution – in societies undergoing rapid change. Suddenly, something new happens, and one finds oneself in a setting with no preordained script to be followed. One is faced with the task of rebuilding the ship at sea.

A typical reaction to this kind of insecurity is withdrawal, but it is equally common to try to redefine the situation to make it resemble something familiar. When Columbus became the first European to set foot in the Caribbean, he was convinced that he had reached India. Later conquistadors were aware that they had arrived in a country which had not been described in the Bible, that is an entirely new land with unknown and undescribed inhabitants. Many of them still tried to interpret their experiences through biblical inter-pretations. In *The Conquest of America*, Tzvetan Todorov (1989) shows that the Aztecs and the Spaniards interpreted each other into their respective pre-existent world-views. Neither group was ready to acknowledge that something entirely new had entered their world, which required new cognitive maps or even an intellectual revolution. In a word, they were not yet modern.

IS INSECURITY NECESSARILY BAD?

The work amounting to making insecure situations secure takes many shapes. Imperialist powers may try to reshape their new lands to make them less threateningly different, or they erect physical boundaries against those they perceive as aliens, as the architects of apartheid did in South Africa and Israel is doing presently. Dominated peoples may either try to imitate their rulers in order to mitigate the sense of insecurity on both sides, or else establish their own boundaries – through separatism, revolution or seeking independence.

Is insecurity a good or a bad thing? That depends. In social anthropological theory, different terms are being used, which provide different answers to the question. Mary Douglas (1966), who belongs to a tradition focusing on the study of social integration and assuming it to be a good thing, regards departures from the existing order as *anomalies*. They are cumbersome since they do not fit in. Many persons who appear as anomalies, besides, become anomic, that is, normless – alienated, confused and unhappy. In the view of Douglas' great intellectual mentor Durkheim (2002 [1899]), anomie was an important cause of suicide.

An opposite approach is found in the early work of Fredrik Barth (1963), who, in the early 1960s, directed a research programme about the entrepreneur in northern Norway. According to Barth's definition, the entrepreneur was someone who bridged formerly discrete spheres; who found new commodities to sell in new locations, new ways of running a business, new niches and so on. He thrived on uncertainty and change. In his purest form, Barth's entrepreneur was a Peer Gynt; poorly integrated into the moral community, but hardly a candidate for suicide. It may perhaps be said that the entrepreneur fares like everybody else in the age of neoliberalism, which values freedom so highly but neglects security: whenever one has success, the range of options and the scope of personal freedom feel fantastic, but the moment one hits the wall, freedom is reinterpreted as insecurity and the choices as a kind of coercive compulsion. The entrepreneur becomes an anomaly the moment he fails to succeed.

As shown in many social science studies, group identities are under many kinds of pressure in the present era, and identifying with a group can be an insecure and unpredictable task. People who formerly had no mutual contact are brought together, new cultural forms arise, and the dominant ideology dictating that life should consist in free choices puts pressure on everyone. Old recipes for the good life may not have been lost, but they are conventionally discarded as reactionary and inhibiting. The result may just as well be frustrated confusion as positive self-realisation.

Even without the aid of this kind of freedom ideology, capitalism is capable of creating insecurity and new social dynamics. It has been a massive force, uprooting people from their conventional ways of doing things, moving them physically, giving them new tasks and bringing them into contact with new others. When mining began in the copper-rich areas of the eastern parts of present-day Zambia, just after the First World War, workers were recruited from all over the colony. They spoke many languages and had many different customs and kinship systems, but very soon, the workers began to sort each other, in a rough and ready way, on the basis of ideas about social distance (see e.g. Mitchell 1956). The people hailing from the western regions were seen as a category apart, likewise the Lozi speakers, the matrilineal peoples and so on. Some of the groups had experienced regular contact before urbanisation, and had conventional ways of dealing with each other. Some even enjoyed an institutionalised joking relationship with each other. (This wonderful African institution deserves to be exported elsewhere. Perhaps Israelis and Palestinians, or Christians and Muslims in Europe, might want to give it a try?)

INSECURITY AND RAPID CHANGE

J. Clyde Mitchell (1956), who studied urbanisation in the Copperbelt in the 1950s, once described a situation in a beer hall. A man and a woman are drinking beer. A second man joins them. He has a few coins which he puts on the table, intending to spend them on beer in a minute. Suddenly, the woman snatches a coin and sings, in a teasing voice, 'An X has lost his money ...' She belongs to the Ys, who have a joking relationship to the Xs. Instead of joining in the laughter, the man becomes angry and says that he is far from being an X; as a matter of fact, he is a Z, and the Zs have no joking relationship whatsoever to the Ys. The woman retorts that, to her, the Xs and the Zs are the same anyway. (Norwegians who are treated as Swedes in Copenhagen, something that happens very often, can relate to the man's reaction.)

This vignette illustrates the social insecurity that arises when societies change quickly. Just as a fish discovers the water only at the moment it is being hauled out of it, so does identification become an explicit problem only when it can no longer be taken for granted. The Bisa, the Lozi and other groups who met in mining towns like Luanshya, developed ethnic identities which they had never had before, but they also immediately began to question the significance of their new ethnic identities. Trade unions were also important in their new lives and, quite soon, Africans began to differentiate from one another through education and achievements in the modern sector of society.

Notwithstanding the rigid racial hierarchy of the Copperbelt, which was sometimes reluctantly bracketed by the anthropologists working at the mercy of the Colonial Service, the newly urbanised Africans were thrust into a post-traditional existence, where their former taken-for-granteds had to be defended, or else could be questioned. Another telling example of this transition is the changing significance of female circumcision among Somali women in exile. Because of the civil war and the near-total dissolution of the Somali state, a considerable proportion of the Somali population is exiled – many of them in neighbouring Kenya and Ethiopia, but there are also many in Europe and North America. In local communities in Somalia, nearly all women are circumcised. Among the few who avoid the knife are, incidentally, daughters of deeply religious men who have studied the Qur'an and thus know that Islam does not prescribe female circumcision.

ENTERING POST-TRADITIONAL SOCIETY

In Somalia, according to the anthropologist Aud Talle (2003), an uncircumcised female body is perceived as imperfect, unappetising and grotesque. Most Somali women in Somalia are oblivious of the fact that most women in the world are not circumcised. Then some of them are dislocated to England, Canada or Norway, and soon discover that the attitudes towards circumcision in their immediate surroundings are different from what they have been used to. The very woman who was pure and perfect on the dry savannah of the Horn is suddenly transformed into a mutilated victim on the streets of London. Nothing has changed except the circumstances. But this is enough for a seed of doubt to be sown. Will she really choose circumcision for her daughters, when nobody except a few Africans has it done in her new homeland? Is circumcision really necessary for a girl to become a proper woman? She may decide not to let her daughters be circumcised, despite the fact that this decision hurls her into cultural insecurity. Suddenly, she no longer follows the hallowed script detailing how to be a good Somali woman; she is forced to improvise and to trust her own judgements.

Cases (and rumours) of female circumcision in Western countries instantly lead to reactions among the majority which are sometimes described as 'moral panic'; but the fact is that, in this case, the path from a traditional to a post-traditional identity can be surprisingly short. As many as half of the Somali women interviewed in a Canadian survey indicated that they did not want their daughters to be circumcised. Some of them had only spent a couple of years in the country. In Somalia, the figure might have been 2 or 3 per cent.

When a Somali woman begins to question her own cultural tradition in this way, a deep ambivalence begins to ferment. If you have been engulfed in an unquestioned tradition your whole life and make a single individual choice contradicting the traditional script, it is as if the entire fabric becomes unravelled. In theory, from that point nothing prevents you from asking other questions of tradition: Why should I accept being subordinate to men? Why are we Muslims? What exactly does it mean to be a Muslim?

Most Somali women in exile may limit themselves to asking a few critical questions of their traditions, but their daughters tend to be less modest. A kind of liberal attitude which is widespread in our societies, not least among those who want to help the new arrivals to become similar to themselves, may nonetheless result in a mixture of pity and resignation when it turns out that many of the women in question are not willing to sever all ties (or chains, according to the liberals) to their dated and oppressive tradition. Sometimes, they are under pressure from their surroundings; perhaps their fathers, husbands and brothers do not want them to learn the language of their adopted country, and they may resort to violence or the threat of violence to prevent 'their' women from becoming 'liberated'. But this is hardly the whole story. Many immigrants – both women and men – remain faithful to tradition because they are familiar with its feel and smell, it gives them a sense of security and a clear, safe identity, and, besides, it offers resources they need to survive, such as work, a social network and the right to be themselves. They feel the cold breath of the chronic insecurity of late modern society, and some of them immediately withdraw into their shell to avoid being infected with pneumonia.

What exactly it is that provides a sense of security varies. You may be an entrepreneur in one place, but then you become a dreaded anomaly in another. There is no simple answer available, to analysts or to citizens. Those who demand the total victory of individualism and free choice forget their own need for security – I have more than once observed Norwegian anthropologists at international conferences, huddled together around their own table and enjoying themselves quite a bit – and they also tend to forget that rights imply duties. Yet, those who romanticise the intimate, tradition-bound communities are guilty of an equally grave error, since they tend to forget that such communities are no more natural than other ways of organising social relations; and that it is by virtue of courageous leaps into the unknown, into risk and insecurity, that the world changes. Humans, in other words, have both roots and boots.

*   *   *

Such is one predicament regarding security that faces us in a world increasingly made up of post-traditional societies. The theoretical questions about individual and society which were raised by the likes of Tönnies and Durkheim a century ago remain valid, but they need to be refashioned in order to fit the requirements of an era of mass migration, global capitalism and hegemonic individualism.

We have considered the literary characters Brand and Peer Gynt, Zambian miners and Somali women in exile. Let me now, in a bid to sharpen the argument, move to a late modern incarnation of Peer Gynt, who does not travel *to* the Orient, but who comes *from* the Orient to make himself a life as an entrepreneur. This man is initially a migrant without worries who regards the world as his oyster.

In the famous opening sequence of *The Satanic Verses* (Rushdie 1988: ch. 1), where the actors Saladin Chamcha and Gibreel Farishta fall out of Air India's flight 420 from Bombay to London, later to be fished out of the English Channel, Gibreel improvises an English translation of an old Hindi film song: 'O, my shoes are Japanese/ These trousers English, if you please/On my head, red Russian hat/ my heart's Indian for all that.' As every Indian over a certain age knows, the source is Raj Kapoor's film *Mr 420* from 1955. (In Hindi, the number 420 has connotations of sin and treachery. The kinship with Peer Gynt is clear!)

In an essay written a year or two after becoming the victim of an Iranian fatwa, Rushdie explained the deeper meaning of the book. It 'celebrates hybridity and fears the absolutism of Purity', he explains (Rushdie 1991: 394). Yet both his great novel and the dramatic aftermath of its publication indicate that Rushdie's penchant for impurity is countered by two formidable antagonists. Both of them can be seen as absolutist, both demand purity, and both prefer simplicity to complexity. It is well known, even among many of those who have not read Rushdie's novel, that it is a sophisticated satire lampooning literalist forms of Islam. It is less known that the book also, and almost to the same degree, makes fun of Margaret Thatcher's Britain. It was during her tenure that Norman Tebbit invented 'the Tebbit test', which implied that people who lived in Britain but did not cheer for a British cricket team at international matches were dangerous fifth-columnists. Cricket is a huge sport in many of the British immigrants' countries of origin, not least in India and Pakistan. Rushdie, thus, does not only criticises religious fanaticism, but also cultural intolerance and nationalist homogenisation. Rushdie might, in the same breath, have criticised multiculturalism, as an ideology which prefers security to insecurity, and which – according to its critics – thereby sacrifices freedom. Rushdie prefers the impure hybrids to the clearly delineated groups, which is not an uncontroversial option in a world where there is a great demand for simplifications. In his seminal book on nationalism, Ernest Gellner (1983) compares the homogenising force of nationalism with Modigliani's paintings, where 'neat flat surfaces are clearly separated from each other, it is generally plain where one begins and another ends, and there is little if any ambiguity or overlap', contrasting them with Kokoschka's impressionist canvases made up of a multitude of tiny specks of colour (the pre-nationalist world). A few years later, Ulf Hannerz (1996) suggested, in a friendly critique of Gellner, that perhaps Kokoschka had a future after all, thanks to the emergence of new, changing cultural mosaics. Whatever the case may be, the contrast between Modigliani and Kokoschka may offer a better metaphor for the tensions characterising group integration and disintegration in the present era, than simplistic contrasts between individualist neoliberalism and fundamentalist collectivism. A world characterised by many small differences was, in the modern era, reshaped into a world consisting of a few major ones – the ethnic, religious and national ones – but the development hinted at by Hannerz shows that the last word is by no means said yet.

Rushdie's appeal to the liberating qualities of post-traditional society has a formidable opponent in another postcolonial author of global significance, namely the Nobel laureate V.S. Naipaul, who is far less sanguine about the actual freedom involved in so-called free choice than Rushdie. Naipaul has repeatedly expressed deep suspicion regarding the term 'exile'. He sees it as a concept of the privileged few, which seems to say that the opportunities of the individual are limitless, that movement is enriching, and that one is somehow placed in an exalted position as judge and jury if one is fortunate enough to be in exile. Sir Vidia regards the condition of the exile as a punishment, not as a release. The condition might give increased insight, but the price is stiff: life-long solitude and lack of belonging.

In Naipaul's books, we encounter a world which appears comical in his early work – the actors are clowns who inadvertently parody the people they try to mimic – but which gradually turns sombre and dark: the actors grapple for something they have lost but will never find: a core, an attachment. Although Naipaul, like many other postcolonial writers, deals with fragmented and dislocated identities in his work, he never celebrates them. To him, the loss of community, security and roots is solely tragic.

In Rushdie, the reader encounters a world where insecurity is just another word for freedom, where the right to create and re-create oneself by mixing this and that is enriching and liberating. The span between Brand and Peer Gynt can easily be recognised in the relationship between Naipaul and Rushdie. It is in the tension between these positions that we should begin to look for an understanding of our era's simultaneous obsession with freedom *and* security. This book is a beginning, showing that the debate not only continues in all continents, but also that human security could be an eye-opener for a social anthropology which struggles to find its place in a post-cultural-relativist, thoroughly disenchanted world.

NOTE

This chapter is partly based on my *Oratie* (inaugural lecture) 'Risking Security', given at the Free University of Amsterdam on 15 March 2005.

REFERENCES

Alkire, Sabina. 2002. *A Conceptual Framework for Human Security*. Working Paper 2. Centre for Research on Inequality, Human Security and Ethnicity (CRISE), Oxford University.

Barth, Fredrik. (ed.). 1963. *The Role of the Entrepreneur in Social Change in Northern Norway*. Bergen: Norwegian University Press.

Bauman, Zygmunt. 2000. *Liquid Modernity*. Cambridge: Polity.

Bauman, Zygmunt. 2001. *Community*. Cambridge: Polity.

Beck, Ulrich. 1992. *Risk Society: Towards a New Modernity*. London: SAGE.

Douglas, Mary. 1966. *Purity and Danger: An Analysis of Concepts of Pollution and Taboo*. London: Routledge and Kegan Paul.

Durkheim, Émile. 2002 [1899]. *Suicide: A Study in Sociology*. London: Routledge.

Eriksen, Thomas Hylland. 2004. *Røtter og føtter: Identitet i en omskiftelig tid*. [Roots and Boots: Identity in Turbulent Times]. Oslo: Aschehoug.

Gellner, Ernest. 1983. *Nations and Nationalism*. Oxford: Blackwell.

Giddens, Anthony. 1991. *Modernity and Self-identity*. Cambridge: Polity.

Hannerz, Ulf. 1996. Kokoschka's Return, or, The Social Organization of Creolization. In *Transnational Connections*. London: Routledge, 65–78.

Ibsen, Henrik. 1972 [1867–68]. *Oxford Ibsen: 'Brand' and 'Peer Gynt'*. Oxford: Oxford University Press.

Mauss, Marcel. 1960. *Sociologie et anthropologie*. Paris: PUF.

Mitchell, J. Clyde. 1956. *The Kalela Dance*. Manchester: Manchester University Press.

Morris, Brian. 1994. *Anthropology of the Self*. London: Pluto.

Rushdie, Salman. 1988. *The Satanic Verses*. London: Viking.

Rushdie, Salman. 1991. *Imaginary Homelands*. London: Granta.

Security Dialogue. 2004. Special section: What is 'Human Security'? *Security Dialogue* 35(3): 345–88.

Talle, Aud. 2003. *Om kvinneleg omskjering* ('On Female Circumcision'). Oslo: Samlaget.

Todorov, Tzvetan. 1989. *The Conquest of America: The Question of the Other*. Oklahoma: Oklahoma University Press.

United Nations Development Programme (UNDP). 1994. *Human Development Report 1994*. New York: Oxford University Press.

Winslow, Donna. 2003. Human Security (inaugural lecture), Vrije Universiteit Amsterdam, 13 May 2003.

Wolf, Eric. 1964. *Anthropology*. Englewood Cliffs, NJ: Prentice Hall.

Part I

The Political Economy of Human Security

2
Taking Risks for Security's Sake: Bolivians Resisting their State and its Economic Policies

Ton Salman[1]

> 'I could have been a giant,' said the bonsai tree,
> 'But someone bound my roots and held me down
> [...and] what's the use of life without adventure?'
> (Brian Bedford and Vin Garbutt, 'Wings')

Human security, I shall argue, can help to re-conceptualise our research topics and questions in fruitful ways, provided it is addressed and applied in a critical, context-sensitive way. Human security, when taken as a perennial attempt, a steady orientation, a never-withering goal of all human endeavour, will obviously not do. In the many cases in which we witness deliberate risk-taking, preparedness to engage in social unrest and decisions to step out of well-trodden routine, it is frankly of little help. Risk-taking is just as much a 'natural' human action as are apparent efforts to increase security for oneself or one's beloved – and the concept of human security should be able to address both. People, for instance, often demonstrate a desire to avoid or escape forms of community and security that they experience as stifling or oppressive. People may, moreover, want to engage in insecure and even dangerous action if they no longer want to tolerate injustice or exclusion. Much individual and group action can be interpreted as conscious risk-taking rather than as a quest for an immovable state of security, and thus invites us to reconsider the taken-for-grantedness of the very dichotomy of security and risk. Risks are often assumed to, for instance, increase compensation or bring about a more 'bearable' (and differently arranged) security. And people's attempts to achieve material, physical and existential security, either collectively or individually, may cause them to clash among themselves, thus creating new arenas of contestation and insecurity. The idea of a one-dimensional 'state of security' or the striving for such is therefore an implausible feature of human conditions and motivations. What we need is a more sophisticated and polyphonic version of human security. Attempts to carve out such a notion are already under way in much of the recent literature (Boholm 2003, Eriksen 2005, Mani 2004, Schwartz 2004). Notions like empowerment, rights, risks, freedom and awareness are, in a critical mode, connected to and confronted by the idea of human security, thus enriching and complementing our understanding of its potentials and limitations.

I believe that recent events in Bolivia are a case in point. Bolivia experienced a persistent series of street protests, especially in the period 2000–05, that exposed many of the participants to considerable danger. Bolivians paid a high price for their perennial protests against successive governments and their policy proposals. The protesters were confronted with tear gas, batons, trigger-happy police (70 victims in October 2003 alone), food shortages in the cities, societal polarisation, political and economic instability, and loss of income.

The participation of many tens of thousands of people in these protests goes against the conventional wisdom in social movement research that people are likely to engage in hazardous collective action only when their options for coping with the existing order and life conditions have shrunk to the point where conditions have become unbearable.[2] In Bolivia, many are poor and their prospects are dim, but few are hungry or completely and utterly desperate about tomorrow's fate (Wodon et al. 2001). So why did so many Bolivians repeatedly take to the streets during these years? Why did the protests not fade away, considering that battles over an unjust tax bill, the sell-off of the country's extensive reserves of natural gas, and the demand for the resignation of a headstrong and repressive president had all been won? Why did so many Bolivians go on endangering their country's future, thwarting their own informal businesses/small-time economy and scaring off international investors, even after power was assumed in October 2003 by the first 'decent' president – journalist and intellectual Carlos Mesa – that they had had for many years? Why did this president's appeasing and compromise-seeking attitude not convince? And why did he, too, have to go on 9 June 2005? What perception of what was at stake, and of what 'the greater risk' was, made them persist in their onslaught on any government that took its turn in power? And from what historical learning process did this perception stem?

I will try to make two points in addressing these questions. The first is that the notion of 'human security' is helpful only when it is acknowledged that both security and insecurity come in many different shapes and forms, and that people's perceptions, appraisals and responses are as crucial as 'the facts' of insecurity. The second point is that the Bolivian case illustrates that these perceptions, appraisals and responses come into being in a process of historical learning/unlearning and thus reflect people's experiences with regard to earlier disasters, threats, violence, discrimination, exclusion and resistance. There is no such thing as a 'natural', transcendental human posture towards the presence of insecurity.

BOLIVIAN POLITICS: PORTRAIT OF AN IMPROPER DEMOCRACY

In January 2006, Evo Morales was sworn in as the country's new president. He broke the spell: for the first time, the country's indigenous majority managed to elect an indigenous president. Morales had been a key figure in the innumerable protests the country had witnessed since 2000. As leader of the coca farmers in the country's central Chapare region, he resisted the US-instigated eradication policies and the region's militarisation (Sivak 2008). Later, in 1997, he gained a deputy's seat, but was forced to step down when he was accused of inciting violence against the military eradicating the crops. However, he regained his seat in the 2002 elections, and three years later won the presidential elections with an absolute majority. After he took office as president, many felt that the protesters had finally taken over, and many had unrealistically high expectations.

To understand this outcome of the events, we need to look back at Bolivia's recent history – a sequence of disillusioning administrations, protests, negotiations, and renewed crack downs and protests, leading to a high toll in terms of the number of deaths and injured persons, damage to the country's economy and image, and damage to the already precarious livelihoods of many thousands of mainly poor Bolivians.

How did this negative spiral start? One of the most often commemorated historical events in Bolivia is the 'revolution' of 1952. In that year, a coalition of indigenous peasants, miners and progressive *mestizo* and 'white' Bolivians led by the Movimiento Nacionalista Revolucionario (MNR), overthrew the oligarchic, authoritarian and racist political system. Under the charismatic leadership of the MNR, Bolivia finally became a 'modern' democracy. It introduced the 'national development model', universal and obligatory suffrage for all citizens over 18, education for all, state influence in strategic economic sectors such as mining, and (somewhat ambiguous) land reforms; it also abolished the terms *indígena* ('indigenous') and *indio* ('Indian', pejorative), and replaced them with that of *campesino* (peasant). This last measure betokened the emancipation of the Aymaras, Quechuas, Guaranís and other smaller indigenous peoples of Bolivia.

Although the 1952 revolution represents a landmark in Bolivian history, the event did not bring about a democracy in which participation was 'natural' and 'equal', and it did not lead to the gradual eradication of poverty or to the promised reduction of the gap between the rich and the poor, or that between the *blanco-mestizos* and the indigenous peoples. What it did lead to was an unstable country: Bolivia has gone through more presidents (both authoritarian and elected) in the twentieth century than any other country in the region. In addition, seven coups d'état and counter-coups d'état were mounted in the four-year period 1978–82. According to many, Bolivia's democracy, which was restored in 1982, is still feeble, as it is in many other Latin American countries (Barr 2005, Philip 2005, Sousa Santos 2004, Tanaka 2002).

The persistent and most salient traits of Bolivia's politics in the years preceding 2000 that might help to explain its current vicissitudes include, to begin with, the failed attempt to eradicate the poverty and exclusion of the indigenous population (Varnoux Garay et al. 2004, Flores 2002, Kohl and Farthing 2006). The MNR position of the 1950s focused on a nationalist rather than a multiculturalist project, and opted to downplay rather than highlight the indigenous identity in order to obtain its emancipation. To little avail: the indigenous difference would not fade away. In the 1970s, a radical indigenous movement – the Kataristas – emerged in Bolivia and advocated the return of the Inca empire (*Tawantin Suyu*). It entered public space by means of some spectacular actions, but soon became caught up in internal frictions and lost most of its appeal. The indigenous peoples' awareness of their difference, however, did not disappear; in fact, it was fostered by persistent poverty and deprivation, as well as, paradoxically, by the indigenous migration to Bolivia's larger cities and the gradual increase in the number of university-educated indigenous individuals.

It was not until 1994 that the country's implicit assimilation policies were replaced by an official, constitutional acknowledgement of the pluri-ethnic and multicultural make-up of Bolivian society. Remarkably, this shift in national self-identification was brought about by the administration of Gonzalo Sánchez de Lozada (1993–97), commonly known as 'Goni', who led the MNR party. By then, the party had become much more conservative and had embraced the neoliberal recipes suggested by the Washington Consensus, the IMF, the World Bank and others. The MNR, however, had also become more sensitive to the multicultural discourse. Goni's vice-president, Victor-Hugo Cárdenas, was one of the inspirations behind the constitutional reform. He was the first indigenous Bolivian to obtain such a high position in Bolivian politics. He was leader of one of the small remaining Katarista parties, the MRTK-L.[3] Cárdenas, however, had become a more intellectualist and thus, to the *blanco-mestizo* electorate, a more digestible, indigenous leader who championed the cause of pluriculturalism and multi-ethnicity. The link between the MRTK-L and the MNR was possible thanks to this second feature of the 'renovated' MNR: it had opened up to ideas related to decentralisation, participation and multiculturalism,[4] and was – in the framework of planning a 'second generation' of neoliberal reforms – willing to implement a 'modernisation' of the state apparatus. But, as we will see below, even these reforms proved incapable of ending the marginalisation of Bolivia's indigenous peoples (who constitute over 50 per cent of the population). The indigenous 'inclusion' remained cosmetic. The subsequent government – that of former dictator Hugo Banzer (1997–2002) – made things worse: his administration was not only equally ineffective in combating poverty, reviving the economy and improving the lot of the indigenous population, but also highly corrupt. The resultant persistent poverty and exclusion of the indigenous peoples over the decades is one of the ingredients of the current disposition to protest in Bolivia.[5]

A second salient trait of Bolivian politics is its elitist and exclusionary party system. The system is characterised by the predominance of a petty intra-party and inter-party logic, and the inability of the political parties to build a bridge to society. Political parties are absorbed in internal and mutual squarings of accounts, and in recruiting their cadres from unrepresentative population sectors. To make things worse, new political contenders are met with chicanery on the part of established parties, which introduce legislation and contrive underhand pacts to protect themselves. Because of these practices, thousands of Bolivians feel that their interests and problems have hardly ever been reflected in the government's deliberations or in parliamentary debates (Albó and

Barrios 1993: 146–8, Salman 2006). They have come to realise that neither governmental nor opposition parties will ever genuinely defend their interests. Although the level of trust in politicians and parties is traditionally low in Latin America (see Camp 2001), it reaches dramatic depths in Bolivia: according to a 1990 survey, 77 per cent of Bolivian respondents expressed the conviction that parties did not work for the good of the country but merely defended group interests (Gamboa 2001: 101; see also Berthin Siles and Ernesto Yáñez 1999: 37–44, Varnoux Garay et al. 2000). 'If about 90% [of the population] feels that it is not participating, or only does so when voting, that means that the parties are practically absent from *the political life of the civil society*, as mediators or articulators of representation' (Tapia and Toranzo 2000: 30, original emphasis). The authors add that the 1.6 per cent who said that they do participate are probably the happy few who obtain jobs in the post-electoral redistribution process.[6]

The most serious effect of this party system modality is that parties can hardly be held accountable for their actions as governing or, for that matter, opposition actors. No political 'identity' is present against which concrete stands can be measured. And the fact that this has characterised the performance of parties for decades means that people have 'unlearned' how to compare parties' self-presentations in terms of political differences and of closeness to their proper interests and grievances (Salman 2004). The effect is twofold: the parties 'forget' to seek a distinct constituency (and instead use populist campaigning strategies), and people's quest for representation in the political realm is smothered (Mayorga 2003). This too contributes to Bolivia's inclination to discard the parliamentary and public political debate as a channel for participation in decision-taking. Instead, people have developed growing confidence that street protests would influence politics and make their demands heard.

A third important feature of Bolivian politics that might help understand its continuous political havoc is neoliberalism. Bolivia returned to democracy in 1982. Its 1982–85 left-wing administration ended in gloomy failure. Hyperinflation and broad protest against its devastating effects forced the government to step down before the end of its term. The government that assumed power in 1985 started on a path of neoliberal reform that has held sway ever since, despite the fact that it was never explicitly put to the ballot. The party culture described above allowed the parties to compete for victory on the basis of populist discourses, charismatic appeal and sweeping promises, and liberated them from the need to present to the electorate a clear-cut blueprint of their policy plans and the associated economic and social consequences. Most of the substantial policy changes initiated since 1985 have been directed at further privatisation, or the granting of natural resource exploitation concessions, the 'modernisation' of the state apparatus or the slimming down of the state's involvement in redistribution models. These actions gave higher priority to a neoliberal free market focus than to an attempt to design some sort of 'national development', or to openness to alternative diagnoses or proposals. There was no consulting of civil society. '[L]ittle, or no, opportunity was given to civil society to discuss and debate the national macroeconomic policy' (McNeish 2004). McNeish suggests that strong international pressure underlay the reluctance of subsequent administrations to really discuss their macro-economic agendas. The neoliberal reforms are thus insulated from debate: they are considered to be 'beyond negotiation' and above public discussion.[7] People's experiences of the negative consequences of these policies in their daily lives, and their realisation that a questioning of the 'basics' of the economic model was impossible, resulted in an attitude of categorical rejection of all governmental discourses and actions. The top-down a priori disqualification of all alternatives to existing policy parameters was a final, strong incentive to give up 'routine democratic procedures' and to resort to other forms of collective action.

To succinctly reconstruct the developments that have occurred since 2000 and to portray the sustained protests and the people's willingness to 'risk' their precarious daily subsistence during that period, I will discuss three features of Bolivian politics: the persistent indigenous deprivation in the economic and political spheres, the dysfunctional and exclusionary party system, and the neoliberal onslaught that was insulated from popular evaluation and influence.

BOLIVIA 2000–05: A COUNTRY IN TURMOIL

'No! No! The adventures first,' said the Gryphon in an impatient tone. 'Explanations take such a dreadful time.' (Lewis Caroll, *Alice's Adventures in Wonderland*)

In 2000 and 2001, the privatisation of the water supply in and around the central Bolivian city of Cochabamba, and the subsequent dramatic increases in tariffs, resulted in massive protests. In the end, the government gave in.[8] The outcome was celebrated as a victory over the neoliberal policies, and triggered both euphoric analysis as well as new organisational and movement-building initiatives. In the protests, various social movement leaders and politicians developed or reaffirmed their national profiles. I will elaborate the adventures of two of them – not to suggest that, individually, they made any decisive difference, but because this allows us to reflect upon the motives and vicissitudes of the protesters and their actions. To begin with, we will look at the 'career' and the social significance of Evo Morales, the incumbent president. Evo Morales, who is of Aymara origin, is the undisputed leader of the coca farmers in the Chapare region, close to Cochabamba. On a ticket of the MAS (Movimiento al Socialismo), he was elected to the Chamber of Deputies in 1997. From that position, he defended the constituency's source of revenue (Sivak 2008) and rejected the US-inspired policies to eradicate all 'excessive' coca cultivation.[9] Pointing at the ongoing clashes between the military and the coca farmers in the region, Morales was accused of fostering 'illegality' and armed resistance, and was ousted from parliament in early 2002. This only strengthened his position. His party – the leftist MAS – became the second largest party in Congress, and Evo Morales became one of the two front runners for the presidency in the June 2002 elections. Since none of the parties won a straight majority, Congress had to choose between the two front runners, the other being the MNR candidate Gonzalo Sánchez de Lozada ('Goni'), who had been president between 1993 and 1997. It was Goni who was eventually selected by Congress. He assumed office on 4 October 2002.

Evo Morales became the catalyst for a new series of protests, but was neither the organiser of nor the main agitator in all these events. The main protagonists were varying coalitions of protesters, most of whom were opposing measures that would affect their livelihoods. On 12 February 2003, for instance, a fatal series of events led to heavy gunfire in the very centre of La Paz, and forced the president to withdraw a crucial tax bill, to change his entire cabinet and to struggle desperately to regain his authority. This all started when – troubled by a large fiscal deficit and the need to obtain a new IMF loan, which would only be granted if the deficit were reduced – Goni's government had designed a tax bill that boiled down to a 12.5 per cent income tax on all salaries above 880 bolivianos (approximately US $115). From the outset, there was widespread protest against the government's failure to contemplate progressive taxation. Goni's proposal meant that ('once again') the poor Bolivians would have to pay the bill for incompetent government – to which it should be added that it was government and large enterprise employees who would be hurt in particular, and that the huge number of people working in the informal economy would be only indirectly affected.

Among the most prominent protesters, not surprisingly, were the police. They took to the streets on 12 February 2003 to reject the proposal and insist on the pay rise they had been demanding for a long time. As usual in situations of street protests, the presidential palace in Plaza Murillo was guarded by a small group of military police. The police were joined in the plaza by a group of secondary school pupils, who were there to demand the dismissal of their school principal and to air their rejection of government policy in general and of the tax bill in particular. When the pupils started throwing stones at the palace, smashing most of its windows, the military opened fire. As the pupils immediately ran away, the first victims were the police demonstrators. They, in turn, opened fire on the palace. In the ensuing chaos, the president was evacuated and rapidly negotiated the withdrawal of the police from the streets of La Paz. The crowd that had meanwhile gathered in and around the plaza then attacked government buildings, including the vice-president's offices and the Ministry of Sustainable Development and the Ministry of Labour. They then progressed to the offices of ElectroPaz, to the customs offices and to the town hall in the adjacent city of El Alto, where they ended up looting shops in the city centre.

Remarkably, in these events the most powerful and consistent opposition party – the MAS – was not the protagonist. Morales's party was reactive, not proactive, in the series of events around 12 February. Immediately after these events, however, Evo Morales's MAS did not hesitate to demand the president's resignation and to threaten to organise new protests.

The MAS was, however, paramount in the events that unfolded in October 2003. A government proposal to export natural gas to the USA via Chile became the flashpoint for weeks of violent protests. As had been the case in February, the roots of the conflict extended beyond the issue at stake – although an earlier sale of gas to Brazil on terms unfavourable to Bolivia certainly made this particular powder keg more explosive. For many Bolivians, the idea of exporting the gas via a Chilean port that had been Bolivian territory until the Pacific War 140 years earlier was infuriating, as Chilean–Bolivian relations have been tense ever since that war. But the measure stood for more. Goni's free-trade policies and his attempt to promote Bolivian membership of the Free Trade

Area of the Americas (FTAA) made him a clear target for an opposition that was convinced that neoliberalism was responsible for the country's hardship. This time, therefore, Morales had a lot to do with the protests – although he was accompanied by the social movements in Bolivia that rejected free trade treaties and by the many thousands who suspected that such 'deals' between the 'mighty' would eventually hurt them. In a way, the general dissatisfaction accounts for the fact that only a spark was needed to ignite the people's fury. In this case, the gas issue culminated in riots first in the city of El Alto, and then in the city of La Paz and other major cities. What ultimately motivated the protesters was their overall rejection of everything the government stood for. They were convinced that 'letting it go' would hurt all poor Bolivians (as previous measures had done), that electoral or other orderly forms of protest would have no effect, and that risking their lives on the streets was now the lesser danger. All this culminated in the demand for the president to step down.[10] The feeling that the country was disintegrating into anomie, together with the 70 deaths that had resulted from the confrontations, gave a devastating, and this time decisive, blow to the government's prestige.

The virulence of the protest led to a crisis within the coalition. When the vice-president, Carlos Mesa, withdrew his support, the president decided to abandon his gas export proposal. He asked for calm and for respect for the democratic institutions, and promised to consult 'everybody' before taking decisions. But it was too little, too late. By then, miners, *campesinos*, coca farmers, teachers, students, intellectuals, and almost every group and organisation that was not committed to the government were demanding the president's resignation, which eventually came on 17 October. Evo Morales, meanwhile, had become one of the major spokespersons for precisely this demand.

The presidency was assumed by Vice-President Carlos Mesa. He was not affiliated to any political party and was a respected journalist and intellectual; as a matter of fact, many wondered why he had agreed to be Goni's running mate in the first place. Mesa's assumption of power, and the way in which the constitution was upheld during the dramatic events, initially met with broad support and acclaim, both within the country and internationally. His immediate decision to form a government of technocrats and 'independents', leaving out the parties, was a remarkable innovation in Bolivian politics. However, it put him in a quandary, because, in the longer run, the parties would not let themselves be sidelined.

Moreover, given the intensity and magnitude of the accumulated anger and frustration, his 'benefit of the doubt' and the breathing space that Morales had promised him soon withered, especially since Mesa vowed to continue coca eradication. The understanding between Mesa and Morales came to a definitive end after a controversial referendum on the issue of the exploitation of Bolivia's rich hydrocarbon reserves and a prolonged political struggle over how to translate the outcomes of the referendum into legislation. The demands for Mesa's resignation and for an even more radical bill on the exploitation of natural gas became louder. On 9 June 2005, protesters won the day: Mesa stepped down and the protests subsided in order to allow the new president, Supreme Court of Justice President Eduardo Rodriquez, to organise 'tranquil' new elections.[11] Morales time and again demonstrated his political talent and his ability to mobilise support. He was a crucial factor in the wave of protests that Bolivia experienced during these years. But, of course, he cannot help us to account for the disposition of the Bolivians to rally, even for the umpteenth time and even though there was increased exhaustion about the ongoing protests in the country. Before we examine this issue of the disposition towards protest, let us first meet another crucial protest leader in Bolivia: Felipe Quispe.

Felipe Quispe participated in the Katarista movement of the 1970s, in a branch that was even more 'Indian' than the one that Cárdenas joined. Quispe is the leader of the rather small, but in the 2002 elections surprisingly strong, Movimiento Indigenista Pachacuti (MIP) party.[12] He is an Aymara leader who never tires of highlighting his ethnic roots and goals. In the 1990s he assumed the Aymara honorific title of *Mallku*. His discourse is fiercely anti-'white', and he is feared by many of the urban *blanco-mestizos* in Bolivia. On the Altiplano (the Bolivian highlands, which are the home of the Aymaras), the Mallku on various occasions mobilised the chronic grief of the highlanders, who are always poor and always outcast. There were efficient, carefully organised roadblocks, and men, women and children mobilised together, sometimes even with a sense of Andean *wayka*, that is, of collective competition to find out which community or organisational unit was stronger and more efficient. As a result of such roadblocks, it did not take long for food shortages to become pressing, mainly in the larger cities along the country's central axis, which runs from Santa Cruz through Cochabamba to La Paz. Several industries had to close down and finally the government agreed to negotiate. The figure of the Mallku was magnified by the mass media.

Quispe also did his part in January 2005, when the series of protests that finally brought down Mesa started. Quispe's confrontational style has given voice to the resentment of a marginalised indigenous population. And his radical brand of Katarism also resonates among sectors of the urban population of El Alto. Quispe is the second most salient opposition leader in Bolivia, who one has to take into account to understand the eruptions of protest in the country. Of course, many more protest leaders emerged during the later years in Bolivia. Jaime Solares, at the time leader of the COB (Bolivia's national confederation of trade unions), and Roberto de la Cruz, a local leader in El Alto, are just two of them. Remarkably, these leaders often clash and call each other every name in the book. Hence, presenting Morales and Quispe is merely to focus on two of the most prominent protest leaders. Although the role of these leaders is important and their moves are followed closely by the media, they do not of course create the protests: protests are created by their participants. More or less independently from these two leaders' 'agitation', Bolivia saw, during the following years, an endless series of demands and protests from pensioners, consumers, entrepreneurs, students, market vendors, taxi drivers, neighbourhood organisations, trade unions, school-teachers, coca farmers, highland peasants and others, and all these demands were, without exception, expressed in the form of marches, roadblocks, hunger strikes and similar means. Although these are, as such, part and parcel of democracies, in the case of Bolivia they have been converted into the sole mechanism of political dealings, and as the only remaining vehicle for state–society 'dialogue'. So who are these people who are willing to risk so much, time and again, to fill the streets with their presence? What is the background to the disposition towards protest?

BEING CERTAIN ONLY OF ANXIETY

By 2003, many Bolivians had grown tired of the protests and unrest. In the eastern part of the country – which has a distinct ethnic make-up and political culture, a notably differently structured economy and a greater geographical proximity to the controversial gas reserves (the rapid exploitation of which it hoped to benefit from) – an outright counter-movement arose. It would therefore be wrong to suggest that *the* Bolivians had made political protest their daily business, or to insinuate that decisions to protest are lightly taken or that the protagonists are a homogeneous group with similar demands and coordinated actions. On the contrary, the ongoing conflicts have created increased controversy, both in the country and in academia, regarding demands and the priorities, leadership, and regarding the range and scale of the disputed issues: are they incidental or structural, are they economic or racial? They have also brought about frictions on strategic questions, on the legitimacy of the pursued 'identity politics', on ethnic polarisation, and about the blurred line between opportunism and 'genuine indignation'. In the end, however, all these qualifications only make more pertinent the question why such a large portion of the Bolivian people continued to reproduce a shaky, unstable situation, if each and every individual and specific group agreed about the troubles and insecurities it created.[13] The only possible explanation is an abysmal series of 'mismatches' between the policies and visions of the governing bodies, and those of the majority sectors of society. Where these majorities begin to envision the governmental plans as downright threats to their livelihoods, and in addition have little confidence in their ability to change these plans by electoral means, at least one precondition for the astonishing preparedness to persist in protests seems to be fulfilled.

In today's Bolivia there are many of these mismatches between the realm of politics and the societal concerns and developments (Drake and Hershberg 2006). The first of these mismatches is the simultaneous ongoing self-enclosure of politics and political parties versus the growing self-awareness of the indigenous population. Like many other Latin American countries, over the last 20 years Bolivia has witnessed an increasingly self-confident indigenous population that is demanding an end to unofficial discrimination, an effort to lessen indigenous deprivation in such fields as education, health care, access to services, etc., and the acknowledgement of cultural identities and territorial claims. In Bolivia, as in most other Latin American countries, various concessions have been won. However, the opening up of the political system did not occur, or occurred only symbolically. It eventually triggered, in 2002, the quite spectacular election to parliament of indigenous representatives on more or less explicitly ethnic tickets (Albó 2002, Assies and Salman 2003, Seleme 2002), and the rather confrontational mode it took: indigenous deputies, expressing their frustration, addressed their *blanco-mestizo* fellow representatives in hostile ways. The indigenous MPs assumed this polarising stance because of the long-standing reluctance of established politics to create room for them – despite proselytising among their ranks during campaigns. This helps to account for the fact that this somewhat nasty tone prevailed in the identity politics adopted by various indigenous voices, and by Quispe in particular. Morales, Quispe and others often spoke of their struggle for their 'brethren' and of the bankruptcy of the 'occidental' models of governing the country and managing the economy. Their threat to 'take over' the country very much disturbed the *blanco-mestizo* audience.

A second mismatch is the already mentioned imposition of the neoliberal economic model without any genuine consultation and against the views that many Bolivians hold of the role of the state in economic development and the protection of the weak. From interviews, surveys (Latinobarómetro 2004, *The Economist* 2002, UNDP 2004) and the appeal of populist discourses, one may conclude that most Bolivians prefer the welfare state they never had. Fragments of such a state have historically been realised in Latin America and also in Bolivia, in populist modes: benefits were reserved for specific sectors (Assies et al. 2005). Rather than being rooted in a code of universal inclusion, access to benefits derived from a system of occupational stratification. Revenues were thus restricted to sectors that have legally defined, recognised occupations. Despite its unequal implementation, the practice has become favoured by many Latin Americans. The 'handouts' had slowly come to be perceived as the standard for a correct state attitude, and an image of the appropriateness of the expansion of these doles began to dominate among Latin American populations. The state's withdrawal not only from influencing the economic sphere, but also from its obligation to 'care', clashed with this popular image.

This takes a more concrete form in the third mismatch, namely that between the political and the societal images of the risks and items that the state ought to cover. Health risks and the risks of old age provision, because of the mechanism mentioned above, have come to be viewed as risks that the state should help to mitigate. Something similar applies to unemployment risks and protection. The state, meanwhile, is moving in the opposite direction (Tironi 2005: 176). This seriously affects many Bolivians, since security in the realm of employment and income is not only extremely precarious in Bolivia, but has also worsened in recent decades because of the state's withdrawal from mining and other formerly nationalised economic sectors. Due to the absence of alternative employment in the brittle national industry, in the small sector of highly industrialised export agriculture (mainly soya) and in the frail subsistence agriculture, Bolivia's economy has since then been one of the most 'informalised' in the world. Only a minority have formal, stable jobs and incomes. Added to the state's growing incapacity to provide health care and universalised, free education, this has produced strong tendencies towards the privatisation and subsequent divergence of the quality of these services. Private education, private health clinics and other privatised services are available to the wealthy; the run-down state services are there for everyone else. In a way, this means that risks have been privatised. No-one will or can cover the risks of the poor. For the have-nots, it simply means higher risks.

A final, closely related mismatch is that between the unenthusiastic attempts by government spokespersons to present 'reasonable', compromise-focused solutions to Bolivia's main politically controversial issues (such as gas exploitation), and the 'unreasonable', 'foolhardy' rejection of those solutions by protesters. The referendum on the hydrocarbons issue organised by Carlos Mesa in 2004 is a case in point. Before the referendum, many protested against it, because it included no less than five, rather half-baked and complex questions. Because of this, many people distrusted the whole affair, and, rather than try to decipher the Byzantine wording of the questions, they preferred to demonstrate. Journalists and international observers often concurred in criticising these protests as being 'for the sake of protest', and for bringing on to the streets people who could not state what was at stake in the referendum. What they missed hearing in the people's angry exclamations were expressions of *systematic* distrust in all governmental propositions with regard to something that has become a poor Bolivian's hope for a better future, namely enormous reserves of natural gas. Their fear of being deceived won out over their awareness (people are not *that* stupid) that they could not answer the question about what precisely could be done about the referendum, or exactly what snake they had discovered in the grass. What many Bolivians had learned from their experiences with politics was: don't trust them, especially when they play the 'trustworthy equanimity' game. To paraphrase interviewees' statements, people feel that, 'every time we did that, especially with regard to the country's rich resources and their exploitation, we ended up empty-handed and poorer'. According to a poll carried out by Ruizmier Consulting and Research in La Paz, El Alto, Cochabamba, Santa Cruz y Tarija in March 2004 (the month in which the first referendum proposals were made public), the government scored only 4.32 out of 10 points on the ICG (*Indice de Confianza del Gobierno*; Government Confidence Scale). In just one month, it had fallen by 0.93 points (17.8 %) – the largest fall in confidence in one month for Mesa's government (source: *La Patria* newspaper, Oruro, Bolivia, 13 April 2004). This suggests that something beyond a single unequivocal confrontation on a specific issue was at stake: the dispute was not about the referendum, but about the government's credibility.

Bolivia was characterised by a political culture in which distrust between the polity and society had become the most salient feature (Drake and Hershberg 2006). This distrust was strengthened in the period 2000–05, during which numerous protests were initially ignored by the authorities, and then often repressed. It was again strengthened when, after having ousted a stubbornly neoliberal president ('Goni') in 2003, the polity again proved unable to win people's trust in the political system, namely when Mesa was unable to reconcile the divided country or to resolve the gas controversy. The latter element brings us to one of the baleful consequences of an illegitimate political system: its inability to convince people encourages different agents in society to defend their interests somewhere else and to turn their backs on the state. Apparently, then, Bolivians perceive the current political and economic arrangements in their country as a greater risk to their livelihoods and futures, than the chancy business of resisting these arrangements on the streets.

DISCUSSION

A straightforward postulate in terms of people's 'natural' tendency to avoid risks clearly does not apply to the complex situation sketched above. Three axes of insecurity infuse the Bolivian configuration. For many Bolivians, and especially for the indigenous Bolivians, their livelihoods are insecure both immediately and in the future. Second, their experience with regard to accessing politics in order to change the economic model, to change state attitudes and to participate in deliberations is one that, time and again, confirmed the frailty and deficiency of the country's democratic system. Evo Morales's recent success might signify a change in that perception – but it is too soon to tell. People were clearly not confident about the effects of their democratic participation. As a result – and this is the third axis – people engaged in other, non-parliamentary and often risky activities in order to try to make a difference. Due to the systematic exclusion, corruption and perfidy of Bolivia's polity, people were inclined to distrust any government initiative. The insecurity produced by this endemic lack of trust led to fierce resistance (which generated new and acute insecurities for the protagonists), which in turn bred intensified insecurity about the country's destiny. Because of the endemic disbelief, Bolivia will encounter great difficulty in returning to a modus operandi in which a minimum of trust guides the sorting out of political controversy: hitherto the fight tended to begin even before the contenders became acquainted with one another's positions, arguments and negotiating spans. A fragmented and, in Bolivia's case, increasingly polarised society, is the outcome of this process.

Bolivia is an example of a worst-case scenario. The persistent deafness, exclusiveness and impenetrability of the party system and governmental institutions, combined with their incapacity to voice the worries, perceptions and proposals for alternatives from below, and the representational deficit that became manifest in a void with regard to the polity's capability to acknowledge and to respond to societal interests, all boiled down to a societal incompetence in building interest-voicing associations, in recognising shared concerns, constructing vital social movements, lobbying or seeing the need for unification, or translating ad hoc frustrations into political choices or ideological identifications: the addressee for all such initiatives is simply absent. The potential for a process of democratic consolidation seemed inverted: instead the country lived through a democratic de-consolidation. Recent events seem to counter this assertion; after all, Evo Morales was elected president because he seemed to embody and unite both discontents and hopes. But, taking into account the 2006–08 developments, it seems too soon to conclude that trust in democratic dialogue has triumphed over generalised frustration.

The Bolivian party system and political culture have affected not only governance but also the opposition to governance. No adequate civil interlocutor has been construed, because no adequate sparring partner at the level of political institutionality was available. Diamond's[14] prescription was reversed: there was no enhancement of the accountability, responsiveness, inclusiveness, effectiveness and hence legitimacy of the political system that would then give the citizens respect for the state and positive engagement with it. Instead, the state, represented by parties and politicians, failed to perform and to convey its viewpoint, and consequently civil society failed to articulate reactions in a politically settled way, failed to enter into politics and has ended up completely disrespecting the state as such.

With regard to the concept of human security, the story reveals that using this concept as an encompassing theoretical frame is not very promising. To state that people, in a transcendental, cross-cultural mode, always strive for security and always try to reduce the degree of insecurity, is only as revealing as it is to state that people always try to fill their stomach or always long for affection. As culturally empty affirmations, they tell us little about the meaning that people attach to these pursuits, or about the concrete shapes of threats or the strategies to assuage these threats. Moreover, such a proclamation tends to suggest that people always strive for calm and immobility. The Bolivian situation, however, suggests that people might just as well opt for risks and 'danger' in order to get some security.

The analysis also suggests that insecurity comes in many different shapes and forms. Structural collective insecurity with regard to livelihood or to political exclusion or slight; insecurity because of globalisation's impact on the authority of traditions; and the insecurity that people take on in the case of risking their necks by participating in protests are only some of these shapes. Therefore, people's perception of what 'insecurity' is seems to constitute an indispensable component of whatever analysis of human security we attempt.

NOTES

1. SCA/FSW/Vrije Universiteit Amsterdam. I thank Marjo de Theije, Ellen Bal, Oscar Salemink, Thomas Eriksen and the SCA staff for their valuable comments on an earlier version.

2. See Raschke (1987), Salman (2000). It is a piece of wisdom that is often criticised nowadays: many authors argue that motivations for collective actions are much more multi-layered and complex, and are more than merely the outcome of a calculus on the stakes. Collective and individual memories, political culture, mobilisation strategies and potentials, the role of media, and peoples' perceptions of rights, of the just and the unjust, and of the dynamics of the group with which they identify, all play important roles in the emergence of protest (see e.g. Eckstein and Wickham-Crowley 2003, Salman 2001a, 2001b, Salman and Assies 2007).

3. In the 1960s and 1970s, the Katarista movement had made a strong case for a reawakened indigenous self-consciousness. In that sense, it went against the policy of downplaying ethnic difference with which the MNR had tried to emancipate the indigenous population since the 1952 revolution. The movement's radical stand, at the time, frightened the country's *blanco-mestizo* population. By the early 1990s, however, the Katarista movement had dispersed and moderated.

4. The commitment to multiculturality, however, was partly merely an electoral strategy. The dedication of neoliberals to multiculturalism is embedded in their specific views on decentralisation and a particular brand of participation that does not necessarily chime with the aspirations of indigenous peoples' movements (Calla 2000, Hale 2002, see also Steur 2005).

5. Much more could of course be said about the problems of political representation of the poor and their 'socially institutionalised incompetence' (Bourdieu 2001, see also Karl 2003), but this is not the place to do so.

6. A redistribution process that also exemplifies the institutional weakness of the state: state dependencies are often 'personalised', often inefficient and incapable, and, in the view of the Bolivians, often whimsical (Sánchez de Lozada 2001, Philip 2003, Salman 2006).

7. The presence of increasingly self-confident indigenous movements questioning Western notions of 'a good life' and sustainability, and the dogma of economic growth and expansion, makes the deafness subsequent governments displayed towards alternative proposals on economic policies extra hard to understand, let alone swallow. It is important to keep in mind, though, that the critique of the monomaniac pursuit of neoliberalisation of the economy was not confined to the indigenous population.

8. That is: after having tried to ignore the protests, after having repressed protesters, after thwarting negotiations, after having brought into action snipers, and after having declared the state of emergency and detained and deported (to a remote sort of concentration camp in tropical eastern Bolivia) many opposition leaders.

9. Coca is a traditional crop in Bolivia, which is chewed in order to optimise energy-use and to counter tiredness, and which is used in small amounts for industrial products. Coca harvests have grown considerably since the 1970s, however.

10. Besides secondary sources, my claims about Bolivians' perceptions of politics in their country are based on a series of street interviews in La Paz, in 2000, 2003 and 2005–08.

11. Which took place in December 2005.

12. Obtaining 6 per cent – which is not bad for a party and a leader considered by the 'established' and 'acknowledgedly democratic' parties as operating on the fringes of political legitimacy. In the run-up to the elections, Quispe and the MIP were regarded as despicable and as disqualified from government, because they ferociously expressed the discontented Indian voices in Bolivia.

13. This is an important reminder that a diverse collective of people, struggling against the authorities but also disagreeing among themselves, produces a result that no single component of the collective initially intended. And that, at the same time, these parties are aware of this and cannot do anything about it, or only at the cost of forsaking their own interest; or they hope fruitlessly the other party will come to the same conclusion. The spell can be broken only if a meeting ground at a 'meta-level' can be established. But the Bolivian state, the obvious entity to facilitate such a development, did not deliver – at least not until Morales took power.

14. Diamond asserted that: '[b]y enhancing the accountability, responsiveness, inclusiveness, effectiveness, and hence legitimacy of the political system, a vigorous civil society gives citizens respect for the state and positive engagement with it. In the end, this improves the ability of the state to govern ...' (1996: 234).

REFERENCES

Albó, X. 2002. La nueva correlación campesino – indígena en el parlamento. *Artículo Primero* 6(11): 9–24.

Albó, X. and R. Barrios (eds). 1993. *Violencias encubiertas en Bolivia*. La Paz: CEDIB/Aruwiyiri.

Assies, W. and T. Salman. 2003. *Crisis in Bolivia – The Elections of 2002 and their Aftermath*, Research Paper no. 56. London: Institute of Latin American Studies, University of London.

Assies, W., M. Calderón and T. Salman (eds). 2005. *Citizenship, Political Culture and State Transformation in Latin America*. Amsterdam: Dutch University Press/ Zamora: El Colegio de Michoacán.

Barr, R.R. 2005. Bolivia: Another Uncompleted Revolution. *Latin American Politics & Society* 47(3): 69–90.

Berthin Siles, G. and E. Yáñez. 1999. *¿Qué sabemos sobre el desarrollo democrático Boliviano?* La Paz: Punto Cero.

Boholm, Å. 2003. The Cultural Nature of Risk: Can There Be an Anthropology of Uncertainty? *Ethnos* 68(2): 159–78.

Bourdieu, P. 2001. *El campo político*. La Paz: Plural.

Calla, R. 2000. Indigenous Peoples, the Law of Popular Participation and Changes in Government: Bolivia, 1994–1998. In W. Assies, G. van der Haar and A. Hoekema (eds) *The Challenge of Diversity: Indigenous Peoples and Reform of the State in Latin America*. Amsterdam: Thela Publishers, 77–94.

Camp, R.A. 2001. *Citizen Views of Democracy in Latin America*. Pittsburgh, PA: University of Pittsburgh Press.

Diamond, L. 1996. Toward Democratic Consolidation. In L. Diamond and M.F. Plattner (eds) *The Global Resurgence of Democracy*, 2nd edn. Baltimore, MD: The Johns Hopkins University Press, 227–40.

Drake, P.W. and E. Hershberg (eds). 2006. *State and Society in Conflict – Comparative Perspectives on Andean Crises*. Pittsburgh, PA: University of Pittsburgh Press.

Eckstein, S.E. and T.P. Wickham-Crowley (eds). 2003. *Struggles for Social Rights in Latin America*. New York and London: Routledge.

Eriksen, T. 2005. *Risking Security: Paradoxes of Social Cohesion* (inaugural lecture). Amsterdam: Vrije Universiteit/Free University Amsterdam.

Flores, V. 2002. *Bolivia: sociedad fracturada*. La Paz: Azul Editores.

Gamboa, F. 2001. *Itinerario de la esperanza y el desconcierto – Ensayos sobre política, sociedad y democracia en Bolivia*. La Paz: Muela del Diablo.

Hale, C.R. 2002. Does Multiculturalism Menace? Governments, Cultural Rights and the Politics of Identity in Guatemala. *Journal of Latin American Studies* 34: 485–524.

Karl, T.L. 2003. The Vicious Cycle of Inequality in Latin America. In S.E. Eckstein and T.P. Wickham-Crowley (eds) *What Justice? Whose justice? Fighting for Fairness in Latin America*. Berkeley: University of California Press, 133–57.

Kohl, B. and L. Farthing. 2006. *Impasse in Bolivia – Neoliberal Hegemony and Popular Resistance*. London/New York: Zed Books.

Latinobarómetro. 2004. www.latinobarometro.org, consulted March 2005.

Mani, D. 2004. *Human Security: Concept and Definitions*. Tokyo: UN Centre for Regional Development.

Mayorga, R.A. 2003. Bolivia: metamorfosis del sistema de partidos. *Íconos* (Quito: FLACSO) 16: 96–105.

McNeish, J.A. 2004. Stones on the Road: The Politics of Participation and the Generation of Crisis in Bolivia. *Bulletin of Latin American Research* 25(2): 220–40.

Philip, G. 2005. Democracy and Development in Latin America. *Latin American Research Review* 40(2): 207–20.

Raschke, J. 1987. *Soziale Bewegungen – Ein historisch-systematischer Grundriß*. Frankfurt/New York: Campus Verlag.

Salman, T. 2000. Politico-cultural Models and Collective Action Strategies – The Pobladores of Chile and Ecuador. In L. Roniger and T. Herzog (eds) *The Collective and the Public in Latin America*. Brighton: Sussex Academic Press, 192–216.

Salman, T. 2001a. Paradigms Lost – An Paradigmen vorbei. Theoriebildung um städtische Organizationen und Bewegungen in Lateinamerika. *Peripherie – Zeitschrift für Politik und Ökonomie in der Dritten Welt* 81/82: 116–37.

Salman, T. 2001b. Investigar movimientos sociales urbanos: viejos y nuevos enfoques y temáticas. *T'inkazos – Revista boliviana de ciencias sociales* 8 (La Paz: PIEB): 9–34.

Salman, T. 2004. Apocryphal Citizenship – Anthropologizing the Citizenship Debate in Latin America. *Journal of Urban History* 30(6): 853–73.

Salman, T. 2006. The Jammed Democracy: Bolivia's Troubled Political Learning Process. *Bulletin of Latin American Research* 25(2): 163–82.

Salman, T. and W. Assies. 2007. Anthropology and the Study of Social Movements. In C. Roggeband and B. Klandermans (eds) *The Handbook of Social Movements Across Disciplines*. New York: Springer: 205–65.

Sánchez de Lozada, A. 2001. Accountability in the Transition to Democracy. In J. Crabtree and L. Whitehead (eds) *Towards Democratic Viability – The Bolivian Experience*. Houndmills: Palgrave, 195–215.

Schwartz, A. 2004. Interview with Bernadette Muthien and Charlotte Bunch. AWID, URL (consulted August 2005): website, http://www.awid.org/go.php?stid=1391.

Seleme Antelo, S. 2002. Elecciones 2002: Se impuso la diversidad. *Artículo Primero* 6(11): 25–32.

Sivak, M. 2008. *Jefazo – Retrato íntimo de Evo Morales*. Santa Cruz: Editorial El País.

Sousa Santos, B. de. 2004. *Democracia de alta intensidad – Apuntes para democratizar la democracia*. La Paz: Corte Nacional Electoral.

Steur, L. 2005. 'On the Correct Handling of Contradictions': Liberal-culturalism in Indigenous Studies. *Focaal – European Journal of Anthropology* 46: 169–76.

Tanaka, M. 2002. *La situación de la democracia en Bolivia, Chile y Ecuador a inicios de siglo*. Lima: Comisión Andina de Juristas.

Tapia Mealla, L. and C. Toranzo Roca. 2000. *Retos y dilemas de la representación política*. La Paz: PNUD-Bolivia (Cuadernos de Futuro 8).

Tironi, E. 2005. *El Sueño Chileno – Comunidad, familia y nación en el bicentenario*. Santiago de Chile: Aguilar/Taurus Ediciones.

UNDP. 2004. *Democracy in Latin America: Towards a Citizen Democracy*. New York/Lima: UNDP.

Varnoux Garay, M., J. Abastaflor Frey and F. Mariaca. 2000. *Construyendo democracia – Estudios de opinión socio-política en las ciudades de La Paz y El Alto*. La Paz: Punto Cero.

Varnoux Garay, M., R. Archondo and J.G. Bautista. 2004. *Líderes y partidos indígenas: el factor étnico en el sistema político boliviano*. La Paz: ABCP/Konrad Adenauer Stiftung.

Wodon, Q., R. Castro, K. Lee, G. Lopez-Acevedo, C. Saiens, C. Sobrado et al. 2001. Poverty in Latin America: Trends (1986–1998) and Determinants. *Cuadernos de Economía* 38(114).

3

State Formation, Imposition of a Land Market and Silent Resistance among the Berbers of the Middle Atlas

Bernhard Venema, with contributions by Ali Mguild[1]

This chapter deals with the Beni Mguild and Ait Ndhir Berber tribes, living in the Middle Atlas of Morocco. The central question posed here is how these people have constructed and used social and cultural repertoires to create security in a globalising world. Competition may develop between different ideas and practices, with one form gradually undercutting and replacing the other. We shall argue that these new perceptions and practices are derived from new power constellations centred on state formation and capitalist market forces. For local Berber societies this implies that security comes to depend on transactions and institutions outside the community. Due to economic and political insecurity local societies feel threatened in their livelihood and therefore they develop defence mechanisms. One 'defence mechanism' is the enforcement of local practices in the light of ongoing globalisation processes (Appadurai 2001: 256, 257, Eriksen 2000: 289, 290). Feelings of economic and political insecurity may lead to the affirmation of autochthony, resulting in boundary-making and a sense of belonging and exclusion (see also Geschiere and Nyamnjoh 2000, Lentz and Nugent 2000).

The emergence of this type of defence mechanism cannot be assumed automatically. Rather, we argue that it is mostly cohesive communities that respond in this way. In fragmented communities there are multiple forms of social control and external forces will be dealt with in different and even in opposite ways; in disintegrated communities integrative mechanisms are absent and society is in crisis. Abbink (2007) shows this process in his study of an agro-pastoral society, the Suri people in Ethiopia. He argues that much of the suffering within Suri society nowadays is generated not only by external forces but also by the exercise of violence by the Suri themselves, both in- and outside their own group, while integrative mechanisms are too weak to redress the crisis. This seriously affects the social structure and cultural norms in their society. As a result Suri culture, as a repertoire of shared values, norms and behavioural rules, is slipping away. He argues that this happens in other East African pastoral societies too. However, in communities which, for one reason or another, are still cohesive, normative systems and methods of control are well established and core notions of tradition reassert themselves more easily. As has been argued by several authors, in such communities the maintenance of or return to traditional practices is rational because it offers protection for all (Salemink 2003, Scott 1976, Wolf 1966).

The aim of this chapter is to identify the threats encountered by the Berber tribes of Beni Mguild and Ait Ndhir, and the countervailing pathways they have developed as a response in order to create security. During the pre-colonial period these Berber tribes were able to maintain a large degree of independence vis-à-vis the central state. The Sultanate had tried to subject the tribal areas in order to gain control of trading monopolies and to levy taxes. The Sultan, as a descendant of the Prophet Mohammed, had traditional religious authority. However, although the successive Sultans sometimes were able to establish garrisons, this was only for quite short periods. The tribal system had to be cohesive and able to defend its autonomy to safeguard livelihood security. The first question is: which factors have contributed to tribal cohesion?

After the French army 'pacified' Morocco, it became a French colony. This chapter deals with the process of state incorporation and the capitalist development of land privatisation to allow the creation of a settler colony. Rural Berber leaders collaborated with the colonial government in its endeavour to build a Berber block against the growing nationalism among the urban Arab elite. This resulted in impoverishment of the common Berbers and the undermining of political security. The second question is: how has colonialism undermined tribal cohesion among the Beni Mguild and Ait Ndhir?

In the postcolonial period the Sultan was able to establish his hegemony in the religious and secular domain. As has been argued by Hefner (1993), it is not only religious 'market forces' that influence religious change but also the various state policies in the domain of religion, forcing people into the mainstream dominant religion. In the secular domain, the state tries to take over decision-making power regarding access to common land and water points from the tribes, leading to great economic insecurity among the rural Beni Mguild and Ait Ndhir. The third question is: what counter-strategies have developed since independence due to the development of a hegemonic state and the imminent danger of the tribes losing economic and political autonomy? Do the the tribesmen remain attached to old institutions and customary land access arrangements? Or do Muslim leaders organise a religious movement because people look for security in religious reform, and this subsequently converts to or merges into a political organisation?

COHESIVE COMMUNITIES

The two agro-pastoral Berber tribes of the Beni Mguild and the Ait Ndhir live in the north-central part of the Middle Atlas, numbering about 345,000 people. The tribesmen have sheep breeding as their main base of existence. They move camp between the highland summer pastures and the lowland winter pastures that can be dozens of kilometres apart. In addition they practise agriculture, most often on plots near the winter camp. From the 1930s they started to sedentarise.

The tribes developed institutions to guard their resources and to provide for security for their members. Ownership of land and water points was collective, emphasising access-rights to land for all and the tribe's cohesiveness in, as will be shown, a politically unstable environment. They had viable political institutions at different levels for a flexible approach towards providing security. The tribal council divided pastures and agricultural land among the tribal segments that had participated in the conquest of the land. The tribal segment dealt with the day-to-day affairs of resource management, such as redistribution of pastureland among lineages and ensuring adequate access to water for the flocks of sheep. At the lineage level decisions were taken regarding the timing of agricultural operations and of moving camp (Bruno 1917, 1918, Abes 1917, 1918).

The lineage was the mutual aid group on a day-to-day basis. The lineage members trekked together to the camps and assisted each other to safeguard their flocks against raids and to ensure an adequate food supply. The lineage council solved local conflicts, imposed fines and offered assistance during life-cycle ceremonies. Large camp circles had a mosque tent, in which the camp's elected Koran teacher held services and gave an education in the Koran to the boys. In addition, he advised the lineage council on religious and legal matters. All members of the tribe had to contribute their share to the upkeep of the Koran teacher and also contribute to the mosque funds, which could be used for mutual assistance as well (Amicis 1985, Huot 1923).

Before Morocco became a French Protectorate, feuding between tribes in the Middle Atlas was the normal state of existence. The feuding and associated feelings of honour and combativeness originated in the pastoral economy. Because there were no clear boundaries of pastures and ownership of flocks, men had to assert their influence in order to maintain access to the resources. Feuding often disrupted economic life because the agricultural activities stagnated. Harris, a correspondent of the London *Times* and an agent of the British government, observed:

> Although the tribes enumerated above [Gerwan, Ait Ndhir and Beni Mguild] came from the same stock and are closely allied, forming a distinct branch of the Berber race in Morocco, it must by no means be thought that they live at peace among themselves. Every tribe, and often the subdivisions of tribes, is at war with its neighbours, and at the 'sok' or market, outside Agurai, which all patronise, so common has become bloodshed and murder, that today only members of one tribe market at a time. (Harris 1897: 645)

Feuding, although involving victims, at the same time was a major force in keeping the tribal system going, by maintaining a balance based on tribal cohesion.

Feuding could involve a decrease in the male population; therefore men from neighbouring tribes were allowed to settle down in a community if they could find a protector. The stranger would sacrifice a sheep at the door of his intended protector as an entreaty; this ceremony was called *tamghrouste*. If the man accepted the offering he became the guardian of the stranger. The ceremony offered dispossessed individuals and their families an opportunity to secure a livelihood.

Due to their sense of combativeness and honour, it was difficult for these tribes to create peaceful alliances with neighbouring tribes. As has been demonstrated by Gellner (1969), holy men played a central religious role, and a political role as well. These holy men were descendants of saints and had much prestige due to their sanctity (*baraka*). Some claimed descent from the Prophet Mohammed and were conceived as having inherited *baraka* as well; this group of holy men was called *shorfa*. They mostly lived near the borders of Berber tribal segments and were sedentary. They helped make peace, arrange the payment of blood money and provided assistance to traders and visitors travelling under their protection. As compensation, the tribesmen granted them land or provided for a shepherd.

The village of Zaouia Ifrane in the Beni Mguild area conforms with the classical example of a *shorfa* group as described by Gellner: they are culturally distinct, Arabic-speaking, settled in a village and under *sharia* regulations. They form the oldest settlement of the tribal segment of the Ait Abdi. When the Ait Abdi arrived they were not chased away; this was because the village was respected being a place of Koran learning. The graveyards of the ancestors served as neutral grounds for negotiation during times of conflict, while the descendants themselves were held in great esteem and, apart from some agricultural and pastoral activities, lived from gifts and sacrifices from visiting Berbers (see also Bakker 1993: 49).

In 1668 an army led by *sherif* Moulay Al-Rachid Alaoui succeeded in defeating some powerful Berber leaders of the Middle Atlas. From that time onwards, this Alaoui dynasty tried to subdue the tribal areas, in order to monopolise toll-money, taxes and trading monopolies. The holiness of the Sultans did not imply that their secular authority was accepted when the autonomy of the Beni Mguild and Ait Ndhir was at stake. These tribesmen regularly attacked the army of the Sultan. The authority of the provincial governors appointed by the Sultan was weak. Most often they were recruited from among the tribesmen and took their authority not from the Sultan but from the latter (Harris 1897: 643, Segonzac 1903: 128).

The conclusion is that the Beni Mguild and the Ait Ndhir formed tribal societies, in which cohesion was maintained through collective ownership of land and a decentralised and flexible political organisation. Autonomy was maintained by force if necessary, while saintly families were looked to for mediation. People from elsewhere were allowed to settle to revitalise tribal society.

LAND MARKET, POLARISATION AND INCREASED INSECURITY

Berber tribes, among them the Beni Mguild, Ait Ndhir, Guerouan and Zemmour, besieged Fez and Meknes in 1911 and 1912 to prevent Morocco becoming a French Protectorate and losing their autonomy. The French army came to assist the Sultan and, confronted with military force, Sultan Hafid signed the Treaty by which Morocco became a French protectorate. However, it took the French army until 1934 to defeat the tribes of the Middle and Central Atlas, who vigorously defended their autonomy. What the French called 'pacification' in reality was a military conquest lasting more than twenty years and resulting in the deaths of thousands of French. After the conquest, the territories of the Beni Mguild and Ait Ndhir became a military region under a French military officer who was assisted by a *caid*, a local tribal leader willing to cooperate with the French authorities. Civil legal affairs were dealt by a tribal judiciary council composed of members of the tribal segment council under the supervision of a French official. Penal affairs remained under the courts of the Sultan, but the French military officer and the *caid* dealt with many cases informally.

Immediately after the First World War there was a massive influx of immigrants from France, all hungry for land. This posed a problem for the French authorities because, in most of Morocco, land was held as collective property and thus was deemed inalienable. Men who had cleared land for cultivation had only permanent usufruct land: land could only be sold after the council of the tribal segment had given its approval, after which the local Koran teacher drew up a paper which was signed by a number of witnesses. However, land titles were not registered due to absence of judges and notaries in the rural areas (Bendaoud 1917: 290, 291, Bidwell 1973: 208).[2]

In order to make land sales possible, the French authorities passed a decree in April 1919 that cultivated land should be treated as joint property, that is to say it was to be divided among the households as private property. Land titles could then be registered at the land registry office or the tribal judiciary council. Vinogradov (1974: 97) formulated as follows what occurred among the Ait Ndhir: 'Ignorant of the value of land, and intimidated by the French army that was pressing the Ndhirs into corvées to clear roads and European farms, the tribesmen were quickly relieved of their newly acquired property.' While they cultivated 250,000 ha in 1925, due to land grabbing they were left with 138,000 ha in 1947 (Bidwell 1973: 316). Among the Beni Mguild, land grabbing by *colons* and traders from Fez and Meknes occurred too: they acquired about a quarter of the land under cultivation (about 20,000 ha).

The authority of the administration over land became a powerful weapon for the punishment of those who were hostile to the regime and the reward for those who cooperated. Many *caids* and their assistants (*khalifas*, *shaykhs*) collaborated with the French authorities to enrich themselves to the detriment of common tribesmen. With connivance of the French administration they not only purchased land but appropriated collective land too, which they registered as private property (Beaudet 1969: 23, 51, 61, Bidwell 1973: 81–4). Among the Ait Ndhir *khalifa* Moha ould Said owned no less than 10,000 ha, among the Beni Mguild *caid* Said ould Haddou ou Akka owned 1000 ha, there were many more. Because tribal leaders manipulated their own tribesmen, there gradually developed feelings of frustration among the ordinary tribesmen; people started to revolt against *corvée* labour and the French army regularly had to come to the aid of the *caids* and their assistants (Bidwell 1973: 82, 83, Venema with Mguild 1992: 150, 2002: 106).

The enforcement of private property and the stealing of collective land weakened the Berber institutions. The tribal leaders had become corrupted due to collaboration with the French administration. The councils of the lineage and tribal segment lost authority because their control over land had been curtailed by force. *Colons* and Moroccans from elsewhere could settle independently, without performing the ceremony of *tamghrouste* by which foreigners were integrated in Berber society. As a result this ceremony fell into disuse. Newcomers seeking to work as labourers for the Berber farmers simply became labourers for the Berber farmers.

During the Protectorate, the role of the brotherhood lodges and saintly families as arbitrators had also weakened because now the French administration and collaborating *caids* were fully in command. Later on, the saintly families started to resist the colonial administration. As stated by Vinogradov: 'Intimidated by the French, confused by the new bureaucracy and manipulated by the tribal leaders, the anxious and insecure Berbers turned to the saintly families who served as religious leaders, teachers and physicians' (1974: 10).

It is clear from the above that during the colonial period both tribes experienced great economic insecurity due to exploitation by French *colons*, Arab merchants and tribal leaders. Forced introduction of private property resulted in the development of a class of rich farmers, among them tribal leaders, and the weakening of the tribal councils and cohesion.

INDEPENDENT MOROCCO: THE STATE APPROPRIATING ISLAMIC SPACE

Headed by the urban educated and religious elite, later on joined by Sultan Mohammed V, opposition gradually developed against the French administration, although it came late to the Beni Mguild and Ait Ndhir due to the collaboration of the tribal leaders with the colonisers. Directly after independence (in 1956) a hegemonic state was created. As well as representing secular authority in Morocco, the Sultan is, as the representative of the *shorfa*, the head of the Islamic community too: the *Amir el Muminine* (Commander of the Faithful). This had been included in the constitution of 1962 and 1992. However, it was especially under King Hassan II that religious leadership was emphasised by the ceremony of alliance (*baya*) through a communication of 12 February 1964 of the Royal Protocol Department of the Palace. This ceremony reproduces the pact that was traditionally established between representatives of a given tribe and the holy lineage they had appointed as their permanent arbitrator (Morsy 1984: 56).

Now, on a variety of occasions, the power of the king is religiously legitimised through the ritual of the *baya* of the Throne Feast and of the religious feast-days such as the Great Sacrifice, Ramadan and the Prophet's Birthday, and during visits to the provinces. High officials, members of parliament, political leaders, guardians of mosques, brilliant students and young investors – all selected by the administration – present themselves. They wear the sacred and unifying white robes, and they bow four times and together call for the divine grace of His Majesty, while the servants of the Palace, wearing red conical hats, call out, giving them the message of the blessing of the Sovereign. This is an occasion for the king to underline his traditional role, not only as head of the state but also as the religious leader who participates in sacred performances.

In this situation actors in the religious periphery have hardly any power left. At present the mosque is under heavy surveillance. It is the Ministry of Habous and Islamic Affairs that appoints imams, after consultation with the regional council of scholars in Islam, which itself is supervised by the Ministry of Interior. Since the decree of March 1958, endowments to the mosque (*habous*) are managed by the state in the person of an official of the Ministry of Habous and Islamic Affairs instead of by the community itself. As a consequence, in the research area the community members have ceased their endowments because of fraudulent practices and loss of control by the community (see also Dilrosun 1993: 23).

Famous saints receive state support and media coverage, among others Moulay Idriss in Fez, or Moulay Idriss of the Zerhoun. Royal gifts are bestowed on their shrines and sometimes members of the royal families grant them visits at the occasion of the annual festival of the saint. However, the state undermines the local religious community. The Ministry of Habous and Islamic Affairs keeps an eye on local lodges and saintly families, and permission must be asked to organise the yearly pilgrimage and to improve the upkeep of the shrine. Since independence, but especially since 1974, this ministry has put a stop to the number of people claiming to be of a saintly family. Below follows an example in the research area.

Case: The Lineage Ait Sidi Moussa (Beni Mguild)
The descendants of Dada Moussa claim that their forefather Dada Moussa was a *shorfa* Idrisside. Many men assured that there had been a paper that confirmed the line of descent ('the tree') to true *shorfa*-hood. It was disappointing that they had lost the paper because they had to deliver to Rabat. Said one informant: 'We are the descendants of Dada Moussa. Before independence we used to have a paper where Dada Moussa came from – it was from the region of Fes and he was a *sherif* Idrisside – and also who his descendants were. You know, it was a complete family tree. But then it was seized by the King and he never returned it to us.' (Bakker 1993: 55, 58)

Led by the king, hegemonic endeavours occurred in the secular domain too. The central government decided that access to tribal land was no longer a matter for the lineage council and traditional overseers but for the government. In fact, the Ministry of Interior declared itself to be the sole representative of the rural population's interests and the sole institution with authority regarding the common pastureland. From now on it was the *caid* and the governor who decided who had access to the commons. Mostly this meant that immigrants who had stayed at least one generation in the area were allowed access to the commons, although the original settlers did not agree with this at all (Venema 2005: 194).

This also meant that forests in the area were regularly closed for grazing in order to allow the king and his friends to have hunting parties. Until 1999 the herders regularly set fire to parts of the forest as protest against this restriction on securing a livelihood. As recounted by locals, the police always responded by rounding up several people in randomly selected villages and putting them in jail for several days. Such measures were characteristic of the authoritarian reign of King Hassan II, which in popular language is referred to as '*les années de plomb*' [the years of lead]. Since the reign of the new King Mohammed VI more no-entry signs and fences have been erected, and although these are respected more than previously, the herders remain dissatisfied with the lack of access to vital pasture land.

The conclusion is that in the postcolonial period the central state was hegemonic in the religious field as is exemplified in the ceremony of *baya*. So the mosque became controlled by the state, and the mosque as a mutual aid institution was undermined. In the secular field, the state as a hegemonic actor has created insecurity by allowing strangers access to land. As will be shown below, the Beni Mguild and the Ait Ndhir developed ways of resistance towards the central state.

PRESERVING AND REVITALISING TRADITIONAL INSTITUTIONS: THE LINEAGE COUNCIL

The political parties failed to put forward an alternative for the hegemonic Moroccan state. The elected representatives are inclined to endorse whatever the government wants endorsed, especially in the rural areas. In fact the municipal and communal elections were the last step in the administration's concerted action to re-establish relations with local notables (Bourqia and Miller 1999: 274, Hammoudi 1997: 31, Seddon 1981, Venema 2002: 113). There is no trust at all in the elections because it is generally believed that votes can be bought. Says an informant:

> Since there are elections there is no trust in the elected members. Those elected in the rural councils are just profiteers and even the *baraka* has diminished in the village. And this is why the members of the *jemaa* (lineage council) believe they can best solve the problems among themselves. And if the *jemaa* decides to take matters into their hands they have to solve the problems whatever the conditions are.[3]

Another farmer said:

> *Caids* come and go, so it is better that we continue our work. We are the ones who know who has the right to graze their cattle and we know the importance of the tribe to manage our affairs and not a youngster at the desk of his office who is going to guide us with papers and pencil.[4]

Actually the lineage council still plays an important role in regulating access to the commons. In the view of the indigenous population, the newcomers have no right to these pastures. The village council has a watchman (*naib*) recruited to supervise access to and use of the collective pastures. His main task is to deny access to newcomers' herds and to see to it that the spring resting period for the grassland re-growth is respected. The line taken by most lineage councils and watchmen is that those who have not been traditionally adopted and performed *tamghrouste*, as well as descendants of those who have not performed the ceremony were not deemed as part of the indigenous population. As such they are barred from membership of the lineage council and from grazing their cattle on the commons. Free and uncontrolled settlement thus came to mean exclusion from the Berber community with its associated rights (Venema 2002: 108, 109, 2003: 45). So the council members argue that newcomers in fact do not belong to the community. Even if they pay all their fees to the lineage council, these fees are considered as a gift (*sadaqa*) but not as a membership fee (*frida*). There are many Arab families who have lived for more than a generation in the area without access to the commons, two such cases are described below.

Mohammed Ali

Mohammed Ali is a sheep farmer who is originally from Missour. In 1937 he bought land from the Ait Mouli, a grouping within the Ait Abdi tribe (of the Beni Mguild), and started rearing sheep. He and his son were not allowed to herd their animals on the collective pastures. The son brought this problem before the *caid* again and again, but because the *caids* were recruited from the Ait Abdi population until the 1970s no action was taken. Only when an (Arabic-speaking) outsider was appointed as *caid* in Ain Leuh was his case brought before the provincial governor and later the Direction des Affaires Rurales of the Ministry of the Interior. Following a successful lawsuit in 1982 he was granted access rights (because he had lived in the area for so long) and the *caid* ordered the Ait Abdi to leave him undisturbed. However, the Ait Mouli continue to work against him, especially because they cannot stand the fact that he has become a wealthy man (he owns 1600 sheep and two lorries). They have therefore decided that he is not allowed to water his flock at the Akadous water point just a short distance from his farm. Now his son must fetch water by lorry from another source, nine kilometres away. This is a government-built water point and the Ait Abdi were not entitled to deny him access. (Venema 2002: 110).

An old man of the Ait Harzallah.

An old man of Áit Harzallah of the Ait Ndhir said: 'In the old days, people came from other tribes, made the *tamghroste* and we let them settle on our land. In time they took their guns and fought along our side and they became our brothers. Now everybody is selfish and people point out this and that *takhamt* [lit. tent, but the term is still used to refer to an extended family] and say: "they are not genuine Harzallawis; we remember their grandfather who came from the Riff and was allowed to squat on our land. He did not even make the *tamghroste*. They cannot be counted on us [meaning they cannot be considered as members of the group when it comes to division of collective land]. This is shame and against the custom. But then things have changed and many of us who never have farmed in our lives are obliged to take up the plough and break the rocks for a living.' (Vinogradov 1974: 59)

The above cases show that the lineage council has reasserted itself and regulates access to common land. The lineage-council is something in the hands of the firstcomers: threats of loosing livelihood security have resulted in 'strangers' not having access to the commons. The conclusion is that people have returned to the familiar in an attempt to counter the threats imposed by the state. The local population bypasses the official rules and uses a traditional institution to create security.

PRESERVING AND REVITALISING TRADITIONAL INSTITUTIONS: THE HOLY MEN

After independence the state propagated a more orthodox version of Islam in the Middle Atlas and elsewhere. In the village El Qebab, studied by Drouin, the reform movement started in 1965 with the appointment of a new imam. At the Friday prayer, he publicly condemned the worship of saints and the privileges of the holy families who live from the gifts of the population. The author continues: 'The people reacted fiercely to such attacks and, during the long period of drought of 1966, at the ceremony held to pray for rain (*lemma*), they killed a sheep at the graveyard of Moulay Mokhtar in the central part of the village' (1975: 155).

Among the Ben Mguild and the Ait Ndhir there is still much respect for the *shorfa* and holy men because they have *baraka*. Tribesmen visit them to ask for talismans to protect their family, their cattle or their crops. In addition, they go there to discuss religious matters, such as how to sacrifice at the Great Sacrifice and how to apply the prescriptions at the *rites de passage*; informants consider them as good people: they give *fatiha*, heal people and help in solving problems. Says an informant:

> Sometimes we invite a *sherif* to help solve a problem together with the members of the *jemaa*. The *sherif* is invited as a sort of religious witness to solve the problem according to the *sharia*, and he who betrays the arrangement between individuals or villages, the *sherif* will shout at him and he will read him texts from the Koran and concludes that God will punish him.[5]

Although prior permission must be obtained from local government officials, who hardly ever cooperate, visits to the holy shrines continue as before. It is an important collective ceremony because it is homage to the lineage or clan cemetery, or the grave of a holy man as is shown in the case below.

Case Sidi Moussa

The Ait Sidi Moussa (of the Beni Mguild) are acknowledged as a holy family; they are pastoralists, speak Berber and live like Berber. They number approximately 330 families. They are given respect as a holy family by surrounding tribes during the yearly festival (*moussem*) of their ancestor Dada Moussa. Especially the fellow tribes Ait Liass, Zayan and Ait Oumnisef honour him. The festival is quite an extensive one. During two weeks the surrounding tribes come and donate their *sadakas* and they are heartily received by the families of the Ait Sidi Moussa. With the *sadakas* sheep are bought and eaten. Visiting families are divided among the Ait Liass.

As has been argued above, newcomers are barred from the commons because they are considered as strangers. Immigrant *shorfa* have access to the commons, however, for reasons of respect. So there are exceptions to this exclusion, and 'outstanding' newcomers might be invited to attend the meeting of the village council, as with particularly pious men such as those organising the ritual sacrifices on the holy days. More precisely, only those were eligible who had behaved appropriately towards the 'original settlers' by helping to solve conflicts, donating to the village fund and, if rich, helping the needy by providing loans (Venema 2003: 45). Below follow two examples of holy men who do not belong to the original settler families but have obtained a good position in the tribe.

Haj Moulay Aziz

Haj Moulay Aziz is a descendant of a *shorfa* family from Tindjad. His father settled in Souk el Had (village of the Beni Mguild) without performing the *tamghrouste* ceremony. He became a seasonal labourer in France, where he worked for many years. He was able to buy a sizeable tract of land, and his sons intensified farm operations by buying a tractor and starting aboriculture. The family is well off: they own a Peugeot 405 and several houses, which they rent out. The cattle are allowed to graze the commons. Haj Moulay Aziz has travelled to Mecca, and thus bears the title El Haj. Whenever he returns from France, he says his prayers in the mosque and organises *sadakas* on the holy days to honour the forefathers. He tries to settle conflicts by applying Koranic law, and even mediates in conflicts between settlers and newcomers over access to the commons.

Moulay Mustapha

Moulay Mustapha too is a descendent of a *shorfa* family from Tafilalt whose father also settled in the area without performing *tamghrouste*. Moulay Mustapha now lives among the Ait Boubker, near the hamlet of Faliba. He is a rich farmer, and has a tractor with which he ploughs the fields of other farmers. He has access to the collective pastures and has even built stables there. He is a religious man, attending all the prayer services, and is much respected for his learning. He is a member of the lineage council of Faliba and helps decide on community affairs and resolve conflicts among families. (both cases from Venema 2003: 46)

In concluding this section, we argue that, in the religious domain, the population has not accepted the modern version of Islam as propagated by the central state. People do not appreciate that local religious institutions like the mosque have become state-run institutions. Therefore holy families continue to receive much respect and are accepted as religious leaders and advisors. As a consequence, the tribesmen interpret the official rules regarding access to land in their own way. Strangers are not allowed to use the common pastures but, because of their authority and prestige, holy families do have access.

ISLAMIC ACTIVISM: SPACE FOR PROTEST?

Islamic revival has become more prominent as a cultural repertoire in Morocco as a reaction to state policies that are perceived as insufficiently opposing the putative expansion of Judeo-Christian culture by Western countries, most notably Israel and the United States. The first popular protest was after the Iranian revolution of 1979, when the fugitive Shah was welcomed by King Hassan II, which resulted in massive protests by infuriated devout people. Many other popular protests were to follow.

But internal factors contributed to Islamic activism too. The industrial and commercial elite, with the royal family taking the lead, has appropriated the benefits of economic development. The contrast between the rich and the poor is very sharp. Estimations of the fortune of the royal family run between $2 billion and $4 billion. At the same time, it is estimated that 70 per cent of the urban adult population has to survive in the informal sector (Obdeijn et al. 2002: 188, 194; see also Pennell 2000: 378). Many of the young and disaffected in the towns feel that economic and social progress never reached the ordinary population and have lost hope.

In this context, Islamist leaders could become their spokesmen. For example, Cheikh El Yacine, a former teacher, was able to attract a large following by attacking the Moroccan state as being non-Islamic and non-egalitarian. What made him popular was an open letter to the king in 1974 entitled 'Islam or the Deluge'. In it he argued that King Hassan II was corrupt, that poverty was widespread, that he propagated Western liberal values and that he was indebted to foreign, particularly Zionist, capital. In 1999 he wrote a letter which argued that the royal family's fortune should be repatriated in order to reduce Moroccan foreign debt, poverty and the unemployment rate. Since the 1970s he has been put in jail, placed in a psychiatric clinic and placed under house arrest. Since 1999, under the reign of Mohammed VI, he has regained some of his liberties.

The number of activists, those organising meetings, religious ceremonies and demonstrations, is unclear because they have to operate secretly: it is very difficult to organise meetings in the mosque and most often the meeting is at home. Estimates run between 20,000 and 50,000 members, mostly to be found among the young and educated in the cities.[6] The number of those sympathising with the movement, participating in specific activities only, is, of course, many times higher.

Among the rural Beni Mguild and the Ait Ndhir, there are hardly any activists and not many sympathisers because they are often not able to read and lack access to other media, and hence are not well informed about this movement. Those who have access to written sources, cassettes or the television are shocked by the point of view of Cheikh El Yacine and his daughter Nadia Yacine, that the king does not have specific divine authority. The Islamists attacking holy families and *shorfa* as heretical did not win converts to their cause. What active members there are live in the towns of Azrou and El Hajeb, each of which has some dozens of active members, who study the *fatwas* of Cheikh El Yacine and participate in meetings in Fez or Rabat.[7] There are more sympathisers, however, as became clear in 1991 when Morocco sent 1500 troops to Saudi Arabia to hold the line against Iraq, and hundreds of people, mainly students, teachers and officials, demonstrated in both towns.

To begin with, the movement was not allowed to create a political party. However, in 1996 the government permitted the creation of a moderate Islamic party, the Parti de la Justice et du Développement (PJD). This party accepts the king as the leader of the Islamic community and the monarchy as a political system. It has as its main goal to propagate a pure Islam; so it wants to apply the *sharia* in legal matters, is against non-Islamic behaviour and it is critical towards 'holy families' because, as informants say: 'before God everybody is equal'. The party leaders were opposed to the introduction of a new personal code, replacing the older code promulgated between 1957 and 1959. In the new code, adopted in February 2004, men and women are treated as equal, repudiation and polygamy are abolished and juridical intervention is required in any division of property subsequent to a divorce. Because it was King Mohammed VI himself who had seen to the introduction of the code, the PJD party has now abandoned its criticism.

Elections in Morocco did not arouse much enthusiasm because the Ministry of Interior manipulated the polls. Turnout is low, even since Mohammed VI became king.[8] In 2002 the PJD became the third largest party in the parliament, although it only put up candidates in 51 of the 92 constituencies. Among the Beni Mguild and the Ait Ndhir this party obtained votes in the urban areas; in Azrou it became the largest party with 20 per cent of the votes, in El Hajeb it obtained 9 per cent.

With the exception of two rural centres (Ait Taoujdate, Ait Bourzoune), this party was not able to present itself among the rural Beni Mguild and Ait Ndhir.[9] The local influential tribesmen were not interested in embracing this party, which was associated with urban economic interests and orthodox religious values, and in which there was no space for local religious practices and beliefs. Local leaders – both members of the lineage council and the holy men – typically represent the local traditions as has been shown above. They try to manage community affairs on their own; it is through them that customary access rights to land and the influence of the holy men are maintained. In addition, they are the leaders of the local ritual offerings by which the cultural identity of the community is reaffirmed. So these local leaders did not present themselves as candidates of this party or put forward associates as candidates, and as a result the PJD party was hardly known among the rural population.

It can be concluded that among the urban population there is a tendency towards the revival of the Islamic community. Here we see space for the PJD party, as the only mobilising structure allowed. Among the rural Beni Mguild and the Ait Ndhir, however, a broad-based militant Islam is absent because it does not fit in with their cultural practices.

CONCLUSION

This chapter dealt with two agro-pastoral tribes, confronted with colonialism and later on with a hegemonic central state, struggling to create human security.

The first question that was posed is how to explain tribal cohesion among Beni Mguild and Ait Ndhir during the Sultanate. Collective ownership of land, and a decentralised political tribal framework, provided a cohesive structure for the distribution of resources and the management of conflicts. Feuding was a major force in keeping the tribal system going, but it promoted violence too. Therefore people from elsewhere looking for a livelihood were able to settle to revitalise tribal society. Due to its cohesiveness the tribal system was able to maintain its autonomy, while saintly families were looked to for mediation.

The second question concerned how colonial rule and land privatisation affected the tribes, especially tribal cohesion. It appeared that, in an attempt to appropriate land, the colonial government disregarded the traditions surrounding access to land. This example was followed by tribal leaders, resulting in the disruption of traditional control mechanisms like the lineage council. As a result newcomers were able to settle independently.

The loss of economic security and the collaboration with the state by tribal leaders undermined tribal cohesion.

The third question was what counter-strategies developed after independence. The king's policies established a monopoly position within Islamic space. The mosque and the mosque's endowments came under heavy surveillance, and the mosque could no longer function as a mutual aid institution. The central state established a monopoly position within the secular domain too. It appropriated the rules of access to what was left of the commons and forests. This weakened the economic security of the tribes, resulting in the reassertion of the lineage council and a stress on autochthony.

The popular perception of the king's religious position is ambivalent. Through his traditional charisma as a descendant of the Prophet, and the sacred performances at the religious and national feast days, he enjoys popular respect. However, people do not appreciate the monopolisation of the religious discourse; for example, that local religious institutions effectively became state-run institutions. Therefore, local saintly families are still much respected, as is evident from the example of newly arrived holy families being granted access to the common pastures. Again, the local population use a traditional institution to counter the threats imposed by the state and to maintain political and economic security.

The cultural repertoire of militant Islam has gained some importance in urban centres like in Azrou. A small part of the urban intelligentsia looks for security in religious reform, due to failure of the state to obtain legitimacy. The rural and lower-class urban population is not attracted, because it is already attracted by the religious charisma of the king. The moderate Islamist party PJD is present in the urban centres of the two tribes too. However, among the rural population this party hardly receives support because it does not coincide with the local traditions and the interests of the local leaders. Here, little space exists for turning religious extremism political.

The general argument then is that disintegrated or fragmented societies with weak or absent control mechanisms are not able to reassert tradition. However, the two agro-pastoral tribes dealt with here create human security by opting for community and tradition. They are able to do so because they have cohesive communities with strong political authority, capable of defending their autonomy. But their present-day tradition is different from the past because the context is no longer traditional but modern. Tradition has become a way of dealing with modernity. Hence what we are witnessing are competing forms of institutionalisation. One is backed by state law and the bureaucracy, encoded in an official accepted version of Islam; the other the enforcement of local practices more or less grounded in values and safety nets embedded in institutions seen as distinct from the colonial and postcolonial state.

NOTES

1. Ali Mguild has been the assistant and interpreter of Bernhard Venema since 1986. He is a municipal officer at Souk el Had (Middle Atlas).
2. Interview with local notary at Souk el Had on 30 September 2001
3. Interview with farmer in Timahdite on 7 February 1991.
4. Interview with farmer and traditional watchman (*naib*) on 11 September 1990 at Azrou.
5. Interview with teacher and inhabitant of Sidi Addi, 24 September 1990.
6. See Pennell (2000: 363); www.maroc.net.ma, accessed 11 April 2004; james. com.wysiwyg, accessed 16 September 2002; *Le Nouvel Observateur* 9 October 2003 ; Obdeyn et al. 2002: 173.
7. Interview by Ali Mguild with two teachers at Azrou, 20 November 2004.
8. During the parliamentary elections of 2002, turnout was 51.6 per cent, and at the communal elections of 2003, 52 per cent.
9. See www.elections2003.ma (accessed 16 July 2002).

REFERENCES

Abes, M. 1917, 1918. Monographie d'une tribu Berbère: Les Ait Ndhir (Beni Mtir). *Archives Berbères* (Publication du Comité d'Études Berbères de Rabat) 2(2): 149–94, 2(3), 337–416, 3(4), 321–45.

Abbink, G.J. 2007. Culture Slipping Away: Violence, Social Tension and Personal Drama in Suri Society, Southern Ethiopia. In M. Böck and M. Bollig (eds) *The Practice of War: Production, Reproduction and Communication of Armed Violence*. Oxford: Berghahn Books.

Amicis, E. de. 1985. *Morocco: Its People and Places*. London: Darf Publishers Ltd. (First published 1882.)

Appadurai, A. 2001. Disjuncture and Difference in the Global Cultural Economy. In S. Seidman and J.C. Alexander (eds) *The New Social Theory Reader: Contemporary Debates*. London: Routledge.

Bakker, J. 1993. *The Lasting Virtue of Traditional Healing: An Ethnography of Healing and Prestige in the Middle Atlas of Morocco*. Amsterdam: Vrije Universiteit/Free University Press Amsterdam.

Beaudet, G. 1969. Les Beni M'Guild du nord: étude geographique de l'évolution recente d'une confederation semi-nomade. *Géographie du Maroc* 15: 1–78.

Bendaoud. 1917. Notes sur le pays Zaian. *Archive Berbères* (Publication du Comité d'Études Berbères de Rabat) 2(3) : 276–306.

Bidwell, R. 1973. *Morocco under Colonial Rule: French Administration of Tribal Areas 1912–1956*. London: Frank Cass.

Bourqia, R. and S.G. Miller (eds). 1999. In the Shadow of the Sultan: Culture, Power and Politics in Morocco. *Harvard Middle Eastern Monographs* 31 (Harvard University: Center for Middle Eastern Studies).

Bruno, H. 1917, 1918. 'Introduction à l'étude du droit coutumier des Berbères du Maroc central. *Archives Berbères* (Publication du Comité d'Études Berbères de Rabat) 2(3): 170–95, 3(4), 297–309.

Dilrosun, C. 1993. Vrouw, moskee en emancipatie. Het streven van vrouwen in Marokko via de Islam hun positie te verbeteren. MA thesis in Social and Cultural Anthropology, Vrije Universiteit, Amsterdam.

Drouin, J. 1975. *Un cycle oral hagiographique dans le Moyen Atlas Marocain*. Paris: Publications de la Sorbonne.

Eriksen, T.H. 2000. *Small Places, Large Issues: An Introduction to Social and Cultural Anthropology*, 2nd edn. London: Pluto Press.

Gellner, E. 1969. *Saints of the Atlas*. London: Weidenfeld and Nicolson.

Geschiere, P. and T. Nyamnjoh, 2000. Capitalism and Autochthony: The Seesaw of Mobility and Belonging. *Public Culture* 12(2): 423–52.

Hammoudi, A. 1997. *Master and Disciple: The Cultural Foundations of Moroccan Authoritarianism*. Chicago: University of Chicago Press

Harris, W.B. 1897. The Nomadic Berbers of Central Morocco. *Geographical Journal* 9: 638–45.

Hefner, R.W. (ed.) 1993. *Conversion to Christianity: Historical and Anthropological Perspectives on a Great Transformation*. Berkeley: University of California Press.

Huot, Cap. 1923. Les terres collectives et la colonisation européenne. *l'Afrique Française* 3: 277–92.

Lentz, C. and P. Nugent. 2000. *Ethnicity in Ghana: The Limits of Innovation*. London: Macmillan.

Morsy, M. 1984. Arbitration as a Political Institution: An Interpretation of the Status of Monarchy in Morocco. A.S. Ahmed and D.M. Hart (eds) *Islam in Tribal Societies. From the Atlas to the Indus*. London: Routledge and Kegan Paul, 39–65.

Obdeijn, H., P. de Mas and P. Hermans. 2002. *Geschiedenis van Marokko*. Amsterdam: Bulaaq.

Pennell, C.R. 2000. *Morocco since 1830: A History*. New York: New York University Press.

Salemink, O. 2003. Social Science Intervention: Moral versus Political Economy and the Vietnam War. In Ph. Quarles van Ufford and A.K. Giri (eds) *A Moral Critique of Development: In Search of Global Responsibilities*. London: Routledge, 169–93.

Seddon, D. 1981. *Moroccan Peasants: A Century of Change in the Eastern Rif, 1870–1970*. Folkestone: Dawson.

Segonzac, Marquis de. 1903. *Voyage au Maroc*. Paris: Librairie Armand Colin.

Scott, J.C. 1976. *The Moral Economy of the Peasant: Rebellion and Subsistence in Southeast Asia*. New Haven, CT: Yale University Press.

Venema, L.B. 1992. Het Ontstaan van een lokale Elite in een Plattelandsdistrict van Marokko: de Relatie met Nationale Ontwikkelingen. *Sharqiyyât* 4(2): 145–60.

Venema, L.B. (with A. Mguild 2002). The Vitality of Local Political Institutions in the Middle Atlas, Morocco. *Ethnology* 41(2): 103–17.

Venema, L.B and A. Mguild, 2003. Access to Land and Berber Ethnicity in the Middle Atlas. *Middle Eastern Studies* 39(4): 35–53.

Venema, L.B. 2005. State Formation, Access to the Commons and Autochthony among the Berbers of the Middle Atlas, Morocco. In S. Evers, M. Spierenburg and

H. Wels (eds) *Competing Jurisdictions, Settling Land Claims in Africa*. Leiden: Brill, 181–201.

Vinogradov, A.R. 1974. *The Ait Ndhir of Morocco: A Study of the Social Transformation of a Berber Tribe*. Anthropological Papers. Ann Arbor: University of Michigan Press.

Wolf, E.R. 1966. *Peasants*. Englewood Cliffs, NJ: Prentice Hall.

4
Flexible Migrants: Brazilian Gold Miners and their Quest for Human Security in Surinam

Marjo de Theije and Ellen Bal[1]

Contemporary Surinam is characterised by an ethnically and culturally diverse population. This heterogeneity is essentially the result of a long history (or histories) of forced (including the mass import of slaves) and voluntary immigration. With the exception of a small number of Amerindian communities (e.g. Caribs and Arawaks), all contemporary citizens of Surinam are descendants of immigrants or migrants themselves. Surinam's history of nation building is one marked by processes of uprooting, departure, creolisation, emancipation, community formation and taking root; each community (and individual) with its own specific trajectory.

Based on a plantation economy since the seventeenth century – some argue that Surinam still is a plantation society (Bruijne 2001: 223) – Surinam has been linked to the outside world through its export of mineral and half-finished products (including sugar, bauxite, some timber and gold) and import of labour. Until the abolition of slavery, slaves from various parts of West Africa formed around 90 per cent of the population.[2] The end of slavery led to a large inflow of indentured workers from British India, and the Dutch East Indies. Together with the original, Amerindian, communities and the 'white' section of the population (who never constituted more than 4 per cent of the total population) composed of Dutch, Belgians, Germans, French, Scandinavians, Ashkenazi and Sephardic Jews, the Dutch colony developed into a highly diverse society. Recent, postcolonial immigrations from China, the Dominican Republic, Haiti, and particularly Brazil, have added to the heterogeneity of the country's population.

Surinamese citizens such as the Hindustanis (of British Indian origin), the Afro-Surinamese or Creoles (descendants of slaves),

Maroon communities (descendants of runaway slaves), and the Javanese and Chinese (offspring of indentured labourers from the Dutch East Indies) have long histories of colonial suppression and of becoming full-fledged citizens of Surinam. The historical trajectories of recent, postcolonial migrants, such as Haitians, Dominicans and Brazilians, are, for various reasons, very different. Whereas the 'old migrants' could not, or did not want to, maintain relations with the place of origin (see e.g. Bal and Sinha-Kerkhoff 2006, 2008), 'new migrants' have many options at their disposal to keep up the linkages with their hometowns, families and friends. These interconnections have an important transformative effect on the process of immigration and integration, on notions of belonging and community constructions, on the way migrants are perceived and received by others, etc. (see Vertovec 2003).

This chapter focuses on the largest category of recent migrants, the Brazilians. We purposely refer to them as a *category* (or network) rather than a community, to emphasise the relatively feeble and instrumental character of the ties they maintain with one another (cf. Eriksen 2002: 41). Since the mid 1990s, tens of thousands of Brazilians have found their way to Surinam in search of work, gold and money. It is estimated that at this moment as many as 20,000 Brazilians are working and living in the country (Algemeen Bureau voor de Statistiek 2006: 439).[3] Our research shows that these immigrants are mostly unschooled or (semi)-literate agricultural labourers from the poorer regions in northern Brazil. They work in small-scale gold mining[4] as miners or *garimpeiros*,[5] in the *barrancos* (mining pits) owned by fellow Brazilians or Surinamese, who have invested in the necessary machinery. While the first *garimpeiros* generally stayed in the rainforest, since the mid 1990s, we find an increasing number in Paramaribo, the capital of Surinam. Local supermarkets have begun to sell Brazilian products, and Brazilians themselves have opened bars, hostels, and shops selling mining equipment for the *garimpeiros*. Nowadays, a part of the Tourtonne neighbourhood is known as Klein (Little) Belem, or Belemzinho, referring to Belem, the capital of the state of Pará, in the north of Brazil. Here, a visitor can imagine her- or himself in Brazil, with the signboards in Portuguese, and Brazilian products sold everywhere.

In Surinamese public discourse, the Brazilians are considered a threat to Surinam's security (economy, ecology, society, etc.) rather than an asset. Newspapers report that the Brazilians are there 'to carry away our gold';[6] they describe them as aliens who do not pay tax and who import criminality from Brazil. Time and again, 'illegal' and 'Brazilian' seem inextricably bound up with one another. Indeed, most *garimpeiros* have no residence or working permit (at the most a temporary tourist visa), no social security number, no health insurance, no permanent address and no guaranteed income. While representing a threat to human security for many Surinamese, the *garimpeiros* themselves live and work under harsh conditions, and face various insecurities on a daily basis. Their illegal status and the absence of a strong sense of community render them physically and existentially vulnerable. They have to deal with (political) marginalisation, health risks, loneliness, isolation, anxiety, etc.

It is tempting for anthropologists, who often study the poor rather than the rich, the weak rather than the powerful, to concentrate on the downsides of illegal migration: the push factors (poverty, deprivation, etc.) that led to the migration and/or the marginal and vulnerable position of illegal immigrants. In this chapter, we adopt an alternative approach that focuses in particular on the flipside of individualism (read solitude) and detachment, and which we sum up with the term *migrant flexibility*. We will show that the absence of a close-knit community, the lack of attachment to Surinam (as a nation, and place) and their position as (frequently) illegal or semi-illegal, also allows for individual freedom and opens up various new possibilities. All miners, Brazilian and Surinamese alike, share an interest in some basic facilities, stability and trust in the field, in order to realise their individual dreams of prosperity (Heemskerk and de Theije forthcoming, Theije 2007a, 2007b). Yet their relative lack of commitment (to one another and to Surinam, its people, soil and even its gold), makes it much easier for the Brazilian miners to 'move on', to find other professions, and to try their luck elsewhere. In other words, while there are many downsides of illegal work in gold mining, their position as aliens implies a certain individualism and detachment that facilitate a readiness to take risks, i.e. to undertake actions that carry some probability for negative consequences (e.g. Boyer in Magar et al. 2008: 10), and an ability to move on, and to create new chances.

The concept of *human security* offers an interesting tool, or lens, to study these Brazilians in their quest for human security (or rather, in their search for gold). It provides a particularly suitable instrument to unravel the many faces and dynamics of migration and belonging, encompassing individual differences and collective similarities at the same time. It helps to uncover (apparently) contradictory manifestations of human (in)security that accompany migration processes in general, and, more specifically, the migration processes of Brazilian gold miners in Surinam. Here we argue that the conditions (such as the lack of a strong collective and binding identity, individualism, illegality), which often mark the lives of these migrants, not only cause physical and existential insecurity, but also facilitate a certain *physical* and *mental* flexibility, that may open up new opportunities.

Hereafter, we will try to demonstrate the complexity of human security in the lives of the Brazilian miners in Surinam by giving a brief description of the various insecurities these miners have to face, followed by an account of the flipsides of many of these same insecurities, which also open up new possibilities for these migrants. We have woven the life story of Helena, a 52-year-old Brazilian female *garimpeiro* through our account. Her life history is particularly revealing of the paradoxes of human security for Brazilian gold miners in Surinam.

MIGRATION TO SURINAM AS A STRATEGY IN THE QUEST FOR HUMAN SECURITY

Most Brazilians in Surinam exchanged a situation of relative certainty (in terms of predictability and familiarity with their life conditions) for a life in an unknown country, where they will have no secure income, where living conditions will be harsh, and where they will be in a vulnerable position in terms of civil rights. However, many *garimpeiros* in Surinam were already experienced (seasonal) migrants before they moved on to Surinam, British Guyana or French Guiana. Many had migrated from rural zones to mining areas, or from southern or north-eastern states to the north, Pará in particular. For gold miners in Brazil, mining often is a seasonal activity (Slater 1994: 720). In southern Pará, for example, rural workers incorporate mining in the 'cyclical logic' of their work (Schonenberg 2001: 399).[7] Most informants estimate that 90 per cent of the Brazilians in Surinam come from northern Brazil, and that some 70 per cent of them are from rural Maranhão. Every day new migrants arrive, while others return temporarily or to never come back again.

From the 1980s onward, gold mining became the most important motive for migration in northern Brazil. In 1980, the discovery of a large gold mine in Serra Pelada (Bald Mountain), in the Brazilian Amazon, triggered a gold rush involving 80,000 *garimpeiros* and ultimately producing 90,000 kilos of gold from a single open pit (Veiga 1997: 10). From here, gold fever spread to neighbouring countries such as Venezuela, Guyana, French Guiana and Surinam, and caused a revival of small-scale gold mining in these countries. The rise in the price of gold since the 1970s, the deterioration of the local economy, the civil war in the 1980s,[8] and the closing of many mining sites in the Brazilian Amazon for independent *garimpeiros* ultimately led to the influx of thousands of Brazilian miners into Surinam. Between 1995 and 1998, gold production in Surinam boomed. The estimated output rose from 10,000 kilos in 1995 to 20,000 in 1998 and 1999, but only part of the production was registered (Mol et al. 2001: 184). This corresponds with the observations of our interviewees, who identified 1997–8 as the peak year for immigration of Brazilians into Surinam. Since then, the production of gold in small-scale mining continued to increase and the official Central Bank of Suriname's purchases from *garimpeiros* and *porknockers* almost doubled to 12,000 kilos between 2000 and 2006. Gold is Surinam's second largest export product (after alumina) and more than half of it is produced by small-scale mining (International Monetary Fund 2007).

The 'business' of small-scale mining is by definition a risky one, and the life of a *garimpeiro* is harsh and unpredictable in various ways. A miner is never certain of his income, and investments may or may not render any profits. Mining in Surinam is usually carried out by a small workforce of four to eight miners, one (female) cook, and an overseer (who may also be the owner), who organises the work. *Garimpeiros* work for a specified share of the production, while cooks, drivers of tractors and all terrain vehicles (ATVs), and operators of excavating machines have fixed wages. All informants agreed that it was becoming increasingly difficult to find gold; in the words of Pedro: 'Easy gold, at the door of your house, near to the city, easy to win … is finishing.' To find gold now requires far greater investments in terms of time, labour and machinery. For small-scale *garimpeiros* this is far more difficult than for the large companies, who are granted concessions in the Surinamese rainforest, because their methods are based on experience and trial and error, instead of scientific research. If no gold is found, the investments are gone.

Another important risk factor concerns the health of the *garimpeiros* and of all others living in gold miner camps. Good sanitation is often lacking, there is a shortage of clean water, and the diet is poor – even though all *garimpeiros* emphasised that it is very important to eat well if one has to work so hard. The job itself is heavy and unhealthy; the men stand in the water under the burning sun, up to 12 hours a day. All informants who had been asked about it stated that they suffered from malaria. Moreover, in order to separate the gold from the soil, miners use mercury, which is known for its harmful effects on health and the environment. Pit workers also suffer disproportionately from accidents with the machines used in mining (Heemskerk 2003: 275).

An additional factor contributing to the insecurity of Brazilian miners is their, often illegal or semi-illegal position. *Garimpeiros* repeatedly complain about the Surinamese bureaucracy causing this problem by not granting them a work permit. This sense of 'deportability' or 'the possibility of deportation' (Degenova 2002: 439) causes anxiety. As citizens without rights, they feel at risk from criminals and corrupt police. Rumours about the police raiding *pensións* and brothels to check documents and to arrest illegal Brazilians abound. Sometimes the illegal worker can pay his or her way out of trouble, but they may also be deported. Some informants argued that it is not impossible to acquire a legal status, even though Surinamese bureaucracy is difficult to tackle.

One important aspect of human security is that of 'belonging'. Here we focus on three particular dimensions of belonging that play a crucial role in the lives of the *garimpeiros* in Surinam: belonging to Surinam as a (nation-)state, to land (as 'sons' and rightful owners, 'of the soil'), and to a local (regional, religious, ethnic, etc.) community. The *garimpeiros* have not developed a strong sense of belonging on any of these three dimensions. Earlier we detailed how their often illegal status causes a sense of insecurity and vulnerability. As illegal immigrants, moreover, they have no legal rights as citizens of Surinam, and can make no claims concerning the mine pit in which they work, no matter the amount of blood, sweat and tears they invest in that soil. Traditional owners of the land or concession holders may suddenly expel these workers from a mining pit.

Yet, there is, as we shall demonstrate hereafter, another interesting side to this: while Surinamese miners, whether they are locals or from other parts of the country, are permanently fearful that the gold will become exhausted, the *garimpeiros* do not share that fear. Once the gold runs out, they will simply move on, unattached as they are to the place. The third dimension of belonging, that of belonging to a community, which provides a sense of identity, a we-feeling, a warm nest that offers support in times of need (cf. Bauman 2001), has not strongly developed amongst the miners. Certainly, a *garimpeiro* network has developed, and the Brazilians know where to find support, advice, comfort, leisure, etc. Nonetheless, many have explained that, when it comes down to it, they are on their own.

FLEXIBLE MIGRANTS: MOVEABLE AND NON-MOVEABLE SECURITIES

'It was well worth the pain.' After working for twelve years in Surinam, the 52-year-old Helena is about to return to Brazil. Satisfied, she looks back on a very successful period in her life. She left Brazil because she did not see any opportunities to improve her economic situation there. 'I have no schooling, so in Brazil I would be a laundress or domestic servant. In Brazil, I would not have earned even 10 per cent of what I earned here.'[9]

Helena was born in Tocantins, in northern Brazil. Already at a young age, in the 1970s, she became involved in the service economy, which the gold mining in this region had generated. Later she moved on to Brasilia, where she married and had two children. When her husband died and left her with two small children, she decided to return to the north to make a living there. In 1981, the gold rush in the Amazon region reached a climax, caused by the discovery of gold in Serra Pelada. Helena then decided to shift to Santarem, where she began a shop for miners and others who swarmed into the region. Ten years later, the mining business in Santarem deteriorated. In 1995, Helena decided to leave her country and to take a chance elsewhere. She accepted the invitation of a friend who had moved to Surinam and decided to try her luck in Paramaribo, Surinam. She opened a restaurant, at a time when many Brazilians were arriving. Some years later, she moved on to the mining area known as Benzdorp, where she started a shop and a restaurant. Benzdorp was growing fast in those years, and her business prospered. After a few years, she sold her house and restaurant, and set up her own gold mining business. She bought a motor and other mining necessities, and became a pit owner.

In many respects, Helena's case is unique and different from other stories. Unlike most *garimpeiros*, for example, she is a woman. And while many *garimpeiros* never had any other professions but gold mining, Helena also was a shop owner, a cook, etc. At the same time, however, her fate is similar to that of other Brazilians, and her life story contains many elements that are crucial to our understanding of the temporary migration of the thousands of *garimpeiros* to Surinam and Guyana and French Guiana.

RAGS AND RICHES

For the various reasons mentioned above, the business of gold mining is risky. At the same time, however, it holds the promise of fortune.

There is always that chance to strike lucky. Since *garimpeiro*s work for a set percentage of the produce – this applies to the pit owners as much as to the miners – this chance, or dream, seems to outweigh the risks. The percentage the workers receive depends on the working techniques used (with the exception of the concession owner, who always receives 10 per cent of the total produce). In a pit where all work is carried out manually, the labourers divide 30 per cent of the remaining produce among themselves (in case of six workers, for example, each worker receives 5 per cent). The remaining 70 per cent is for the owner to pay all the operation costs, including the salary of the cook and food for the whole crew. In pits where the service is (partly) mechanised with excavator machines and sometimes bulldozers, the percentage for the workers drops (down to 12 per cent) but more terrain is processed and output thereby increased. In any case, the higher the production, the more gold the workers receive.

Yet not all Brazilian migrants are directly involved in the mining business and these migrants do not earn a fixed share of the turnover. However, the industry attracts all sorts of entrepreneurs, who seize the opportunity to benefit from the business (if only the attraction) of gold. A worksite, or *barranco* (literally gully, artisanal mining pit), is often located at a great distance from a village. Hence, the workers live in camps, sometimes with workers from nearby *barrancos*. In this way, the gold industry generates many auxiliary economic opportunities, such as the trade in Brazilian products (ranging from clothes to cigarettes to perfumes), jobs as cook for the work teams in the gold fields, and prostitution. All these activities have in common that they can easily be practised somewhere else.

Helena narrated her life story as if her success as a mine owner was entirely coincidental. However, she had worked hard and lived sober, which allowed her to save a part of her earnings. And when she wanted to invest her savings, she did not open yet another restaurant or shop, nor did she import goods from Brazil to sell in the mining camps. Instead, she bought the necessary equipment and began digging for gold herself. After one unsuccessful attempt, with gear she had partially bought on tick, she hit a good spot, rich in gold. This was 'where everything started, and where I bought another machine, my ATV, excavator – the first one – the Caterpillar'. For Helena, her switch to the gold mining was the best thing she has ever done. It is interesting to note that she does not describe her venture as particularly risky, although she took many chances and encountered various problems in the years that followed. Although she was grateful to God, who 'was always blessing me (...) when things got really difficult', she also explained that '*garimpo* is good business, because you can start with something small', and that it may provide 'good money so that you can grow.'[10] In short, gold mining is risky and attractive at the same time. It involves many hazards but also holds the promise of becoming very successful one day. In addition, it provides the possibility to earn money in various ways, not only by means of the gold digging itself. It requires flexible, resourceful, hardworking individuals, who are ready to take risks, to respond to new opportunities, and to move on when business declines.

ADVENTURE

Gold miners expect to prosper one day. This is an important motive for the Brazilians to engage in gold mining. However, the expectations of economic affluence may simply connote a modest desire to become financially self-sufficient, to be able to buy one's own clothes, to become independent of parental support. Many *garimpeiros* entered the profession as young boys and they related how difficult it was to get used to the circumstances in the *garimpo*. Yet, in retrospect, they also point out that they got used to it, even ended up liking this kind of life. Some expressed this by saying that the *garimpo* is a vice to which they have become addicted. In other words, risk-taking has become more than a strategy; it has become a lifestyle (Nooteboom 2003: 223).

Working in the *garimpo* is an exciting activity and definitely less boring than working on the land, which is not only tedious, but also offers few perspectives on a better life. In the words of Leonardo: 'What counts is the hope, the expectation that you can achieve the goal you have. Adventure dominates. Working on the land, as a labourer, you will never achieve what you want.' As a *garimpeiro* you have more chances: 'Sometimes you are lucky, quickly, in four to five months, maybe a year, you accomplish what you want.... That is why we opt for this adventure.' Leonardo, now in his early forties, had followed his older brothers to work as a *garimpeiro* when he was a young man, back in Pará, in the 1980s.[11]

The women who join as cooks or sex workers, or who take up jobs in the commercial trade, make similar calculations. Some female informants framed their motives in a discourse of need back home, but others also underscored their desire to try something different; they explained that they saw no future back home, while working for minimal wages, without a husband to provide for them and their children, for example. Once in the *garimpo*, some discovered that the adventure was not quite as pleasant as they had imagined it, and that the work was not as easy as they had expected. They began repenting their choice and could only think of earning enough gold to return as soon as possible. However, for young women, an additional aspect of their migrant life is the opportunity to meet a man from another background, with financial means, who may become their husband. Many (ex-) sex workers dream of marrying a Dutchman, although most of them hardly know any Dutch people in Surinam. In general, women in the *garimpo* communities do not stay single for a long time.

The adventure of the *garimpo* is expressed through stories of success and failure that are told and retold again and again; anecdotes about the kilos of gold found and again lost due to bad management, or about the kilos dug up while working for others and for which they never received their rightful shares. Many migrants never find the anticipated riches, and have to work hard to make ends meet with their mining activities. Brazilians from the first hour, in the Benzdorp/Antino area, recount romantic stories about their contribution to the infrastructure in the gold field, about how they spent weeks constructing paths into the bush, making shortcuts to the creeks further inland; men with simple tools and a lot of courage. This courage they still need. Zito and his wife live in a camp four hours inland, and with their old pick-up car have to pass through a dangerous, mountainous area to get there. 'I have lost three babies there already,' Zito said, referring to the accidents and near-accidents they had had, to explain the miscarriages his wife suffered in the past years.[12] They are still longing for a child but their risky and adventurous life does not seem to allow for a fulfilment of this dream.

For a number of *garimpeiros*, the decision to go after gold, even as far as the goldfields in Surinam, seems motivated by the desire to be free, to travel, to escape, more so than by the aspiration to strike it rich one day. Many of the life stories show that the miners decided to join the gold mining business at times in their lives when many things went wrong; when they faced bad luck in business, ended a relationship, were in discord with their parents, etc. Gold seemed to offer a way out of these troubled lives.

Apart from the adventurous life and the dreams of riches, several other attractions keep the Brazilians in the *garimpo*. Social life in the bush is full of temptations, such as drink, drugs and sex. The pit owners who strike it rich share their fortune with others in the brothels of the *garimpo*, and the workers who are less prosperous spend their earnings and hang around near luckier ones to get drinks and women. Quite a number of Brazilians get hooked on these temptations of the *garimpo* life. 'Even when you had not planned to go to the *currutela* [brothel],' says Vander from Maranhão, 'a colleague comes along and invites you, and then another passes by, and you end up spending a gram of gold as if it is a *Real*.'[13] 'You end up losing a lot, spending all you earned during one or several months of hard work in the *barranco*,' he concludes.

In all life histories, independence stands out as a significant characteristic of the *garimpeiro* life in Surinam. A pit owner is free to move to another region, whenever he expects to find more gold there. The worker can leave the pit owner when he does not like the management, his co-workers, the food, or when he finds that the *currutela* is located too far away, or for whatever reasons that frustrate him. In the *garimpo*, a kind of sociability is created, in which courage, risk, luck and conspicuous consumption are central elements. In this social environment, a once landless peasant from Brazil may now be an independent, successful miner, his own boss. Although once the objective of migration was to earn money, *garimpo* life is highly appealing, even addictive, and keeps many workers involved in the *garimpeiro* business in Surinam.

HOME AWAY FROM HOME

'We Brazilians are like compulsory tourists,' said Chico. 'We create our home away from home, wherever we go.'[14] With these words, he explains the growth of the mining village Benzdorp, with its Brazilian bars, Brazilian products put up for sale and Brazilian atmosphere. He also points to the adaptable nature of the population of Surinam's gold fields, and to the (intended) temporariness of their presence in the country. Tourists are merely visitors, they may settle for a while but they do not root. Chico's comparison provides some key explanations for the absence of a strong sense of belonging to Surinam.

The Brazilian migrants see many opportunities to earn money in Surinam but they do not intend to settle in the country on a permanent basis. Most of them express the desire to return to Brazil one day, to set up house near their families, and to resume their lives over there. They will use their savings to build a house, to begin a shop, restaurant or something else that should guarantee a decent income. Helena was earning a lot of money for quite some years, but wanted more, 'because it would not have been worth the pain, if I merely returned to the life I used to live before Surinam. I want to go back to a different life.' Hence she stayed several years longer, in order to return as a rich woman. Many migrants, however, never achieve this goal and quite a number end up being 'stuck' in Surinam. Nevertheless, even these men and women continue trying to materialise their dream to return to Brazil one day and to start a business there.

Brazilian migrants invest much more in their links with Brazil than in personal relations in Surinam. Most workers maintain their emotional ties to Brazil, facilitated by ever improving telecommunication facilities in both countries. Those who can afford it, return for some months every one, two or three years, to visit their families. Many then have a medical check-up, and, if they have enough savings, make some investments. Those with rural backgrounds buy some livestock to start a cattle farm. Others purchase a motorcycle to begin a taxi service. The ones who used to live in towns and cities generally purchase a plot for the construction of a house.

Workers and work sites in Surinam are of a temporary nature. People are constantly on the move. Work places are deserted after some months of work, when the gold is finishing, and camps are thus frequently relocated. Often, machine owners find new locations nearby, but when they do not, they may move their camps to far-away gold fields, in Surinam itself or in neighbouring French Guiana. Now and then, camps become more permanent, when machine owners construct proper houses for themselves and only move workers and camps to new gold fields. For individual workers the shifting between locations is relatively easy since they generally have very few belongings in Surinam and do not need to bring much equipment to the next workplace. These men and women travel light, with one or two bags only, adapted to the temporary nature of their migrant lives.

As urban Paramaribo is difficult to reach from many of the gold fields – only by expensive air connections or by strenuous boat trips – most *garimpeiros* only go there to board their flights to Brazil. Pit owners and shopkeepers in the *garimpo* make the trip more frequently, to purchase mining equipment, mercury, fuel, radio-telephone stations and food supplies for their crew, for prices far cheaper than in the *garimpo*. They also visit the capital to sell their gold, to recover from malaria, to take some rest and to find *divertimento*. Many however have an 'agent' – mostly Surinamese men who speak Portuguese – who does the shopping for them and who sends the purchases to the *garimpo*. In other words, for most Brazilians in *garimpo* areas in Surinam, the jungle is their most permanent abode.

In this situation of constant shift, a need for some sort of community or 'familiar (read: Brazilian) company' arises. Wherever the migrants go, they create home away from home. In this context, home may simply refer to a shelter, where they can hang their hammocks and secure their scant belongings. Yet in villages such as Benzdorp at the Lawa River, or those around the Brokopondo Lake, 'home' also includes shops, hairdressers, bars, *cabarés* (brothels), one or two Brazilian Pentecostal churches, some basic medical assistance (in the form of Brazilian medicine), Brazilian music, a satellite TV connection with Brazil. Hence, these villages offer a feel of home: Brazil in a nutshell. Surinamese dwellers in such places form a minority. They have adapted to the Brazilian environment, speak Portuguese, dance to Brazilian music and drink Brazilian beer.[15]

NO RIGHTS, NO TIES

The (transnational) focus on Brazil alone does not explain why Brazilians remain indifferent to Surinam and the Surinamese. Several other factors fuel their lack of engagement. An obvious one is the fact that few workers are in the possession of an official permit. Many enter Surinam by crossing the Maroni River, which separates Surinam from French Guiana. Here, border authorities are entirely absent. Those *garimpeiros* who obtained a visa upon arrival at Johan Adolf Pengel international airport, or in one of the border towns, do not bother to have it renewed in Paramaribo. According to the representative of the Brazilian consulate in Paramaribo: 'They have enough other problems to deal with and no time to worry about their legal rights and documents.' To be undocumented renders the Brazilians vulnerable. When they are victims of crime, for example, or become involved in a conflict with the Maroons, they cannot call in the police. However, the Brazilians also know that they are never asked for these documents, and in the *garimpo* such documents are of no use at all. Here, other rights matter, such as customary rights to the land (held by the Maroons), or the regulations drawn up by the concession owners.

Land claims by local Maroon and indigenous populations are most troublesome for the Brazilians. Not because *garimpeiros* are against such rights, but because claimants are unpredictable and one can never be sure who may rightfully make a claim. In most gold fields, local chiefs (*gaaman* or *kabiten*)[16] grant permission to Brazilians to carry out their mining activities in exchange for a regular payment of gold, or for a specified percentage of the production (usually 10 per cent). However, sometimes other claimants appear, and the Brazilians end up making payments to several persons. It may also happen that a local person shows up to order the *garimpeiros* to leave the pit, causing the Brazilians to lose their investments. This also happened to Helena once. Even though she knew that the claimant had no legal basis for taking her place, she – in retrospect – said rather acceptingly: 'he may not have been the owner, but he was from this land, from this soil.... And, as the Surinamese say: "You [Brazilians] did not bring even a handful of soil from Brazil."'

The position of concession holder seems much clearer to the migrants, partly because some of them have introduced a registration system and employ staff who not only collect the produce, but also maintain peace and order. However, concessionaires may suddenly change their rules, and evict workers or demand bigger payments, etc. This also happened on the Antino property. In 2006, the owner of the concession entered an agreement with Reunion Gold, a Canadian gold company, to carry out systematic explorations of the field. Several Brazilians had to quit their mining activities on those locations where professional geologists anticipated significant gold reserves. In other words, Brazilians are never sure how long they will be able to stay on a certain site. This, in combination with their orientation towards Brazil and their often illegal position in the country, means that the *garimpeiros* do not become involved with Surinam, its nation and its soil.

This does not mean that the Brazilians make no efforts to legalise their positions at all, however. When, by the end of 2007, the Surinamese government ran a 'pre-registration' campaign, Brazilians cooperated in large numbers. Furthermore, in the Benzdorp/Antino area, where mining takes place on the concessions of two city-based companies, the Brazilians considered registration with one of these firms as a legal permission to work there. Every owner of a pit, shop or bar in the settlement carefully guarded the receipts of his or her monthly payment to the permit holder. To them, such receipts proved that they paid tax, even though this probably would not be of much help if the immigration and tax authorities brought a case against them. Yet, owing to the overall lack of state control – or 'government void' (Kruijt and Hoogbergen 2005: 200) – it is relatively easy to live and work in Surinam for many years without ever getting into administrative trouble.

Helena had all her paperwork in order and she paid her annual income tax. She could have easily refrained from doing so, however, because 'nobody ever asked me for my documents'.

SKILLS

Even though the first Brazilians did not have at their disposal the infrastructure that was available ten years later, they encountered an environment that was very similar to what they were used to back home. Brazil is 'Amazonian' as well and, hardly hindered by state borders, the Brazilians can quite easily move between countries (Heemskerk and Theije forthcoming). Take the case of Chico, for example, who began working as a *garimpeiro* in Rondônia, Guajará-mirim, moved on to Rondônia, Boa Vista ('I picked up some gold there'), and from there to French Guiana, where he worked for several companies in Cayenne. After his deportation from that country for the fifth time, he crossed the river into Surinam.[17]

Once in Surinam, many Brazilians continue to move around, from workplace to workplace. They travel in the jungle for hours, days, or even weeks, to search for a good place to work. Although they depend on the gold for their subsistence, for the reasons discussed earlier, they do not become attached to the ground, the place, the soil where the gold lies hidden. Instead, they keep moving and, wherever they go, they take their skills and work ethos with them. In fact, their very success in small-scale gold mining in Surinam is contingent on their knowledge and experience with different techniques. They introduced the hydraulic methods of mining, which nowadays prevail in the small-scale mining business in Surinam. They brought their equipment to the region and shared their technical knowledge with the local population. Even those Maroons who were not directly involved in the mining business also profited from the economic activities of these *garimpeiros*. The Brazilians have given a boost to the local economy and they pay informal taxes to the local authorities. They are generally more productive than other workers, and concessionaires favour them over others, both as investors and as workers. Their success has also brought some basic economic security for themselves, and at least a relative command over their own lives. Their skills and knowledge are their principal assets. Wherever they go, they will always have those, adding to their flexibility and readiness to move.

CONCLUDING REMARKS: 'THE DESTINY OF AN ADVENTURER IS TO WALK'

'The destiny of an adventurer is to walk.' This is how Helena described her fate and that of her fellow *garimpeiros* during her last conversation with Marjo, while she was waiting for the buyer of her excavator to hand over the gold. After this, she would return to Brazil. Together, they were contemplating Helena's plans, of staying put somewhere in Brazil for three months or so, and of next moving on to set up a new business in Brazil or somewhere outside the country. Helena was sure of one thing: she would not return to Benzdorp, where the gold reserves are coming to an end. Other places in Surinam, so she had heard, are offering a similar prospect. She would probably continue her 'walk' and head for Guyana, or Venezuela, or maybe to one of these new *garimpos* in Brazil.

In this chapter, we showed how the various insecurities, uncertainties and risks, which lie at the core of the lives of Brazilian gold miners in Surinam, also allow for a certain flexibility of minds and hearts, and mobility of bodies, enhancing their chances and even certain pleasures in life. By applying human security as a tool, or lens, to study this particular type of migration, we tried to show how the different dimensions of human security and insecurity are interconnected: how they may cause pain and pleasure, anxiety and fortune, loneliness and freedom, at the same time. We also pointed out that risk-taking should not (only) be conceptualised as the negative side of human security, as the opposite of the security which people desire, but also as a road to security (gold), or even as a desire in itself (a continuous craving for the adventurous life of a *garimpeiro*). In this sense, risk-taking gives expression to individual ambitions, dreams, and the ability and readiness to create new chances in life.

The circumstances under which the Brazilian *garimpeiros* in Surinam live and work are harsh, and encompass serious health hazards and various uncertainties, including that of being without a proper legal position. Notwithstanding these downsides to their lives, our informants showed great appreciation of the economic opportunities, adventure and autonomy, which come with their migrant lives. *Garimpeiros* have, in fact, become quite attached, even addicted to both their individual and shared lifestyles. To many *garimpeiros*, the positive dimensions of risk seem to outweigh the negative dimensions of insecurity and, for some, risk-taking has even become a lifestyle. Illegality, individualism and uprootedness have resulted in a certain physical and mental flexibility that opens up new opportunities. This renders them less dependent on Surinam and the Surinamese, and probably less vulnerable to exploitation than previous immigrants to the country were, in times when transnational connections could not be maintained. We by no means suggest that all migrations follow a similar kind of logic. We want to argue that those insecurities that characterise the lives of migrants, provide chance and agency at the same time. Contemporary gold mining (and the necessary migration) offers highly individualised strategies to get something more out of life. Only by means of close scrutiny of specific migration trajectories can we uncover these particular dimensions of human securities and insecurities, and their intricate interrelations.

The Brazilians prove to be flexible workers, possessed of a flexible mindset and of working skills and technical knowledge which are useful in many places. Based on these insights into their lives and minds, we predict that these migrants will move on, to risky places, opening up various new opportunities to improve their individual lives.

NOTES

1. This chapter is co-authored by Ellen Bal and Marjo de Theije, and based on fieldwork in Surinam since 2001. From 2001 to 2005, Ellen Bal conducted research on Surinamese and Dutch Hindustanis and their linkages with India. She worked closely together with Kathinka Sinha-Kerkhoff. Marjo de Theije began her research on Brazilians in Surinam in 2004. She has paid several research visits to Paramaribo and mining areas in Surinam, and has worked in total for eight months in one of the largest mining areas of the country. She collected the empirical data on which this chapter is based. Both authors work at the Department of Social and Cultural Anthropology of Vrije Universiteit/ Free University Amsterdam.
2. One-third, the Loangas, came from the area between Cameroon and Angola. One-third (Kromanti) came from the Gold Coast (Ghana). Some 25 per cent came from present-day Guinea, Sierra Leone, Liberia and Ivory Coast, and the rest came from Togo, Benin, Western Nigeria (Hoefte 2001: 7).
3. Neighbouring French Guiana and Guyana witnessed a similar influx of Brazilian migrants (Arouck 2000, Cleaver 2005, Colchester 1997, Herman 2003, Simonian and Ferreira 2006).
4. 'Small-scale gold mining' means all mining that uses rudimentary processes to extract gold from secondary and primary ore bodies (Heemskerk 2002: 327).
5. *Garimpeiro* is the Brazilian word for miner and is used almost exclusively for gold miner. In this chapter we use the word only for the Brazilians, not for other gold miners. In Sranan tongo (Surinamese language) gold miners are called *gowtuman*.
6. It suffices to look at forum pages of Surinamese newspapers to see this opinion expressed. See e.g. http://www.waterkant.net/suriname/2007/09/17/brazilianen-in-suriname/

7. This was also reported by Macmillan (1995: 73), who shows that miners are not necessarily landless peasants, as is often thought, and that for many small landowners mining offers an additional source of income (see also Menezes 2004).

8. In 1986, Maroons revolted against the military government, and a peace treaty between the Jungle Commando and the government was signed only in 1992. The 'inland war' caused a severe disruption of the social and economic life of the Maroons and a dislocation of 10,000 Surinamese to French Guiana, across the Maroni River, where many of them still live. The Jungle Commando relied on gold mining for their survival in the interior, and it was during this period that the first Brazilians were invited to work on dredges (*ponton*, *balsa*) in the Maroni River.

9. Over the course of 18 months, de Theije conducted four taped interviews with Helena (born in Tocantins, in 1953), the first in February 2006, the last on 1 July 2007, all in the mining camps where she was living at the time of the interview. Apart from these interviews there were many conversations during encounters at Helena's camp, the landing strip and in the miners' village nearby.

10. She continued: 'That is why I say that he also puts the gold, you know. Because he is the owner of the gold, the silver, he can do all things, he is the God that transformed water in wine ....' For an analysis of the relation between religious beliefs and gold mining, see de Theije (2008a, 2008b).

11. Interview 12 February 2006. Leonardo visited his brother who works on the Antino camp, a few hours walk from the place where he himself was working at the time.

12. Zito, born 1960, Tocantins; in Surinam since 1993; interview 25 May 2007.

13. *Real* is the Brazilian monetary unit. At the time of the interview a *Real* was worth €0.37. Vander, born 1975, Maranhão; in Surinam since 2003; interview 19 May 2007.

14. Chico, Benzdorp, 22 July 2006. Chico came to Benzdorp in 1995 and never left again.

15. For the Brazilians living in Paramaribo on a more permanent basis, Klein Belem is the area where they spend most of their time, not least because many work in the shops, restaurants and bars (including night clubs and brothels) that furnish services to the Brazilian community. But also because they rarely socialise with the Surinamese, since, as they themselves explain, they do not speak the local languages sufficiently well.

16. A *gaaman* (or *granman*) is the paramount chief of an indigenous or maroon tribe; a *kabiten* is a village headman of a tribal village.

17. Chico, Benzdorp, 22 July 2006.

REFERENCES

Algemeen Bureau voor de Statistiek. 2006. *Landelijke Resultaten vol. 1: Demografische en sociale karakteristieken*. Paramaribo: Algemeen Bureau voor de Statistiek Suriname.

Arouck, R. 2000. Brasileiros na Guiana francesa. Novas migrações internacionais ou exportação de tensões sociais na Amazônia? *Lusotopie* 7: 67–78.

Bal, E. and K. Sinha-Kerkhoff. 2006. British Indians in Colonial India and in Surinam: A Tale of Transnational Identification and Estrangement. *Focaal. European Journal of Anthropology* 47: 105–19.

Bal, E. and K. Sinha-Kerkhoff. 2008. Religious Identity, Territory, and Partition: India and its Muslim Diaspora in Surinam and the Netherlands. *Nationalism and Ethnic Politics* 14(2): 155–88.

Bauman, Z. 2001. *Community: Seeking Safety in an Insecure World.* Cambridge: Polity.

Bruijne, A. 2001. A City and a Nation: Demographic Trends and Socioeconomic Development in Urbanising Suriname. In R. Hoefte and P. Meel (eds) *Twentieth-century Suriname: Continuities and Discontinuities in a New World Society.* Kingston: Ian Randle Publishers/KITLV Press, 23–47.

Cleaver, A.J.T. 2005. 'Ni vue, ni connue': A construção da nação na Guiana Francesa. Mestrado em Antropologia Social, Departamento de antropologia, PPGAS. UnB Brasília.

Colchester, M. 1997. *Guyana, Fragile Frontier: Loggers, Miners, and Forest Peoples.* London: Latin American Bureau.

DeGenova, N.P. 2002. Migrant 'Illegality' and Deportablility in Everyday Life. *Annual Review of Anthropology* 31: 419–47.

Eriksen, T.H. 2002. *Ethnicity and Nationalism,* 2nd edn. London: Pluto Press.

Heemskerk, M. 2002. Livelihood Decision Making and Environmental Degradation: Small-scale Gold Mining in the Suriname Amazon. *Society & Natural Resources* 15(4): 327–44.

Heemskerk, M. 2003. Risk Attitudes and Mitigation among Gold Miners and Others in the Suriname Rainforest. *Natural Resources Forum* 27(4): 267–278.

Heemskerk, M. and M. de Theije. Forthcoming. Moving Frontiers in the Amazon: Maroon and Brazilian Small-scale Gold Miners in Suriname. In T. Grätz and K. Werthmann (eds) *Mining Frontiers: Comparative Perspectives on Property Relations, Social Conflicts, and Cultural Change in Boom Regions.* Reno: University of Nevada Press.

Herman, M. 2003. *Searching for El Dorado: A Journey into the South American Rain Forest on the Tail of the World's Largest Gold Rush.* New York: Vintage Books.

Hoefte, R.M. 2001. Development of a Multiethnic Plantation Economy: An Introduction to the History of Suriname from circa 1650 to 1900. In R. Hoefte and P. Meel (eds) *Twentieth-century Suriname: Continuities and Discontinuities in a New World Society.* Kingston: Ian Randle Publishers/KITLV Press, 1–22.

International Monetary Fund. 2007. Suriname: Statistical Appendix. *IMF Country Report No. 07/179.* Washington, DC: IMF.

Kruijt, D. and W. Hoogbergen. 2005. Peaceful Relations in a Stateless Region: The Post-war Maroni River Borders in the Guianas. *Tijdschrift voor Economische en Sociale Geografie* 96(2): 199–208.

Macmillan, G. 1995. *At the End of the Rainbow? Gold, Land and People in the Brazilian Amazon.* London: Earthscan.

Magar, E.C.E., L.H. Phillips and J.A. Hosie. 2008. Self-regulation and Risk-taking. *Personality and Individual Differences* 45(2): 153–9.

Menezes, M.A.D. 2004. Migration Patterns of Paraiba Peasants. *Latin American Perspectives* 31(2): 112–34.

Mol, J.H., J.S. Ramlal, C. Lietar and M. Verloo. 2001. Mercury Contamination in Freshwater, Estuarine, and Marine Fishes in Relation to Small-scale Gold Mining in Suriname, South America. *Environmental Research* 86(2): 183–97.

Nooteboom, G. 2003. A Matter of Style: Social Security and Livelihood in Upland East Java. PhD thesis, Katholieke Universiteit Nijmegen, Nijmegen, The Netherlands.

Schonenberg, R. 2001. New Criminal Domains in the Brazilian Amazon. *International Social Science Journal* 53(169): 397–406.

Simonian, L. and R.D.S. Ferreira. 2006. Brazilian Migrant Workers in French Guyana. In R. Gowricharn (ed.) *Caribbean Transnationalism: Migration, Socialization, and Social Cohesion.* Lanham, MD: Lexington Books, 99–116.

Slater, C. 1994. All that Glitters – Contemporary Amazonian Gold Miners' Tales. *Comparative Studies in Society and History* 36(4): 720–42.

Theije, M. de. 2007a. 'De Brazilianen stelen al ons goud!' Braziliaanse migranten in stad en binnenland. *OSO, Tijdschrift voor Surinamistiek en het Caraïbisch Gebied* 26(1): 81–99.

Theije, M. de. 2007b. Insegurança próspera: as vidas dos migrantes brasileiros no Suriname. *Revista Anthropológicas* 18(1): 71–93.

Theije, M. de. 2008a. Migration and Religious Transnationalism: Recent Research and the Case of the Brazilians in Suriname. In P. Birle, S. Costa and H. Nitschack (eds) *Brazil and the Americas: Convergence and Perspectives.* Madrid/Frankfurt am Main: Iberoamericana/Vervuert Verlag, 151–70.

Theije, M. de. 2008b. Ouro e Deus: sobre a relação entre prosperidade, moralidade e religião no garimpo de Suriname. *Religião e Sociedade* 28(1): 69–83.

Veiga, M.M. 1997. *Introducing New Technologies for Abatement of Global Mercury Pollution Deriving from Artisanal Gold Mining.* Rio de Janeiro: UNIDO/UBC/CETEM/CNPq.

Vertovec, S. 2003. Migrant Transnationalism and Modes of Transformation. Social Science Research Council/International Migration Review Conference on Conceptual and Methodological Developments in the Study of International Migration. Princeton University.

Part II

Security, Identity and Belonging

5
'Bharat-Wasie or Surinamie?'[1] Hindustani Notions of Belonging in Surinam and the Netherlands

Ellen Bal and Kathinka Sinha-Kerkhoff

During our research into notions of belonging among Surinamese and Dutch Hindustanis (from 2001 to 2005), we were struck by the wide variety of notions of belonging and ensuing identities displayed by these citizens in the Netherlands and Surinam. This variety is not easily explained by the ever increasing literature pertaining to migration, ethnicity, etc. Having been introduced to the concept of human security, we realised that this might be a useful tool, in itself or along with other existing theories on migrants and their senses of belonging, to understand the wide variety of notions of belonging.

Hence this paper focuses on *existential security*, and is, more specifically, narrowed down to ways in which people construct *notions of belonging*, against the background of migration. We concentrate on Hindustanis (descendants of British-Indian indentured labourers) in Surinam and the Netherlands.[2] Hindustani Surinamese (or Surinamese Hindustanis) displayed more uniformity in the ways they perceive themselves than Hindustani Dutch (or Dutch Hindustanis), among whom we observed a much wider variety of identifications. Yet social reality is far too complex and individual variation far too large to make a simple differentiation. Moreover, the links between Surinam and the Netherlands are tight and manifold, and the two communities interconnected. Here we try to employ the human security perspective to analyse the multiplicity of narratives of belonging, rootedness and home, among these descendants of British Indian migrants to Surinam, and among those who later moved to the Netherlands, and try to connect them to collective processes of migration, detachment and relinking. But before we expose and analyse these narratives, further elaboration of the study of 'belonging' and the concept of 'human security' is needed.

NOTIONS OF BELONGING THROUGH A HUMAN SECURITY LENS

When the United Nations Development Programme (UNDP) proposed the concept of 'human security' in 1994, it was argued that 'the concept of security was too narrow and focused on threats to the state and national sovereignty' and that a broader view of security that placed the individual or the community at its heart was needed. Alongside two other key elements, 'freedom from want' and 'freedom from fear' were introduced (Winslow 2003: 5). In her inaugural lecture at the Vrije Universiteit/Free University Amsterdam, Donna Winslow further proposed looking at human security as a continuum, with 'freedom from fear' at one end and 'freedom from want' at the other, without forgetting their interconnectivity.

> At a minimum, human security can be determined by people's ability to be protected from the physical destruction of their lives and way of life. At its maximum it can mean a totally threat-free environment as defined by the peoples and communities themselves. (2003: 31)

This new understanding of security has to its advantage that the focus has shifted from the state towards communities and individuals, and allows us 'to examine processes of signification and meaning in relation to other issues, thereby connecting the quest for security to issues of identity' (Winslow and Eriksen 2004: 362).

However, while from a political and activist perspective human insecurity needs to be perceived as a problem that can be defined and overcome (given the right support and means), from an analytical perspective there seem to be many problems with such an approach. For example, it suggests a hierarchy of insecurities (but who determines which insecurity is worst?); it implies that human insecurity is always a bad thing (cf. Eriksen 2005: 11), and that it relates to problems that can be solved – (hence Winslow's position that 'human security' can both be a concept as well as 'end destination' [2003: 31]). However, when one problem is solved, another might arise. Moreover, human security for one person might bring insecurity for another, or, worse, might cost the security (or life) of someone else. Or, what is perceived as insecurity for one might not be for another. We are evidently not suggesting that people should not stop their wars, diseases should not be cured or the hungry should not ask for food. Yet, when a war is ended and refugees return, they may find the roads to their homes destroyed, their neighbours hostile, their lands barren. In the war against terrorism, some are protected through the killing of others. And migration out of economic necessity (even despair) results in economic security, but might lead to loneliness, alienation and psychological insecurity at the same time (and/or highly appreciated freedom and opportunities). In other words, new securities come with new insecurities, are perceived differently by different people, and are context related (and thus also shift in time).

In this chapter, we perceive human security as a state of being that can never be reached, as a 'paradise lost' (cf. Bauman 2001). We use it as a perspective or a lens that allows us to understand what makes people tick, without suggesting that everyone, always and everywhere, is driven by this 'quest for human security'. This perspective of human security takes into account that securities and insecurities go together, that they are two sides of the same coin. It perceives human security as a goal rather than an end destination, as a driving force for many (yet not all), and it underlines the significance of an individual and contextual approach (whereby the individual is related to the social); 'human security has at its core the individual as object' (Newman 2004: 358). In order to be meaningful, human security needs to be narrowed down to individual senses of insecurity on the various dimensions (economic, cultural, psychological, physical, etc.) that matter to people.

For the purpose of this chapter, we found Jennifer Leaning's understanding of human security particularly helpful. Leaning suggests that 'human security calls for a focus on individuals and communities rather than states and nations, and on social and psychological well-being'. Besides, in order to allow for a transition from a conceptual level to one of practical assessment, she argues, these needs can be grouped under the three following headings: (1) relationships with *location* (sustainable sense of home and safety – providing identity, recognition, and freedom from fear); (2) relationships with *community* (network of constructive social or family support – providing identity, recognition, participation, and autonomy); (3) relationships with *time* (acceptance of the past and positive grasp of the future – providing identity, recognition, participation, and autonomy) (Leaning 2004: 354–55, italics ours). Leaning therefore both stresses the relational dimensions of human security and provides a direct link between human security and notions of belonging. We feel that her definition and these three dimensions are very useful for an explanation of the wide variety of discourses of belonging among Hindustanis analysed here. Yet we first have to elaborate on yet another concept, that of 'belonging'.

STUDIES OF IDENTIFICATION AND BELONGING

Collins English thesaurus describes *belong* as 'attach to, be connected with, be fitting, be part of, go with, have as a proper place, pertain to, relate to'; and *belonging* as 'acceptance, affinity, association, attachment, fellowship, inclusion, kinship, loyalty, rapport, relationship'. These descriptions refer above all to positive feelings, social relations and recognition, and activity. The flip side of belonging is *exclusion*, and belonging only matters when it cannot be taken for granted.

Psychologists have concerned themselves extensively with senses of belonging. Other social scientists, in particular those working on migration, transnationalism and diaspora, have followed and elaborated on these theories. While working on people who did not stay put, they realised that *belonging* becomes an issue when it cannot be taken for granted (cf. Malkki 1992). This pertains in particular, though not solely, to people on the move, whether defined as refugees, displaced people or migrants of various kinds. Since the early 1990s, studies of transnationalism and diasporas have mushroomed to such an extent that we can hardly keep track of all ongoing publications. They differ from earlier studies of migration in that they provide:

> ... a new analytic optic which makes visible the increasing intensity and scope of circular flows of persons, goods, information and symbols triggered by international labour migration. It allows an analysis of how migrants construct and reconstitute their lives as simultaneously embedded in more than one society. (Caglar 2001: 607)

This quotation is also illustrative of the fact that studies on transnationalism generally tend to qualify the role of *place* or locality in identity politics. Instead, the focus has shifted to so-called *transnational arenas* of activity (e.g. Appadurai 1995, Glick Schiller et al. 1992, Hannerz 1996). Global capitalism, mass migration and mass communication, it is argued, have created 'transnational social fields' (Basch et al. 1995), 'transnational social space' (Pries 1999) or a 'multi-local life world' (Vertovec 2001: 578), and enabled diaspora communities to participate in homeland politics (long-distance nationalism), for example (Anderson 1992). These days, migrants live 'in social worlds that are stretched between, or dually located in, physical places and communities in two or more nation-states' (Vertovec 2001: 578). The 'portability of national identity' (Sassen, quoted in Vertovec 2001: 575) among these migrants 'has combined with a tendency towards claiming membership in more than one place' (Vertovec 2001: 575).

This chapter is concerned with such groups of transnational migrants who, as will be shown, have more than one sense of belonging. We do not deny that border-crossing social practices and networks often negate the significance of national borders and identities. Yet here we wish to stress the significance of the local. We argue that transnational alliances (whether real or imagined) are often responses to the local, and informed by a basic need to belong. Migrants (whether 'internal' or international) and their descendants have a larger repertoire of places and people at their disposal with which and with whom they can claim a connection, than those who stayed put. Hence they have more narratives of belonging at their disposal. These connections are by no means natural, as the terms, which are often used to describe feelings of belonging suggest, i.e., *being rooted, motherland, fatherland, of the soil*, etc. (see Malkki 1992). At the same time, their choices are also limited and/or regulated and/or informed by the process of migration (reasons for migration, migration companions, place of destination) and of settlement (local – colonial – policies racism, employability, etc.).

Contemporary politicians often deny immigrants dual citizenship, for example, arguing that this would prevent a commitment to the country of settlement. Yet a denial of a 'free choice of belonging' might in fact initiate or further processes of disconnecting and reconnecting to 'the land of origin'. In other words, transnational identifications are not multi- or trans-spatial by nature, but informed by local situations (in the countries of departure and of settlement), and influenced by other global processes and discourses of belonging. In the case of 'belonging' the question therefore arises how both local and ever changing (imagined or real) transnational relations, and changed relations between them, influence notions of belonging.

As with transnationalism studies, there has been a 'veritable explosion of interest' in diasporas since the late 1980s (Brubaker 2005: 1). While diaspora studies have come to include a wide variety of communities/people ranging from victim diasporas, 'trade diasporas', 'labour migrants who maintain ties with their homeland', to all kinds of dispersed communities, some reference to a conceptual 'homeland' seems to be a constant in diaspora studies (though not in all; references are also made to diasporas without a homeland, such as a Muslim diaspora, or even to gay and lesbian diasporas). Two other core elements besides homeland orientation, that generally underlie definitions of diasporas are 'dispersion in space' and 'boundary-maintenance' (Brubaker 2005: 5). The question is how these three connect to the wish to 'belong', and moreover, how a diaspora approach can explain the multiplicity of narratives of belonging.

Brubaker argues that diaspora can be seen as an alternative to the essentialisation of belonging; but it can also represent a non-territorial form of essentialised belonging (2005: 12). And, further, that 'talk of the de-territorialization of identity is all well and good; but it still presupposes that there is "an identity" that is reconfigured, stretched in space to cross state boundaries, but on some level fundamentally the same' (2005: 12). In order to overcome this problem of essentialisation, Brubaker proposes thinking of diaspora not in substantialist terms, as a bounded entity, but rather as an idiom, a stance, a claim. In this perspective, diaspora is a category of practice that allows for individual choices, needs and claims, and also explains the wide variety in reflections on where people belong and where not, even within an ethnic community (defined as such by its members).

THE CASE STUDY: HINDUSTANI NOTIONS OF BELONGING

Surinamese and Dutch Hindustanis can be perceived both as a migrant and diasporic community (here diaspora is not defined as a bona fide actual entity but as a stance; Brubaker 2005). We refer to them as a community or *ethnic* community since, both in the Netherlands and in Surinam, Hindustanis generally consider themselves members of the same, clearly distinct, transnational ethnic grouping, despite differences and occasional frictions among and between them. They can be perceived as *transnational* since many not only maintain linkages across the ocean – between the Netherlands and Surinam – but also in a variety of ways with people of Indian origin in other parts of the world, and particularly with India itself. Finally, they can be referred to as *diasporic* because India, as the 'ultimate land of their origin', informs in some way or the other, how Hindustanis perceive themselves, their lifestyle(s), culture and community.

We have divided the rest of the chapter into two sections. Hereafter, we present a broad outline of the (migration) history of Surinamese and Dutch Hindustanis and try to pinpoint a few distinct moments or periods in which collective perceptions of belonging changed fundamentally. In this section, we try to connect collective, community developments with individual migration experiences. What may seem necessary for the community to endure (as perceived by its members) is evidently not necessarily similar to individual needs, longings, dreams, and ambitions. Collective needs may support the individual but can also limit them, and grand large-scale ambitions may affect personal potentials.

In the following section, we present a variety of narratives of belonging. Here, the focus lies explicitly on the individual, which gives much space for diversity, inconsistency, and conflicting perceptions and ideas. It is by no means our intention to give a comprehensive overview of all existing narratives. Instead, we try to show how the search for some kind of security, especially the need to belong, is shared by many but informs narratives of belonging in various ways, according to individual needs, in different contexts, at different moments of time.

HUMAN (IN)SECURITIES IN MIGRATION AND RETURN

When it became clear that the 'emancipated African slaves' in Surinam were unwilling to continue working on the plantations on the terms set by the planters, a totally new population was brought in as plantation labourers (Goslinga 1990: 499). In 1872, an agreement was signed between England and the Netherlands on the subject of emigration from Calcutta to Surinam. Between 1873 and 1916, when all British Indian immigration ended officially, 34,000 British Indians arrived in Surinam with contracts (Goslinga 1990: 509). After five years of contract work, the labourers could return to British India and free passages were officially granted. Some, however, found alternatives, by extending their contracts for another five years or by receiving a plot of land and becoming small-scale farmers. The latter became permanent residents. These immigrants maintained their British nationality, even if they stayed on in the colony, and, in accordance with British law, their children and grandchildren were also 'British'.

These days Surinamese and Dutch Hindustanis constitute a distinct ethnic community, but also seem involved in a process of gradual separation. Official figures are not available, but they are estimated to number approximately 160,000 people in Surinam, thereby forming the largest ethnic community (besides Afro-Surinamese, Javanese, Chinese, Amerindians, Brazilians, etc.), and 170,000 in the Netherlands, thereby making up 1 per cent of the total Dutch population.[3]

The first generation of British Indian migrants did not share a single ethnic identity. Historical sources (e.g. Grierson 1883) show that the indentured labourers who ended up in Surinam[4] mostly came from the Bhojpuri area of British India, now covering the western part of Bihar and eastern Uttar Pradesh (and part of a region designated by the Muslim rulers as *Hindustan*). This was by no means a linguistically, ethnically or culturally homogeneous area. Thus the migrants came from a variety of cultural, regional and caste backgrounds, sometimes sharing a language but often not even that. Moreover, they left at a time when national (British-Indian, Indian or Pakistani) identities had not crystallised. Men and women had themselves enlisted as singles; family migration was rare. These migrants came with dissimilar ambitions and personal histories, and they were variously equipped physically as well as mentally, to face the long journey and the new circumstances in which they had to live and work.

Already during their stay in the depots or during the long journey to Surinam, which lasted for months, some kind of shared identity developed. Some 'singles' became 'couples', and strangers became 'brothers',[5] and those friendships or even marriages were long-lasting. On arrival in Surinam, the immigrants were allotted to different plantations, sometimes far away from each other. Combined with long working hours, these conditions hindered intensive contacts between workers from different plantations. During the entire immigration period, transport and communication facilities remained badly developed. For example a boat trip from the capital of Paramaribo to the western-most district of Nickerie took three days. It has been argued that only after the Second World War did the Hindustanis come to form one distinct ethnic community.

Hindustani informants often told stories about kidnappings, or their ancestors being lured into contracts under false pretexts by local contractors. Many stories go around about the abduction of women and children, who by no means intended to migrate, or about promises of a land of milk and honey.[6] In reality however, migrants left for various reasons, not seldom out of poverty or despair, sometimes fearing for their lives (also as criminals, or after family trouble). We were told stories about a grandfather fleeing from Muslims attacking the village, or about another grandfather fleeing from his home after beating his brother, and again someone else after hitting his sister-in-law. Yet another ancestor left with his brother during a huge crisis in the cotton industry in 1888, and another out of dire poverty and unemployment. Hence, for some, migration meant an escape from an insecure situation and Surinam provided a refuge. For others, migration was the road to employment or economic security, and again for others it meant independence and adventure.

After five years of very demanding work on the plantations, the contract labourers could make use of a 'free passage' and return to Calcutta. Between 1878 and the end of 1926, over 11,000 British Indians went back to India (De Klerk 1998: 159). By 1912, already 8800 had returned.[7] The desire to return seemed particularly strong amongst the first batches of migrants. Of the first 537 immigrants who had the right to return in 1880, only three decided to settle in Surinam (De Klerk 1998: 162). For them, Surinam had clearly been a temporary phase in their lives. They must have found it very difficult to stay in touch with their relatives during their contract period,[8] but the enormous distance between the two countries was no impediment to their return to *Bharat Mata*, Mother India. According to a Dutch Protestant missionary report about Surinam, life was particularly hard for the British Indian immigrants. They could not understand the languages spoken, some foodstuffs they wanted – vegetables and fruits – were not available, and they hardly had any kind of family life (also because of great gender imbalance – there were far more men than women among the immigrants). It was also hard to practise their religion as there were no holy places for worship, few spiritual leaders and priests, and no holy streams to bathe in (Steinberg 1933: 275).

According to De Klerk (1998) the most important reason to go back was homesickness. Indeed, on arrival in India, returnees expressed their satisfaction about Surinam, and explained that 'only a strong yearning for their relatives in British India had induced them to leave' (De Klerk 1998: 154). Apparently the longing and homesickness was so strong that British Indians were called 'the people of the great longing' ('*de menschen van het groote heimwee*').

Hence, 'the one who speaks to them in their own language, sings their songs, tells them of their fatherland, will find the way to their hearts' (Steinberg 1933: 275). Among these workers, economic security had come with feelings of alienation and loneliness.

Not everyone wanted to return however, or wanted their old life back. The grandfather of one of our informants had enjoyed his life in Surinam enough to stay. But, when, two days after the death of his small son, the body of the boy disappeared from the grave, and his wife lost her mind, he decided to return with his family to India. Since he had fled from home after family quarrels, they could not return to their village. They spent the following eleven years in Calcutta, while he always looked at the ships departing for Surinam. When he learned that no more boats would leave for Surinam, they boarded the very last ship. Life in Surinam was better and more peaceful, according to his grandson.

Hence, while among returnees there was nostalgia and a genuine longing for home, clearly not everyone who returned had the desire to go back. Many were repatriated because they were 'sick', 'unable to work', 'feeble in mind', 'paupers', 'beggars', 'destitute' or of 'undesirable character', and might have returned against their own wishes and most likely had been 'expelled' from the colony. Others were wives and children of male labourers – some born in Surinam – and did not have much of a choice when their husbands or fathers decided to return. Others returned in order to escape debts, an unsatisfactory marriage or other family problems. Some hoped to be able to live a life of plenty and peace with the money they had saved during the period of indenture, others went home in search of wives for themselves or for their sons, or to collect as many family members and people from their village as possible to take them back to Surinam, where 'they would enjoy a freedom and well-being rarely experienced in the land of their birth' (*De West*, 28 November 1920).

'A Diaspora in a Diaspora'

Clearly, the migration experience meant different things for different people. For many it meant an income, a new family and new chances. For others it meant loneliness, hardship and homesickness. And so did returning to India. When the Indian nationalist leader G.K. Gokhale asked for the abolition of indentured emigration in 1912, he referred to 'the desperate urge of Indian labourers to return to their homeland' (Mohapatra 1995: 6). Reports on these returnees – work by other scholars (e.g. Mohapatra 1995), as well as our own fieldwork – show that in the actual encounter between those who returned and those who had stayed put, mutual processes of 'othering' followed. While separated by space, people had adhered to the same collective identity as British Indians, but in the actual encounter during the 'homecoming', disenchantment, the construction of 'the other' and estrangement surfaced. The home no longer offered the warmth and security people had so dearly missed.

Stories from offspring of people who had migrated and of people who had returned to their villages in British India reveal alienation on the part of the returnees who had longed to come back, and of family members, acquaintances and village elders (Mohapatra 1995: 4). Families and 'friends' had either forgotten all about the person, or pretended to have done so; or they had moved away or had died leaving no one to receive the 'lost husbands, sons, daughters or cousins'; or these relatives and 'friends' had taken over the land and were unwilling to part with it, or simply felt it a nuisance to have to feed another mouth (or more mouths!) once again. These family members had also been after the riches of the returnee and, if there were none, they felt that the returnee should not expect their hospitality but rather take one of them overseas, away from the misery in which they lived. Rarely did these returnees think that the conditions of the place they or their ancestors had left behind had improved. More often than not, they felt that the place had deteriorated during their absence. Besides, some returnees complained that the prices in British India had increased so much that it was difficult to manage with the money they had brought back. They also grumbled that wages were so much lower than they used to receive in the colonies. Furthermore, they could not adjust to the 'heat in India' and suffered social ostracism for having crossed the 'black waters' and mixed with other castes and religions. They were disliked because of their different habits regarding food and drink, their language, their changed traditions, as well as their dress and general behaviour, or because they had had mixed marriages and had brought along their 'bastard children'.

As a consequence, the shores of Calcutta (from where the boats departed and where they returned) were flooded with stranded returned Indian labourers and an increasing number of family members who depended on them. These returnees wrote a petition in 1922 to the government of India desperately pleading to be sent back to their respective colonies as 'they found the conditions in their "homeland" utterly unbearable' (Mohapatra 1995: 7).[9] Actually, they had become 'a diaspora within a diaspora' (Mohapatra 1995:

33). They no longer identified with residents in British India but increasingly with those in the colonies overseas, to which they wanted to re-migrate. Some 700 of these stranded and alienated migrants, who could not identify themselves with their 'homeland' any longer, were accommodated in the Akhra Camp at Metiabruz. In 1934, they too wrote a petition in asking for their 'repatriation to the colonies from which they had returned', as 'we are starving along with our wives and children'. Among these disappointed and alienated migrants there were those who had returned from Surinam and who now decided that the best option was to go back (for a more elaborate account see Bal and Sinha-Kerkhoff 2006). In short, migrants had departed for various reasons and returned for various reasons. Sometimes personal experiences informed their choices, others had no choice. For some returnees life turned out all right, others felt estranged, or circumstances prevented them from settling down. And of all British-Indian migrants to Surinam, two-thirds opted to stay put.

'Rooting' in Surinam: Becoming Hindustanis by Ethnicity and Surinamese Nationals

Quite a number of excellent studies have discussed the migration and settlement process of Hindustanis in Surinam (Bhagwanbali 1996, De Klerk 1998, Gobardhan-Rambocus 2001, Hoefte 1998). These studies, however, often ignore the developments that took place in (British) India simultaneously. They do not take into account that developments in India may have also affected the situation in the diaspora, or vice versa. Hence, little attention has been paid to the linkages between the sending and receiving country, not only in terms of ideology and imaginings about the homeland, but also in terms of factual relations between the two. Elsewhere we have demonstrated how homeland politics and notions of belonging among Hindustanis have been intimately related ever since their departure and how these links have varied greatly over time (Sinha-Kerkhoff and Bal 2003, Bal and Sinha-Kerkhoff 2003, 2005, 2006, 2007, 2008). Initially, repatriation facilities and the continuation of the indentured labour system were essential for the migrants to maintain their relations and possibilities to return to India. Later, fresh 'import' of new migrants was perceived as essential for the survival of British Indians as a local community in Surinam.

One example, which we have elaborated on elswhere (Bal and Sinha-Kerkhoff 2006), illuminates interlinkages between the nationalists' battle for independence in British India, and processes of settlement and local identity formation among the immigrants in Surinam. In their struggle for independence, these Indian nationalists drew from a discourse of suppressed exploited overseas Indian migrants, who they included in their idea of the nation, to serve their own political interests (i.e. India's independence). They perceived the abolition of the indentured labour system as an essential step towards independence of the 'Indian nation'. At the same time, however, overseas British Indians, in this case in Surinam, advocated the continuation of the emigration system in order to strengthen the position of their community locally. Transnational identification served local (national) interests on both sides.

When the indentured labour system was discontinued, British Indians in Surinam suddenly found themselves cut off from their land of origin. Many among them had settled as small agriculturists, who thought that for their 'social and moral development' the 'import of families, in particular those with daughters, was of utmost importance' (*De West* [newspaper] 22 October 1920). The Surinamese Immigration Union (Surinaamsche Immigranten Vereeniging *Bharat Oeday*) requested the colonial authorities in Surinam as well as the Dutch government in the Netherlands to take their demands seriously, and argued that their community was still too small to survive in the new 'fatherland',[10] as they did not support 'racial mixing' and wanted to preserve their old cultural heritage, which they would continue to cherish (*De West* 19 November 1920).[11] They appealed for a continuation of some form of immigration (*De West* 19 November 1920). Despite their attempts – they even sent a delegation to India – no system of migration was organised again.

Hence policies designed by British Indian nationalists, who fought for an independent India, caused an estrangement between the British Indians in the 'homeland' and British Indians in Surinam. At the same time, however, the estrangement simultaneously provided the space for these 'overseas Indians' to find their own solutions during their local struggle for social justice and equality in the new country they had made their 'fatherland'. These British Indians in Surinam identified less and less with Indians in the 'homeland', but instead opted for the local (national) and ethnically based identity of 'Surinamese Hindustanis' in their new 'fatherland'.

The abandonment of the indenture system in 1916 also led to the end of colonial politics of segregation and to the acceleration of integration.[12] From 1927, all British Indians born in Surinam received the Dutch nationality (became 'Nederlandsche onderdanen'). This was in the same years when Nehru, who later became the first prime minister of independent India, drafted a foreign policy for the Congress Party urging Indians overseas to identify with their adopted countries (Tinker 1976). One more bond with British India was therefore broken and the main concern for these, now Dutch, colonial citizens, who had settled in Surinam permanently, became the preservation of their traditions and separate identity (Hajary 1937: 103). After India received its independence, Nehru officially adopted a non-alignment policy, which was very different from the concept of a 'Greater India' which the nationalists had adopted earlier. He requested the overseas Indians to adapt to their adopted countries and respect their national sovereignty, and thus dissociated himself from Indian settlers in the (ex-)colonies. He urged them 'to completely identify' with the people in whose midst they lived. He also felt that these overseas communities: 'should realize that they cannot continue to be Indian citizens and at the same time demand or expect citizenship rights in the countries where they live' (Lall 2001: 35).

When the Hindustanis officially stopped being British-Indians and became Dutch citizens in the colony, they needed to invent new identities that helped them to achieve and maintain their legitimate place in Dutch-Surinam vis-à-vis other local migrant groups and the Dutch colonial power.[13] Some scholars have argued that 'the Hindustani competition with Creoles for scarce socio-economic and political resources' (Brinkerhoff and Jacob 1994: 637) produced a strong tendency, 'within the Hindustani group to neglect the internal socio-religious differences and to stress the fact that Hindustanis were a group originating in India, having a common history and therefore a common identity' (Van der Burg and Van der Veer, cited in Brinkerhoff and Jacob 1994: 637). Differences among Hindustanis were under-communicated, and differences with other communities articulated. It is important to note, however, that at the very same time, the contrary also happened, triggered by personal ambitions and strategies for socio-economic and political mobility.

In Surinam in the late 1920s, education, employment and religion (and gender) seemed the primary prerequisite for the enhancement of the socio-economic status of Hindustanis. 'The urge for a better societal position, to belong to the intellectual elite, to acquire possessions and social respect, formed the basis for a breakthrough in Hindustani attempts to emancipate in our country' (Ramsunders-ingh 1998: 93, translated from Dutch).

By the end of the 1920s, differences between the 'educated' and 'uneducated' caused great schisms, and the peaceful cohabitation between the various religious groups had started to erode. Some, Hindus *and* Muslims, chose religion as the main source of identification, and in this context the so-called reformers, who had come from India to the Caribbean, became quite successful in their efforts to introduce new religious, sociocultural outlooks and lifestyles among both Hindu and Muslim Hindustanis. A period of some 15 years, also know as *the Boycott*, followed. In various places all over the country where Muslims were relatively numerous[14] Hindus boycotted Muslims. This divide did not last. In the course of time Hindustanis united under the banner of a shared ethnic identity vis-à-vis other ethnic communities.

When the British left India in 1947, people welcomed Indian independence but were also disappointed about the partitioning of 'their Hindustan' into India and Pakistan.[15] At the same time, some Hindustanis believed that an independent India would have a positive impact on Hindustanis throughout the world:

> It is, furthermore, the firm conviction of all Hindustanis ... that a free and independent Hindustan – here we do not think of the deplorable partion – will positively influence the social position of Hindustanis all over the world. (*Vikaash*[16] June 1947; translated from Dutch)[17]

They also hoped that 'the new Government in Hindustan would allow free emigration of Indians to Surinam' (*Vikaash*, June 1947). At the same time, *Vikaash* (June 1947) reported that this interest of Hindustanis in matters related to Hindustan should not make 'others' think that Hindustanis are not Surinamese, or that they identified as 'aliens' in Surinam, or that they wanted to return to Hindustan. To the contrary, it was emphasised that, 'though not at the costs of others', Hindustanis wanted to get an equal place in the Surinamese society with the right to show interest in happenings in Hindustan, the 'land of our ancestors' and to nourish 'our age-old culture'. It was especially reported that, during the independence celebrations, non-Hindustani participants were also present, and, along with the Hindustanis, they proposed a 'toast' to 'free Hindustan' as well as on their 'beloved Suriname' (*Vikaash*, June 1946, March–April 1947, June 1947, January 1948, May 1948).

In 1949 many Hindus and Muslims organised themselves into one political party, the VHP (United Hindustani Party) to stand in the elections together. Ethnic identity proved stronger (and more instrumental) than religion at the time. This still pertains to Surinam these days, as could be witnessed during recent elections, though not everywhere and not to the same extent for everyone. Some informants made it a point to stress inter-ethnic mixing, pointing to their own mixed marriages, for example, and articulated their Surinamese identity. Among Hindustanis in the Netherlands, however, both ethnic and religious identities seem to play a different and more significant role in the way they construct identities and notions of belonging.

'THIS LAND HAVE I CHOSEN'

In 1968 the well-known Hindustani poet Srinivasi published the following poem.

> This land
> have I chosen
> planted here
> in the tide of
> the days and nights
> my life
> near the ravenous sea
> that eats into the shore
> of my heart
> and shatters it, at times
> but also forgivingly plants
> between the roots of despair
> a coastline
> for future generations
> (Shrinivasi 1979: 51 [first publ. in 1968],
> translation ours)[18]

The poem reflects the personal commitment and choice for Surinam; it refers both to hardship *and* hope. Our interviews with Surinamese Hindustanis suggest a similar commitment to the country. Nevertheless, the period leading up to the independence of Surinam, but also subsequent years, show much variety in feelings of commitment, ambitions, experiences and perceptions of the future. An increase in ethnic tensions, especially between Hindustanis and Afro-Surinamese, or *Creoles*, coupled with economic problems in the country, resulted in the emigration of large numbers of Surinamese to the Netherlands. Today more than half of all Hindustanis are living in the Netherlands. The relationship between Surinamese and Dutch Hindustanis is an uneasy one. There are many stories about arrogant Dutch visiting Surinam in winter coats, showing off their Dutch background. At the same time, every single person we talked to has some friends or relatives living in the other country. Transnational relations are many-sided and still quite close.

Most Surinamese we talked to expressed commitment to Surinam: 'Culturally I am Hindustani, nationally I am Surinamese.' Or: 'I will never leave Surinam for another country. I do not like to live anywhere else in the world than in Surinam, where I have built up my whole life. If I leave that place, I would feel like a refugee.' Or:

> Fortunately we are here. It's important that we root here. Many people here live with one leg elsewhere. As long as Surinam is not strong economically, the love will grow slowly.... But it will be alright.

Many had left for the Netherlands to study, and some stayed on for many years, but still returned to Surinam. One person, a 63-year-old businessman, told us how he went to study in the Netherlands in the late 1950s (as one of the first), but found the country gloomy and poor. After his studies he returned to Surinam and found himself a good job.

'My Body is in the Netherlands, My Heart in Surinam and Soul in India'

> Tricky, even when you are born in the Netherlands, in the eyes of the Dutch you will always be a foreigner. But it is a matter of standing up for yourself. If not, *bakras* [Dutch people] will run you over! People say about me that I have more *bakra* blood in me than Hindustani, because I grew up among the Dutch. Well, that might be so, oh well, too bad, I am catching up. (Posting on 19 June 2002, on www.Indianfeelings.com; trans. by author)

On 5 August 2005, the Dutch free daily newspaper, the *Spits*, reports in a small article that an increasing number of young people from ethnic minorities do not consider themselves Dutch. Among people with a Surinamese background – no reference is made to ethnicity – that feeling has increased by 53 per cent since last year. The afore-mentioned quote reveals that the feeling of not being accepted as an equal citizen of the Netherlands is not new. The same article also mentions that (still) 69 per cent of people from ethnic minorities (here referred to as '*allochtonen*') feel closely related to Dutch society. This applies in particular to the more educated Surinamese.

After their migration to the Netherlands, Hindustanis had to begin a new struggle for citizenship and a process of rooting. Here I will not go into that process of rooting. Instead, we wish to illuminate that contemporary notions of belonging among Hindustanis in the Netherlands are extremely diverse, and can only be understood by relating them to (1) individual sentiments, self-perceptions, needs and ambitions; (2) collective processes of community construction and identity formation vis-à-vis other ethnic communities in the Netherlands and (3) global developments and changes in the 'homeland(s)'.

'India, Surinam, the Netherlands ... ?? What Difference Does It Make?'

The following quotations (translated from Dutch) are derived from postings on the website of the Hindoe Studenten Forum Nederland (HSFN, Hindu Student Forum Netherlands, www.HSFN.nl). They do not represent all notions of belonging among young Dutch Hindustani students but demonstrate the variation in the discourse of belonging. Moreover, they illuminate the influence of global and transnational developments, such as the influence of cinema, on the different narratives of belonging.

> We should not forget that our ancestors came from *Bharat Mata* (Mother India). We are their descendants. When I went there for the first time, I instantly felt that it was my country. I have plans to go there, hopefully for good! (13 February 2002)

> To my mind, India has been quite romanticised; many Hindus in the diaspora are troubled by homesickness and nostalgia, even though they have never been to India and only know it from films. And films are not very realistic! I myself have never been in India, but the country does not attract me. I would, evidently, like to visit it a few times, and find my 'roots' if possible.... Of course I also follow news on India and get angry when injustice is being done to it, but distance remains. And frankly, I feel good about that distance.... To get back to the notions of homesickness and nostalgia: you speak of homesickness when you yearn for an earlier experience. Nostalgia refers to a romanticised longing. For example, I often long for the Surinam of my youth, because I really experienced that. I feel nostalgic over the Surinam of

my grandparents (1950s). I did not experience those days, for I am only 30 years old.... I believe that many think of India nostalgically, in this same way, thereby evoking 'wrong sentiments' (dreamy and too romantic!). Finally, the influence of Bollywood on this nostalgic longing should not be under-estimated: how about films such as *Indian*, which really stir up nationalist sentiments. (14 February 2002)

Every Hindu feels an attachment to India, you can't disagree on that. There it originated, developed and is most dominant. But when I see slogans such as *'saare jahan se achha: Hindustan hamara!'* [of all worlds, my India is best] I get the feeling that Surinam is being neglected.... The Hindustanis who went there did not go there for nothing, nor did they stay there for nothing. They knew they had no future in Indian. They were all poor people. Had they returned, we all would have lived in a developing country, poorly educated, because there was no money for studies. What I mean to say is that, when we honour our ancestors – which is important according to our religion – we should not forget those from Surinam. They worked hard for their children and grandchildren, and did their best not to forget their *dharm*. OK, they might think we have become too Dutch, because we speak without Surinamese accents, but the Indians must have thought the same of the Surinamese Hindustanis. (18 February 2002)

My body is in the Netherlands, my heart in Surinam and soul in India. My body, heart and soul make me who I am, so without the *dharm* from India, the nice experiences in Surinam, and my youth in the Netherlands, I would not be who I am. (18 February 2002)

Each student perceives of himself as Hindustani but explains his or her identity in different terms. On this website, particularly religion seems to provide an important identity marker. Often the 'Hindu connection' is referred to as one of the most important linkages to India. For many, however, religious similarity does not mean that India is also the true homeland. Some feel connected because their ancestors were born there, while for others that does not mean that India still represents their motherland. Bollywood plays a significant role in the ethnic identification and informs the imaginings of India, but here again, differently for different people. Apart from the ancestral and religious connection, notions of a shared 'culture' provide a sense of connectedness.

The following quotations are derived from one of the very first interviews we conducted. It summarises the story of Ellen's 'Bollywood dance' teacher, Nandrani, who was born in Surinam but migrated to the Netherlands in 1970 for the purpose of (arranged) marriage. The quotations show how India has played an important role throughout her life. Her story touches upon various dimensions of the relationship between identity, place and notions of belonging, and was particularly interesting because it underlines the interconnection between belonging and identification:

N: As a child in Surinam, with so many communities, I did not feel I belonged there. Why it was like that I did not know, but something was just not right. As a child you do not realise but later you start pondering over those feelings. We lived in different communities. And then you are not yourself.
E: What do you mean?
N: There you find people from Africa, Indonesia, Java, China, so we lived with different communities, which means ... there was no time for integration because everyone was living in one's own group. And then you have neighbours who are different, and I am different, and he is different. And I always wondered where I belonged.... I did not have many friends and acquaintances either, because something was just not right, and later I understood.

I think it was different with the elder generation. They had more contacts among themselves. But the children went to school with children from different backgrounds, and they did not know how to interact. Here [in the Netherlands] we are confronted with similar problems these days. But here we have developed projects, with children, to learn how we can cooperate in this society. But no such things existed in Surinam, we had work it out ourselves. To learn to accept each other's arts, culture, traditions, learning to accept through talking, arts, songs and so on. Then you start understanding each other and learn how to relate to one another. You know, he is like this, and she is like that. Hey, he speaks that language, I will try to remember some words. But in Surinam we did not have this. It was hard enough to make ends meet, let alone to develop projects or to work on integration ...

And then we went to India with the whole family. Fortunately my husband loves culture. And from then onwards I followed dancing classes every time I went there. The first time I stayed for six months.... Initially, they could not understand me, because I came from the West and must have been westernised. That is how they think. But they also realised I am Hindustani. I still have newspaper articles about me, coming from Holland to study classical dance. They appreciated that. They also interviewed me, about why I came to search for that [dance] there. I told them that dance is important for me, it is my roots, my culture, part of my identity. And I want to bring it back to the Netherlands, for the Hindustanis, for society: hey! That is me, that is us! If I had to choose between Surinam, the Netherlands and India ... it would not be Surinam, but choosing between the Netherlands and India is hard ...

'Eternal Call from the Ganga?'

Since the late 1970s and 1980s, Indian governments have altered their policies towards 'Indian' communities living abroad (see Sinha-Kerkhoff and Bal 2003). They now favour transnational options for nation building and try to forge alliances with 'overseas Indians', who are looked upon as the solution for India's problems. Accordingly, economic, political and social policies have been designed that enable so-called People of Indian Origin (PIOs) to participate in the national development process from afar, or even facilitate their 'return'. These efforts to woo 'its (recreated) diaspora', as part of the new policies designed to solve India's internal problems, are mediated by national-level dynamics in the 'homeland' as well as in the countries overseas.

In this chapter we have shown that only those who believe something good can come from it – in terms of socio-economic, cultural, religious or other benefits – seem inclined to embrace the new collective identity and start building such transnational partnerships between them (identifying as 'an Indian diaspora', part of the Indian family) and the 'homeland'. Our Hindustani Surinamese informants were by no means inclined to accept such transnational relations on India's terms. They were explicit about their interests in India as the country of their ancestors, and/or origin of their religion (both Hindus *and* Muslims), *and* of their disapproval of the Indian government to bring back the so-called People of Indian Origin to their motherland. The Indian perceptions of PIOs as children of Mother India, members of a global Indian family, or part of the same rainbow, do not comply with their notions of 'self' as Hindustani Surinamese, which have developed over the past 130 years. While their different connections with India are based on various mixtures of notions of historical roots, religious connections, cultural and linguistic interests, and a variety of personal ambitions (the want to help 'the poor', to start a business, to travel, etc.), these descendants of British Indian immigrants seem rather successfully rooted – culturally, economically, politically and nationally – in Surinam. This does not pertain to all, to the same degree, and in the same ways.

In recent times, modern means of communication and mass media have significantly enhanced the possibilities both of imagining, and (re)connecting with, faraway people and places. The various new means to take notice of those others have also allowed people to form new transnational relations, and transnational and diasporic identities. In contrast to the Surinamese Hindustanis, many Hindustanis in the Netherlands are making full use of the various new possibilities to establish linkages with India and the so-called Indian diaspora, after a long period in which contacts with India were almost absent. The renewed diasporic identification, however, applies to some, while others identify with Surinam(ese), with the Netherlands (Dutch), or with a mixture of all these. At one end of the continuum there are those who want to have nothing to do with that, who feel Surinamese, or Dutch, or both. On the other end there are those who perceive of India as their motherland, consider themselves members of the Indian diaspora and dream of 'returning' to India one day.

CONCLUSIONS

While the recent shift in migration and diaspora studies allows for an analysis of the ways in which migrants and their descendants construct and reconstitute their lives as simultaneously embedded in more than one society, it does not so easily explain the wide variety of notions of belonging among certain migrant or diasporic populations. In this chapter we have attempted to show how a 'human security lens' (alongside the diaspora and transnational perspective) offers a better understanding of the many ways in which people construct notions of belonging. The human security focus zooms in on the individual, and on the many faces and dynamics of belonging.

It thereby uncovers similar, disparate and sometimes conflicting requirements of individuals and communities, which are informed by personal, local, transnational and global developments, and which never stop changing. When the context (local, national, transnational) changes, one might feel more secure on some dimensions, or feel less at home and attach oneself to an imagined homeland. Or, alternatively, one might feel less secure, and so articulate community boundaries and fight for an equal place in the adopted homeland, or leave all options open (for the time being).

India, Surinam, the Netherlands ... ?? What difference does it make ... love them all ... perhaps the one more than the other ... but could not miss out any one of them! (13 February 2002, www.HSFN.nl)

NOTES

1. The title refers to a discussion on the website of the Dutch Hindu Student Forum (HSFN), in 2002. It means: 'Indian or Surinamese?' (in Sranang Tongo, a creole language spoken by most Surinamese). Interestingly, no reference is made to a Dutch identity.

2. This chapter is based on our fieldwork in India as well as in Surinam and is one of the outcomes of the research project (2001–05) entitled 'A Diaspora Coming Home? Overseas Indians Re-establishing Links with India', sponsored by the Netherlands Foundation for Research in Tropical Countries (WOTRO). This project was carried out by Kathinka Sinha-Kerkhoff and her research assistant Alok Deo Singh (ADRI, Ranchi) and concentrated on so-called People of Indian Origin (PIOs) in Mauritius, the Netherlands and Surinam. Ellen Bal carried out research among PIOs in the Netherlands and in Surinam, and worked in close collaboration with Sinha-Kerkhoff. She received two travel grants from WOTRO, and one from the Department of Social and Cultural Anthropology of the VU University Amsterdam to carry out fieldwork in Surinam. This chapter is based on aforementioned research efforts and on other publications from our hands.

3. Preliminary results of the last population census in Surinam (Censuskantoor 2004) show that the country now has 487,024 inhabitants, of whom almost 70 per cent reside in the capital Paramaribo and its bordering district Wanica. The report makes no reference to either religion or ethnicity, but other data shows that, in 1991, Hindustanis formed the largest community (37.0 per cent), followed by the Afro-Surinamese (31.3 per cent), the Javanese (14.2 per cent), the Maroons or inland Creoles (8.5 per cent), Amerindians (3.1 per cent) and 1.7 per cent 'other' (Brinkerhoff and Jacob 1994: 637–8).

4. Indentured labour was also recruited from other regions such as Maharashtra, Tamil Nadu and Andra Pradesh. Yet, most of the migrants who landed up in Surinam were from the North Western Provinces, Oudh and Bihar (McNeill and Lal 1915).

5. Known as 'depot brotherhood' (*dipua bhai*) and 'ship brotherhood' (*jahazia bhai*) (Gautam 1995: 3).

6. For a detailed account of one such experience see the autobiography of Munshi Rahman Khan, who wrote down his own personal migration history – the only existing autobiography by an indentured labourer (see Sinha-Kerkhoff et al. 2005: xiii).

7. Memorandum of Indians in Surinam, File No. 169-13/34-L & O, 1934. State Archives of West Bengal in Kolkata.

8. It is interesting to note that, since 1896, the Immigration Department took care of the correspondence of contract labourers (De Klerk 1998: 133).
9. See also: Petition of Certain Destitute Repatriate Emigrants from Fiji, B.G., etc. for Return to their Colonies, File 2P-1, Pro. 40-77, November 1922, Branch: Emigration (Dep. Revenue). State Archives of West Bengal in Kolkata.
10. Interestingly, these British Indians looked upon 'Hindustan' (in Dutch spelled as 'Hindostan' or 'Hindoestan') as their 'motherland' and referred to Surinam as their new 'fatherland' (in Dutch: 'moederland' and 'vaderland').
11. The original (Dutch) text states that the community was too small: 'om voortbestaan onvermengd en hoewel zich aanpassende aan de toestanden in het nieuwe vaderland, toch met behoud van veel wat den Indiër met zijn aloude beschaving en rasgevoelens, altijd dierbaar zal blijven'.
12. De Klerk refers to the first decade of the twentieth century as the start of Hindustani participation in civil society. In 1910 and 1911, the first two British (competing) associations, to represent the British Indians in Surinam, were founded: in 1910, De Surinaamsche Immigranten-Vereeniging and, in 1911, the Surinaamsche Britsch-Indiërs-Bond: Ikhtiyār aur Hak (see De Klerk 1998: 173–4).
13. Gautam writes that: 'the enactment of the new law (1927) which forced all newly born children to be Dutch citizens and to acquire Dutch nationality, encouraged the colonial policy of assimilation of Indians in Surinam' (1995: 15).
14. Of all British immigrants, an estimated one-fifth were Muslim.
15. For example, in July 1947, a group of young Hindustani intellectuals wrote in their monthly newsletter *Vikaash* about India's independence and subsequent Partition:

> The moment has arrived.... Freedom that has taken many years of furious fighting has finally been regained. It already has been determined that the remaining 15,000 British troops will leave Hindustan on 15 August. Energetic men who have given everything for the good cause can now look back on what they have reached for Hindustan. But alas! It could not be what they would have wanted so much: their ideal of a United Hindustan has been destroyed, their hope has gone up in smoke.... Yet! There is hope for the future! Especially the circumstance that Hindus and Muslims are not strictly separated gives reason for hope. One expects that both states will cooperate intimately, as they share *so* many interests. (Liga van Hindostani's. *Vikaash (Evolutie)* 12(2), 14 July 1947)

16. This newsletter *Vikaash*, published in the years 1946–48, refers to Surinam 'as our beloved country' (*'ons geliefd land Suriname'*) (May 1947, 1(12)), or 'our dear Surinam' (*'ons aller dierbaar Suriname'*) (June 1947, 2(13)), 'our dearly beloved and dear Surinam' (*'ons innig geliefd en dierbaar Suriname'*) (May 1948, 2(24)). *Vikaash* also refers to the soil of Surinam as 'holy' (May 1948, 2(24)).
17. The original text was published in Dutch and states that: 'verder is het de vaste overtuiging van alle Hindostani's ... dat een vrij en onafhankelijk Hindostan – hierbij denken we niet aan de jammerlijke verdeling – de maatschappelijke positie van Hindostani's over de gehele wereld gunstig zal beïnvloeden.'
18. Dit land/heb ik gekozen/hier geplant/in het getij van/de dagen en nachten,/mijn leven,/bij de schrokkerige zee/die het strand/van mijn hart/aanvreet en/stuk slaat/op gezette tijden,/maar in een vergevingsgebaar/legt tussen de wortels/ van wanhoop/kust voor de latere geslachten.

REFERENCES

Anderson, Benedict. 1992. *Long-distance Nationalism: World Capitalism and the Rise of Identity Politics.* Amsterdam: CASA.

Appadurai, Arjun. 1995. The Production of Locality. In Richard Fardon (ed.) *Counterworks: Managing the Diversity of Knowledge.* London: Routledge, 204–25.

Bal, Ellen and Kathinka Sinha-Kerkhoff. 2006. British Indians in Colonial India and in Surinam: A Tale of Transnational Identification and Estrangement. *Focaal. European Journal of Anthropology* 47: 105–19.

Bal, Ellen and Kathinka Sinha-Kerkhoff. 2003. Hindostaanse Surinamers en India: gedeeld verleden, gedeelde identiteit? *OSO. Tijdschrift voor Surinamistiek* 2 (November): 214–35.

Bal, Ellen and Kathinka Sinha Kerkhoff. 2005. Muslims in Surinam and the Netherlands and the Divided Homeland. *Journal of Muslim Minority Affairs* 25(2): 205–29.

Bal, Ellen and Kathinka Sinha-Kerkhoff. 2008. Religious Identity, Territory, and Partition: India and its Muslim Diaspora in Surinam and the Netherlands. *Nationalism and Ethnic Politics* 14(2): 155–88.

Bal, Ellen and Kathinka Sinha-Kerkhoff. 2007. When Muslims Leave ... Muslims in British India and their Migration to and Settlement in Mauritius and Surinam. In Gijsbert Oonk (ed.) *Global Indian Diasporas: Exploring Trajectories of Migration and Theory.* Amsterdam: Amsterdam University Press, 75–97.

Bauman, Zygmunt. 2001. *Community: Seeking Safety in an Insecure World.* Cambridge: Polity Press.

Bhagwanbali, Rajinder. 1996. *Contracten voor Suriname: arbeidsmigratie vanuit Brits-Indië onder het indentured-labourstelsel 19873–1916.* Den Haag: Amrit.

Brinkerhoff, Merlin B. and Jeffrey C. Jacob. 1994. Racial, Ethnic and Religious Social Distance in Surinam: An Exploration of the 'Strategic Alliance Hypothesis' in a Caribbean Community. *Ethnic and Racial Studies* 17(4): 636–62.

Brubaker, Rogers. 2005. The 'Diaspora' Diaspora. *Ethnic and Racial Studies* 28(1): 1–19.

Caglar, Ayse. 2001. Constraining Metaphors and the Transnationalisation of Spaces in Berlin. *Journal of Ethnic and Migration Studies* 27(4): 601–7.

Censuskator, Algemeen Bureau voor de statistiek. 2005. Suriname census 2004: voorlopige cijfers.

De Klerk, C.J.M. 1998. *De Immigratie der Hindostanen in Suriname.* Den Haag: Amrit. (First published in 1953.)

Eriksen, Thomas Hylland. 2005. *Risking Security: Paradoxes of Social Cohesion* (inaugural lecture). Amsterdam: Vrije Universiteit/Free University Amsterdam.

Gautam, Mohan. 1995. Munshi Rahman Khan (1874–1972), An Institution. Unpublished paper presented at the ISER-NCIC conference on Challenge and Change: The Indian Diaspora and its Historical and Contmeporary Contexts, University of West Indies, St Augustine and the National Council of Indian Culture, St Augustine, Trinidad and Tobago, 11–18 August.

Glick Schiller, Nina, Linda Basch and Christina Szanton-Blanc. 1992. Transnationalism: A New Analytical Framework for Understanding Migration. In Nina Glick Schiller, Linda Basch and Christina Szanton-Blanc (eds) *Towards a Transnational Perspective on Migration.* New York: New York Academy of Sciences, 1–24.

Gobardhan-Rambocus, Lila. 2001. *Onderwijs als sleutel tot maatschappelijke vooruitgang: een taal- en onderwijsgeschiedenis van Suriname, 1651–1975.* Zutphen: Walburg Pers.

Goslinga, Cornelis Ch. 1990. *The Dutch in the Caribbean and in Surinam 1791/5–1942.* Assen/Maastricht: Van Gorcum.

Grierson, G.A. 1883. Report on Colonial Emigration from the Bengal Presidency, Appendix to File 15-20/21. Calcutta State Archives, India.

Hajary, H.N. 1937. De verwacht wordende groote gebeurtenis onder de Britsch-Indiërs in Suriname. *De West-Indische Gids* 19(20): 1–3.

Hannerz, Ulf. 1996. *Transnational Connections: Culture, People, Places.* London: Routledge.

Hoefte, Rosemarijn. 1998. *In Place of Slavery: A Social History of British Indian and Javanese Laborers in Surinam,* Gainesville: University Press of Florida.

Lall, Marie-Carine. 2001. *India's Missed Opportunity: India's Relationship with Non-Resident Indians.* Aldershot: Ashgate.

Leaning, Jennifer. 2004. Psychosocial Well-being over Time. In J. Peter Burgess and Taylor Owen (eds), *Security Dialogue* 35(3): 354–5.

McNeill, James and Chimman Lal. 1915. *East India (indentured labour:) Report to the Government of India on the Conditions of Indian Immigrants in four British colonies and Surinam.* London: His Majesty's Stationery Office.

Malkki, Liisa. 1992. National Geographic: The Rooting of Peoples and the Territorialization of National Identity among Scholars and Refugees. *Cultural Anthropology* 7(1): 24–44.

Mohapatra, Prabhu P. 1995. Longing and Belonging: The Dilemma of Return among Indian Immigrants in the West Indies 1850–1950. Paper presented at the ISER-NCIC Conference on 'Challenge and Change: The Indian Diaspora in its Historical and Contemporary Contexts', Trinidad and Tobago: University of West Indies, St Augustine and the National Council of Indian Culture, St Augustine.

Newman, Edward. 2004. A Normatively Attractive but Analytically Weak Concept. In J. Peter Burgess and Taylor Owen (eds) *Security Dialogue* 35(3): 358–9.

Pries, Ludger. 1999. *Migration and Transnational Social Spaces.* Aldershot: Ashgate.

Ramsundersingh, Karan. 1998. Hindostanen in het onderwijs. In Benjamin S. Mitrasingh and Marita S. Harpal (eds) *Hindostanen: Van contractarbeiders tot Surinamers.* Paramaribo: Stichting Hindostaanse Immigratie.

Shrinivasi. 1979. Suriname. In Shrinivasi (ed.) *Wortoe d'e tan abra: Bloemlezing uit de Surinaamse Poezie vanaf 1957.* Paramaribo: Bureau Volkslectuur.

Sinha-Kerkhoff, Kathinka, Ellen Bal and Alok Deo Singh (trans./eds). 2005. *Autobiography of an Indian Indentured Labourer: Munshi Rahman Khan (1874–1972).* New Delhi: Shipra.

Sinha-Kerkhoff, Kathinka and Ellen Bal. 2003. 'Eternal Call of the Ganga': Reconnecting with People of Indian Origin in Surinam. *Economic and Political Weekly* 38(38): 4008–21.

Steinberg H.G. 1933. *Ons Suriname: De Zending der Evangelische Broederge-meente in Nederlandsch Guyana.* 's-Gravenhage: N.V. Algemene Boekhandel voor inwendige en uitwendige zending.

Tinker, Hugh. 1976. *Separate and Unequal: India and the Indians in the British Commonwealth, 1920–50.* Delhi: Vikas Publishing House.

United Nations Development Programme. 1994. *Human Development Report 1994.* New York and Oxford: Oxford University Press.

Vertovec, Steven. 2001. Transnationalism and identity. *Journal of Ethnic and Migration Studies* 27(4): 573–82.

Winslow, Donna. 2003. *Human Security* (inaugural lecture). Amsterdam: Vrije Universiteit/Free University Amsterdam.

Winslow, Donna and Thomas H. Eriksen. 2004. A Broad Concept that Encourages Interdisciplinary Thinking. In J. Peter Burgess and Taylor Owen (eds) *Security Dialogue* 35(3): 361–2.

6
Cultural Identity as a Key Dimension of Human Security in Western Europe: The Dutch Case[1]

Edien Bartels, Kim Knibbe, Martijn de Koning and Oscar Salemink[2]

HUMAN SECURITY AND CULTURAL CERTAINTY

This chapter deals with cultural identity as related to human security. We will argue that conceptualising the tensions between groups, in this case between Dutch Muslims and 'native' Dutch, in terms of human security adds much to understanding why emotions, suspicions and disquiet run so high between these two groups. The most common conceptualisation of human security – in terms of 'freedom from want' and 'freedom from fear' – seems to justify the assumption that human security pertains to developing countries only and would not be relevant for Western Europe. Taking issue with this complacent notion, we suggest that the concept of human security might be highly relevant for understanding contemporary processes in Europe, depending on its definition and contextualisation.

Although the concept of human security emerged in the United Nations (UN) *Human Development Report 1994*, the notions of 'freedom from want' and 'freedom from fear' hail from US President Franklin Delano Roosevelt's 1941 State of the Union speech, entitled 'The Four Freedoms' (the two other freedoms being freedom of expression and religious freedom). In the *Human Development Report 1994*, on the other hand, human security was defined in much more complex ways, broken down into seven main categories (economic, food, health, environmental, personal, community, political security). Some of these categories have been largely forgotten. For our discussion of human security in Western Europe, however, the dimension of community security seems most relevant:

116

Most people derive security from their membership in a group – a family, a community, an organization, a racial or ethnic group that can provide a *cultural identity and a reassuring set of values.* (UNDP 1994: 31, emphasis added)[3]

The report goes on to state that communities can also be highly oppressive, both for their members and for outsiders, especially in the form of ethnic conflict; and that many traditional forms of community 'are breaking down under the steady process of modernization' (UNDP 1994: 31).

This dimension of human security seems largely forgotten since 1994. Even the post-9/11 situation of rising ethnic and religious tensions – with the 'War on Terror' increasingly fought on domestic European soil – did not lead to a revaluation of the cultural and existential dimensions of human security, with the exception of the anthropological research programme *Constructing Human Security in a Globalizing World* of the Department of Social Anthropology, Vrije Universiteit/Free University Amsterdam (2004), with which the present authors are affiliated. This research programme stretches the meaning of human security to include cultural, cognitive, emotional, religious and symbolic dimensions as well, which are here glossed under the concept of 'existential' and which are bound to processes of signification.

Existential security is sought in the human attempt to make sense of this world and people's place in it, in relation to family, community, society and the wider cosmos. The quest for existential security can be linked with and expressed through issues of national, ethnic, gender and religious identity as ways in which people create collective meanings. These subjects have traditionally been within the purview of cultural anthropology. If the concept of human security is to be meaningful, then those (social, cultural, psychological, existential) dimensions of life that make individuals truly human can only be left out of the equation at great cost. The examples of the 9/11 attacks in New York, the 11 March 2004 bombings in Madrid and those of 7 July 2005 in London, as well as the 2 November 2004 murder of Theo van Gogh in Amsterdam, show that any attempt to analyse these assaults on the physical security of these inhabitants of Europe and the US without looking at the religious motives and ways of identifying of the perpetrators would be misguided. Without identifications and classifications such as 'Muslim' and 'infidels', the arbitrary violence of the attacks cannot be understood (Department of Social Anthropology 2004).

Outside the economic ('Freedom from want'), physical ('Freedom from fear') and ecological ('Freedom for future generations to inherit a sound natural environment') domains, human security is not yet well theorised (Burgess 2004, Chen et al. 2003, but see Eriksen 2005). An important reason is that human security is more often defined negatively in terms of threats, risks or violations (see Fukuda-Parr 2003) than for what it is supposed to mean in positive terms. Eriksen (2005) points to the other possible opposite of (human) security, namely freedom (see also Bauman 2001), because freedom and risk are often two sides of the same coin. For example, the openly gay, right-wing politician Pim Fortuyn in particular claimed that Muslims posed a threat to the tolerant and liberal nature of Dutch society, and paradoxically advocated the abolition of Article 1 in the Dutch Constitution (that forbids discrimination on the basis of gender, race, sexuality, etc.). This example shows the relation, sometimes paradoxical, between freedom and human security.

So how to conceptualise 'existential security' positively (rather than in negative terms)? This requires us to think about the types of social and cultural needs, anxieties, desires, ambitions and projects to which 'existential security' would correspond, and what other notions could be used in the same context. For the English language we could think about the notions of 'certainty' and 'safety' as bearing a strong family resemblance to security. However, as the meanings and uses of these terms are as much a matter of style and context as of definition, we should not venture into an abstract discourse on these three related concepts, separate from the specific cultural meanings these concepts have for people involved. At the same time, given the methodological individualism implied in the concept of human security – as 'people-centred', with individuals as *subjects* of security – we shall have to theorise how to relate individual experiences and projects to structural social and cultural processes. Already in 1991 Anthony Giddens enriched our sociological thinking in this regard with the concept of 'ontological security' (1991: 36–42), which he related to 'identity' conceived not as a 'thing' but as a – largely routine – process of identification linking the person with a group or category (Giddens 1991; see also Jenkins 1996).

In spite of the anthropological fascination with ethnicity over the past two decades, other forms of identification matter just as much. Whereas nation, region, locality, community and 'race' are often seen as 'variations on the basic ethnic theme of collective identification stressing perceived cultural differentiation' (Jenkins

2001: 8), other identifications may follow class, gender or religious lines. Normally, identification is a dynamic and variable process dependent on context and circumstances. In this process of identification the distinctions and connections between security, certainty and safety are not clear, but it is often assumed that people seek some degree of certainty in their (class, gender, religious) identity, while simultaneously striving to create some measure of security through their notion of belonging to a particular collective (social category, group, 'community'). This is perhaps brought out best in Zygmunt Bauman's (2001) connection of security with his nostalgic notion of the 'ethical community' (*contra* 'aesthetic community'), consisting of a 'warm circle' of people having durable responsibilities and commitments to one another against the backdrop of 'liquid modernity'.

According to the French sociologist Danièle Hervieu-Léger, the rise of new forms of more or less fundamentalist 'ethnic religions' in Western Europe has to be understood against the backdrop of loss of traditional community security and hence 'structural uncertainty symptomised by the mobility, reversibility and transferability of all markers' (2000: 164):

> Such manifestations of ethno-religious compensation for the loss of collective identity are variously present in all western countries. Economic uncertainty or social and political crisis may make them assume more acute, perhaps more threatening, forms; and because religious institutions, which profess to be the sole legitimate guarantee of the authentic reference to tradition, have little or no influence over this appropriation of their role, this threat may appear the more real. (2000: 160)

This means that such ethno-religious religious beliefs and practices can be interpreted as attempts to reinvent community against the backdrop of the fragmentation and atomisation that is threatening social cohesion in Western countries. This is not to say that 'modern' life now is necessarily more insecure than 'traditional' life forms in the past, but that the notion of high modernity is characterised by the omnipresence of risk and uncertainty peculiar to today's fast-changing and mediated societies (Hervieu-Léger 2000: 165, see also Giddens 1991, Sennett 1997). It is in such conditions of flux and mobility that attempts to create new collective forms of 'community security' can produce the type of ethnic or religious conflict described in the *Human Development Report 1994* (UNDP 1994).

OPERATIONALISING HUMAN SECURITY IN CONNECTION WITH CULTURAL IDENTITY

But how to operationalise this ambiguous dimension of community security, which can offer comfort and support and produce hardship and conflict at the same time? In the general way that the term 'human security' is used by the UN as a condition that should be promoted for everybody, it applies to the macro-level of societal structures and physical conditions. But on the micro-level of culture, this concept is difficult to operationalise. The existential anthropologist Michael Jackson suggests ways to bridge collective macro- and individual micro-levels when he argues that 'notions of shared humanity, human equality, and human rights always come up against the micropolitical exigencies of ethnic, familial, and personal identity …' (Jackson 1998: 5). For the purpose of this chapter, we will distinguish between two dimensions of creating security and certainty: the level of signification and the level of actually creating groups, delineating identities and defending them.

With regard to the first level, we can again turn to Jackson. According to him, control over the relationship and balance between nature and culture; between the world of the gods and the world of human struggle; between the public domain and private domains is a central human preoccupation (1998: 21):

> … in every human society concepts such as fate, history, evolution, God, chance, and even the weather signify forces of otherness that one cannot fathom and over which one can expect to exercise little or no ultimate control. These forces are given; they are in the nature of things. In spite of this, human beings countermand and transform these forces by dint of their imagination and will so that, in every society, it is possible to outline a domain of action and understanding in which people expect to be able to grasp, manipulate, and master their own fate. (1998: 19)

In terms of power, *how* to control, and *how* to know, and who is authorised to draw these boundaries often emerge as issues between different groups of people (Knibbe 2005: 3). We can expect this to be even more the case in the confrontation between groups and cultural notions that always underlies processes of identification and the search for security and certainty through identity. This would suggest that the emergence of ethno-religious conflicts all over Europe in recent decades can be read as motivated by attempts to create new religious and quasi-secular certainties and communities which coincide with shifting boundaries of controllable domains in the life-world experience of various groups and populations.

So we argue that creating certainties or securities is not the core activity of human security *per se*. Rather, it is the negotiation and ascertaining of the *boundary* between security and insecurity, certainty and uncertainty, which is required for some level of existential or cultural security. Individual experiences, historical shifts in the religious imagination, changing socio-economic circumstances, or sudden shocking events like political murders or terrorist attacks, may require a renegotiation of this boundary. In the case of ethno-religious conflicts in Europe, it is the negotiation of the boundaries between national, ethno-religious groups and movements, and the identities marked by these boundaries that must be the focus of our research and also the focus of the conceptualisation of human security in relation to cultural identities. This brings us to the second level, of actually creating and maintaining group boundaries to construct a sense of community.

Identity construction always occurs in interaction with others, inside and outside their own religious, ethnic or peer-group. Within and between these divergent groups there is a balance of power. That is why the term *identity politics* (Eriksen 1993) is useful here. Identity politics, in this view, should be taken to mean the negotiations over the definition and interpretation of ideas, practices and experiences that constitute a certain identity.

Identity politics also introduces the notion of power and strategic action which can in turn affect processes of signification within certain religions. Considerations of power and control will lead groups to emphasise certain values from within their own religious and cultural repertoire, and downplay others. In this regard, Thomas Eriksen (1993: 21) writes about 'overcommunication' and 'undercommunication' of certain identity *cum* boundary markers.

In the following sections we will elaborate on these rather theoretical considerations of human security, using examples from the Dutch context with which we are most familiar. Although the Dutch situation is idiosyncratic, there are also many similarities with other countries in Western Europe where tensions between ethnic groups increased during the last decade, partly in response to structurally similar conditions in these countries and partly because of transnational networks and influences. Despite a legacy of regional diversity and of 'pillarisation' of society along politico-religious lines, Dutch identity was hardly emphasised, problematised or questioned until the arrival of – especially Muslim – migrants and of course the European Union (EU) integration began to be felt. It was in this context that negotiation and profiling of the boundaries between white Dutch native identities – in Dutch: *autochtoon* – and Dutch Moroccan Muslims – as a segment of the larger group of 'non-natives' (*allochtonen*) – took place. Many people experienced a necessity to express their identity in relation to a presumed or imagined threat, emerging from the (failed) process of integration of migrants. Distinctive for identity politics of Dutch Moroccans in the Netherlands is that they refer to experiences, beliefs, practices and symbols that constitute 'Islam', and not to other identities such as ethnic, urban, etc. This identity construction is different from that of Muslims in their home country (see Eickelman and Piscatori 1996: 20–21).[4] The concepts of identity politics and negotiations are useful here in the sense that they make clear that people make choices in the construction of their identity in relation to other people. It makes clear that people are active agents but are also constrained by larger contexts and by interaction with others. However, adding Jackson's insight on the importance of defining the boundary between the domains one can and cannot control helps us focus more sharply on issues of control and power: who defines how you belong to one group or the other, what means of control do people have? As we will see in the case of Dutch Muslims, they take a concept which the Dutch find to be very important to their own identity, namely 'tolerance', and use it to promote their own identity. But at the same time, in the name of their Muslim identity, some of them preach intolerance against the freedoms that 'native' Dutch value.

The process of constructing cultural identities in interaction and negotiation with other categories implies a struggle for the definition of the situation, especially when identities are experienced as opposing, as in the case of 'native Dutch' identity and 'Muslim identity'. When a particular identity is profiled and the position of a corresponding group in society becomes more visible, the existing balance of power shifts. This changing balance creates feelings of loss of control over one's environment, which is seen as disorderly and threatening. A struggle to restore the old power balance may then ensue, resulting in reinforcement of the boundaries between categories in the process of interaction and negotiation about the identities. The consequence of this reinforcement is that people tend to essentialise the nature of their identity which, in turn, implies the essentialisation of the identities of others and reifying the boundaries between 'us' and 'them' (Baumann 2004). The 'others' are excluded and the boundaries between groups are hardened.[5] Briefly, it is this process that can be seen in the history of the presence of Mediterranean migrants in the Netherlands.

The first generation Mediterranean migrants – 'guest workers' – were ethnically and religiously defined in contrast with 'native' Dutch people, but they were thought of as under control and hence non-threatening because they were supposed to stay for only a couple of years. Therefore, at first their presence did not require a negotiation of the boundary and an adaptation of the self-definition on the part of the migrants nor on the part of Dutch society. It was only with the second-generation migrants that boundaries between the groups began to be blurred and started shifting. Although most are Dutch citizens and supposedly integrated into society, many started profiling their distinct ethnic and religious background.

This paradox between being Dutch yet being distinctly different questions the very category of 'Dutch-ness'. To the Dutch, this raises issues of human security: the boundary between 'us' and 'them' becomes unclear. They fear domination from within their own society by 'others' who claim to be part of their own group yet seem different or strange. They fear that they are, or will be, no longer in control of their own environment or their supposed cultural self, and that they will be forced to change themselves in ways experienced as contradictory to their cultural 'essence'. 'Other' people suddenly shift the boundaries and change the rules.

'TOLERANCE' AS A BONE OF CONTENTION BETWEEN DUTCH AND MUSLIM IDENTITY

Our contribution concerning the issue of cultural identity and the boundary between security and insecurity in connection with the relationship between Moroccan Muslims (born in the Netherlands) and native Dutch people is based on four different studies. The first involves PhD research by one of the authors regarding the construction of religious identity among Dutch youth of Moroccan descent (usually identified as 'Moroccans' in public discourse).[6] The second study is called the Ethnobarometer research project.[7] The third study was a research project among migrant Muslim organisations in the predominantly immigrant neighbourhood of the Amsterdam city district Slotervaart.[8] The fourth study concerns an inaugural lecture which analysed the ways in which the ethnic and national boundaries of 'autochthonous' Dutchness are being ritually constructed (Salemink 2006). All these studies focus on the categories of 'native' Dutch and of Moroccan Muslims (with the exception of the Ethnobarometer project that also focuses on native Dutch people). Most of the Moroccan Muslim men came in the 1970s as 'guest workers'. At the end of the 1970s many brought their families to the Netherlands. Many Moroccan men and other labour immigrants of those days tell stories that they were warmly welcomed by the Dutch. As it was thought that these guest workers would stay only temporarily in the Netherlands, they were not seen as a threat to the existing social order or to Dutch identity in the Netherlands. In fact they more or less confirmed the existing social order and Dutch identity because of this aura of 'temporariness' and because of their contribution to Dutch economy. This changed in the 1990s. It became clear that Moroccan guest workers would not leave the country, that they would stay and that their children would grow up here. In the 1990s a public accommodation of Islam took place by, for example, the building of mosques and Islamic schools. At the same time, studies and media reports pointed to grave problems concerning Moroccan youth: poor results in school, relatively high crime rates, intimidation in public areas and aggression towards (native Dutch) women and homosexuals. Events such as '9/11', the election campaign of the right-wing populist politician Pim Fortuyn (assassinated in 2002), the short film *Submission* about the position of women in Islam (by former parliamentarian Ayaan Hirsi Ali and film director Theo van Gogh) and the assassination of Van Gogh in 2004, all caused huge unrest.[9] They also put young Moroccans in the spotlight as Muslims, at the same time as they were creating a more distinctly Muslim identity to escape from the stereotypes attached to Moroccans.

One of the main questions that surfaced in our studies among 'native' Dutch was, 'What do Muslims stand for?' This question is related to three aspects. First, Muslims are not excluded upfront from the Dutch community. According to this discourse, when Dutch Moroccans adjust to native Dutch 'norms and values', they could be included (which automatically puts the blame for failed integration on the migrants themselves). In other words, the incorporation of Muslims in Dutch society depends on criteria that are used by the Dutch to stay in control over the environment and to maintain a degree of certainty over their identity by demanding conformity on the part of Muslims. The problems related to Moroccan youth are, for 'native' Dutch people, the main reason for wanting to exclude them from the Dutch community. This is interpreted as a problem of not abiding by the prevailing norms and values in Dutch society.

The Slotervaart research project shows that in police, judicial and pedagogical circles, questions are asked about the 'quality of conscience' in Moroccan 'shame culture' which is contrasted with Dutch 'guilt culture'.

The second aspect is mainly related to events such as 9/11 and the assassination of Van Gogh. These events triggered the question of loyalty. Are Muslims 'the fifth column in society' (as Van Gogh suggested referring to radical Muslims)? Many appeals to Muslims and Muslim organisations were made to distance themselves explicitly from terrorist attacks. In the eyes of many native Dutch people it is unclear where the loyalty of Muslim immigrants lies. In other words, it is not so much the terrorist act in itself that counts, but the question as to which side of the boundary Muslims situate themselves on publicly and privately – are they on the side of the native Dutch (who stand for 'Dutch society') or on the side of the terrorists (who wish to annihilate Dutch society)?

The third aspect concerns the presence of Muslims in the public sphere. This is experienced as a real threat as is brought out by the following remarks from one of the Ethnobarometer meetings, when people talked about women's headscarves, mosque construction and so on:

> 'That is the fear!' 'It is not directed against Islam: you are fighting with yourself. What do I feel is important, what people have taught me about what is important and is that affected now? And that insecurity ...'

On the question what is affected one of the non-Muslims answered:

> My culture. My culture, a new culture enters into that, and their culture grows and grows and grows and mine is getting smaller and smaller and smaller. And my culture is my identity, so I am being forced to change my identity and I really don't want that, but I have to.

These remarks illustrate the boundary metaphor very well. It is not Islam in itself, but the feared dominance by Islam and the consequences thereof, the perception of its growing influence and of a changing environment that caused these feelings of insecurity.

This raises the question: what is it that is experienced as threatened and threatening? In terms of the quote: what is the '*core*' of the culture or identity that is threatened? And in what terms do people 'fight' or negotiate to protect the boundary surrounding that '*core*'?[10] In the Ethnobarometer project, it became clear that the main concept used by 'native' Dutch people in their relation to Muslims was the concept of tolerance. There are differences, but for most Dutch people 'tolerance' seems a popular and typical Dutch virtue, and an essential part of Dutch identity. In the relations between Muslims and Dutch tolerance seems a core boundary marker of Dutch identity for Dutch people. Muslims are seen as intolerant towards white/native 'Dutch people', while Muslims and other immigrants – but especially radical Muslims – would enjoy all possible fruits of tolerance, at the expense of native Dutch people. All the freedoms Dutch people have fought for since the 1960s, such as women's emancipation, sexual freedoms, liberation from religious constraints, are assumed to be at risk from Muslims who would not agree with these freedoms. Again, there is a paradox: the Dutch are becoming less tolerant towards the presence of Muslims exactly *because* tolerance is a core value for them.

The Ethnobarometer project shows that the concept of tolerance is a core element of Dutch identity. At the same time, the results show that the concept of tolerance is a core concept in the negotiations of the boundary between the domains under control and those one cannot control, coinciding with the boundary between native Dutch identity and Muslim (non-Dutch) identity. As mentioned in the introduction, human security and freedom are two sides to the same coin. Negotiations about identity are not just driven by a quest for human security but at the same time by evocations of and desire for freedom. This is illustrated by the phenomenon that some Dutch people, who, even though they feel that Dutch tolerance is not fully compatible with Islam, blame the present atmosphere of intolerance and xenophobia and polarisation between Dutch 'autochthones' and Dutch Muslims on the former. They blame some actors and issues for the breakdown of tolerance and the tensions in society, in particular politicians such as Hirsi Ali and Wilders and the sensationalism of the media, the proposed tough measures such as the proposed 'prescription' to speak Dutch in the streets, the protests against big mosques and Islamic schools, the question of 'double nationality',[11] prohibition of the *burqa*, etc. *This means that tolerance is not only part of the core of Dutch identity, but it also marks the boundary between native Dutch and Muslims.* Combined with concrete events such as '9/11' and 'Van Gogh', and the increased visibility of Muslims in the public sphere, this leads to a feeling among many Dutch people that their existence is uncertain. Some native Dutch feel that the boundaries protecting their own group and their environment are blurring. Essentialising these boundaries may be a way to overcome this threat, as it makes clear who the enemy is and what is needed to contain the threat. In his inaugural lecture for instance, Oscar Salemink (2006) analysed how ritualised public events drew and embodied sharp national boundaries between white Dutch 'autochthones' and 'others'.

On the other side, we can see different trends among Moroccan Muslim youth. There are those who seek to actively engage with and belong to Dutch society. Their message, however, about a tolerant and peaceful Islam, compatible with Dutch society, is ignored or disbelieved by many native Dutch people (De Koning and Bartels 2006). But they still claim the right to be acknowledged as full citizens, with the right to decide what standards should apply for their inclusion into Dutch society. At the same time, we see that more and more young Moroccan Muslims call for action against what they perceive as 'a battle against Islam'. Their actions can take various forms but mostly these are individual acts.

Striking in both of these two trends is that, although people feel threatened, they realise that their future is in the Netherlands. In order to secure a prosperous future they have to try to belong. They stand up for their own Muslim identity, demand respect and are less inclined to accept any form of restriction. They try to negotiate the boundary between their own Muslim identity and Dutch national identity by using the same concept as the Dutch, the concept of tolerance. But this concept is transformed. It is not the notion of space for minorities that is central any more. Tolerance is related to the concept of respect. Tolerance and respect are no longer virtues directed at others, but a claim for space for themselves, by saying to others 'Back off, don't interfere with me' (Bartels 2005, De Koning 2005, Pels 2003). Tolerance and respect are not only related to what they see as essential to Islam but also as connected to a kind of universal right to their own identity and to core values of Dutch society. So the boundary between Dutch and Muslim identity is essentialised by the use of the same concepts, albeit interpreted in different ways.

A third trend is emerging among *salafi* Muslims. These young Muslims are transnationally engaged but tend to isolate themselves socially and spiritually from society. By means of clothing and outward appearance (e.g. by wearing a beard) they can distinguish themselves, thus creating a visible, embodied marker. Certainly in these cases we can speak of a withdrawal into a self-created fortress of purity. Some of them are dreaming about moving to Saudi-Arabia, or in a few cases actually going to Saudi Arabia. A fourth trend is a small group of young people calling themselves Muslims but who do not really practise their religion. They have a secular lifestyle and are not interested in politics or in society. Some of them reconsider their faith. The murder of Van Gogh shocked them and they wonder if Islam still is the right way. Also in this group we can find the conviction that Muslim youth feel disappointed about the Dutch not living up to their own standards of tolerance.

CONCLUSION

The fact that Muslims are not excluded upfront suggests that it is not the presence of a new group in society that makes human security and cultural identity an issue. Immigrants – e.g. Muslims – can be included. But in recent years the Dutch have started to formulate criteria for inclusion. This is connected to the shift in discourse from 'political correctness' to a frank expression of fear and disquiet about the presence of Muslims in Dutch society. When Muslim identity can be controlled there are few problems in terms of human security, as brought out by the brief history of Dutch multicultural society in the 1980s and the 1990s. However, the questioning of the terms of their cultural integration by second-generation Muslims, the debates about core – Dutch or Islamic – norms and values, the doubts about their loyalties and the increased visibility of Muslims in society leads to a reflection on Dutch identity.

On the other side, young Muslims not only claim the right to be acknowledged as full citizens but also the right to be fully included as Muslims, claiming the traditional rights and privileges that go with being religious in Dutch society. Both 'native' Dutch and Muslims refer to tolerance as a core value of their identity. At the same time. this concept of tolerance is central in the negotiations to control the boundary between 'us' and 'them', between security and insecurity. In the negotiations for clear boundaries, Dutch people fear the loss of the core of their own identity: tolerance. Muslims of Moroccan descent, on the other hand, tend to use the concept of tolerance to create their own space. Some of them do this in order to be able to participate as Moroccan Muslims in Dutch society, while others isolate themselves from Dutch society. Both 'native' Dutch and Moroccan Muslims try to restore their own human security in competition with others. The result, however, is that their own identity as well as the other's is essentialised and the boundaries between groups are rendered impermeable.

In this chapter we focused on the Dutch case, which obviously is idiosyncratic, but to some extent also exemplary for recent movements in Western Europe. Given the rapid and rather extreme shift from a public discourse of cultural relativism and tolerance to a discourse emphasising integration and assimilation and the closing of state borders for migration, the Dutch case might constitute a magnification of tendencies under way in other countries in Western Europe as well. The situation in different European countries is not only comparable on an academic level, but is also often compared 'in the street', in discussion within and between groups through transnational networks. Events and developments in one country may affect the situation in other countries as well. The transnational and international fuss about cartoons published in Denmark is a case in point. Finally, the threat of terror attacks (Madrid, London, political murders in the Netherlands), and the public and political responses, make it clear that the present insecurity over identity issues has a deep impact on people's sense of physical security, thus violating the 'freedom from fear' dimension of human security.

In other words, the way that people define their cultural identity is part and parcel of their subjective sense of human security – first and foremost in terms of cultural security, but eventually also in terms of their physical safety.[12] In this chapter we have argued that this sense of cultural security is linked with the definition of the boundaries between cultural categories, between 'us' and 'them', between zones under control and zones outside one's control. When once 'secure' cultural boundaries start to shift, this may create anxiety, fear and resentment.

NOTES

1. This paper was originally written as partial basis for a UNESCO report on human security in Europe. That report appeared under the following title: J. Peter Burgess, with Anthony Amicelle, Edien Bartels, Rocco Bellanova, Alfio Cerami, Erik Eggum et al. 2007. *Promoting Human Security: Ethical, Normative and Educational Frameworks in Western Europe.* Paris: UNESCO Section of Human Security, Democracy and Philosophy (see http://unesdoc.unesco.org/images/0015/001511/151144e.pdf).

2. Edien Bartels, Kim Knibbe and Oscar Salemink are affiliated with the Department of Social and Cultural Anthropology of the Vrije Universiteit/ Free University Amsterdam. Martijn de Koning received his PhD from VU University Amsterdam and is currently affiliated with the Radboud University in Nijmegen.

3. Although this definition introduces a cultural dimension into the notion of human security, it should be noted that in this chapter we will take a more dynamic view of groups and processes of identification than the UN.

4. Eickelman and Piscatori (1996) make no mention of experiences in their definition of identity. Most of the time this is left out of the concept of identities and identity politics. Eriksen (1993), Bentley (1987, 1991) and Yelvington (1991) point out, in different ways, why identity is more than just an instrument for the realisation of one's interests, and that experience is an important basis for emerging identities.

5. Paradoxically, when identity constructions are opposed, this does not mean that they are not under control. The early twentieth-century Dutch pillarisation system was based on the segregation of groups of Catholics, Protestants, and secular liberals and socialists, with fixed, opposed identities and a carefully guarded balance of power. They had created a network of organisations in which people were taken care of within their own group from the cradle to the grave (see Goudsblom 1967). This created a 'security' that many babyboomers found stifling, and indeed to be the opposite of 'freedom' as Eriksen suggests.

6. In 2007 Martijn de Koning defended and published his PhD thesis based on research among Moroccan Muslim youth in Gouda, a middle-sized town of 70,000 inhabitants in the western part of the Netherlands (equidistant from Rotterdam, The Hague and Utrecht), which is in many respects representative for many such towns – a Dutch 'Middletown'. Almost 10 per cent of the population has a Muslim background: the 6000 Moroccans constituting the largest group. The research group consisted of boys and girls between 10 and 20 years old who visited one of the mosques for religious and/or social and cultural activities.

7. In 2005 and 2006 a research team of the International Institute for the Study of Islam in the Modern World (ISIM) in Leiden, the Netherlands, conducted research in order the assess the relationship between Muslims and non-Muslims in the Netherlands. This research was part of the Ethnobarometer programme. The Ethnobarometer Programme is a programme of social scientists providing independent and research-based reports on levels of racism, xenophobia and ethnic conflict in selected countries of Europe. It aims to monitor events, highlight areas of tension and identify relevant topics for further research and inquiry. The programme serves as a tool for generating scientific information on inter-ethnic relations where these are taken to encompass both territorial minorities and communities of recent migrant origin, and is coordinated by the director of Ethnobarometer, Alessandro Silj. The latest Ethnobarometer project is called 'Europe's Muslim Communities – Security and Integration Post-11 September'. The project is operational in six countries: Italy, France, Belgium, Germany, the UK, and the Netherlands. ISIM is the Dutch partner for this project. The objective was to assess the consequences of the various responses to 11 September 2001 and the murder of Van Gogh in November 2004 for both the Muslim communities and European societies at large, and, in particular, the relations between Muslim communities and the rest of the population. The material used here is based on the Dutch project carried out in Gouda using five focus groups, four of them with Moroccan Muslims and native Dutch people and one with only Dutch people. The material for this chapter is based upon the first four groups The principal researcher was Martijn

de Koning, under supervision of Professor Martin van Bruinessen of the ISIM. See also www.ethnobarometer.org and www.isim.nl

8. The Slotervaart research project into migrant originations and identity formation of Muslim young people is carried out by Edien Bartels and Master's students in social and cultural anthropology (Vrije Universiteit/Free University Amsterdam) in the Amsterdam city district of Slotervaart.

9. A recent (12 April 2006) study of the scientific council of government policy states:

> A climate of distrust and fear has arisen between Muslims and non-Muslims, and also within the Muslim community itself at times. Communication about 'Islam' now only takes place through intemperate images and inflated words, such as 'clash of civilizations' or an 'irreconcilability of Islam with democracy and human rights'. (page 1 of the summary)

The summary, *Dynamism in Islamic Activism: Reference Points for Democratization and Human Rights* is available at: www.wrr.nl/english

10. Likewise, Sabine Alkire's (2002) definition of human security refers to a vital *core* of all human lives that has to be protected from critical pervasive threats in a way consistent with long-term human fulfilment.

11. During one of the Ethnobarometer meetings, a Dutch non-Muslim posed: " If you choose only for the Dutch nationality, you join the club."

12. The relation between existential security and physical security should be further explored in research.

REFERENCES

Alkire, Sabine. 2002. *A Conceptual Framework for Human Security*. Working Paper 2. Harvard: CRISE.

Bauman, Zygmunt. 2001. *Community: Seeking Safety in an Insecure World*. Cambridge: Polity Press.

Baumann, Gerd. 2004. Grammars of Identity/Alterity: A Structural Approach. In Gerd Baumann and André Gingrich (eds) *Grammars of Identity/Alterity: A Structural Approach*. New York: Berghahn Books, 17–50.

Bartels, Edien. 2005. Guilt and Shame in Relation to the Formation of Conscience. Lecture for the Forensic Psychology and Justice Section of the NIP (Nederlands Instituut voor Psychologen, Dutch Institute for Psychologists). Eefde/Zutphen.

Bentley, G. Carter. 1987. Ethnicity and Practice. *Comparative Studies in Society and History* 29: 24–55.

Bentley, G. Carter. 1991. Response to Yelvington. *Comparative Studies in Society and History* 33: 169–75.

Burgess, J. Peter (ed.). 2004. Special Section: What Is 'Human Security'? *Security Dialogue* 35(3): 345–88.

Burgess, J. Peter, with Anthony Amicelle, Edien Bartels, Rocco Bellanova, Alfio Cerami, Erik Eggum et al. 2007. *Promoting Human Security: Ethical, Normative and Educational Frameworks in Western Europe*. Paris: UNESCO Section on Human Security, Democracy and Philosophy (URL: http://unesdoc.unesco.org/images/0015/001511/151144e.pdf).

Chen, Lincoln, Sakiko Fukuda-Parr and Ellen Seidensticker (eds). 2003. *Human Insecurity in a Globalizing World*. Cambridge, MA: Harvard University Press, Global Equity Initiative.

Commission on Human Security. 2003. *Final Report of the Commission on Human Security*. URL: http://www.humansecurity-chs.org/finalreport/FinalReport.pdf

De Koning, Martijn. 2005. 'Dit is geen poep wat ik praat': De Hirsi Ali Diss nader belicht. *ZemZem* 1: 36–41.

De Koning, Martijn and Edien Bartels. 2006. 'For Allah and Myself': Religion and Moroccan Youth in the Netherlands. In Petra Bos and Wantje Fritschy (eds) *Morocco and the Netherlands: Society, Economy, Culture*. Amsterdam: VU Publishers.

Department of Social and Cultural Anthropology. 2004. *Constructing Human Security in a Globalizing World* (research proposal). Amsterdam: Vrije Universiteit/ Free University Amsterdam.

Eickelman, Dale and James Piscatori. 1996. *Muslim Politics*. Princeton, NJ: Princeton University Press.

Eriksen, Thomas Hylland. 1993. *Ethnicity and Nationalism*. London: Pluto Press.

Eriksen, Thomas Hylland. 2005. *Risking Security: Paradoxes of Social Cohesion* (inaugural lecture). Amsterdam: Vrije Universiteit/Free University Amsterdam.

Fukuda-Parr, Sakiko. 2003. New Threats to Human Security in the Era of Globalization. In Lincoln Chen, Sakiko Fukuda-Parr and Ellen Seidensticker (eds) *Human Security in a Global World*. Cambridge, MA: Harvard University Press, 1–14.

Giddens, Anthony. 1991. *Modernity and Self-identity*. Cambridge: Polity Press.

Goudsblom, Johan. 1967. *Dutch Society*. New York: Random House.

Hervieu-Léger, Danièle. 2000. *Religion as a Chain of Memory*. Cambridge: Polity Press.

Jackson, Michael. 1998. *Minima Ethnographica: Intersubjectivity and the Anthropological Project*. Chicago: University of Chicago Press.

Jenkins, Richard. 1996. *Social Identity*. London: Routledge.

Jenkins, Richard. 2001. The Limits of Identity: Ethnicity, Conflicts, and Politics. Sheffield University, Sheffield Online Paper 2000, URL: http://www.shef.ac.uk/socst/Shop/2jenkins.pdf

Knibbe, Kim. 2005. Certainties and Uncertainties in Moral Reasoning in Religious Contexts in Limburg, the Netherlands. Unpublished paper for the conference 'The Anthropology of Human Security', Vrije Universiteit Amsterdam, URL: http://www.fsw.vu.nl/images_upload/C8D3F976-C29B-6850-4F93E8A20B4E3D14.pdf

Pels, Trees. 2003. Respect van twee kanten: Over socialisatie en lastig gedrag van Marokkaanse jongens. *Migrantenstudies* 19(4): 228–39.

Roosevelt, Franklin Delano. 1941. The Four Freedoms. State of the Union speech. URL (consulted September 2009): http://www.hcbi.com/~tgort/fdr.htm

Salemink, Oscar. 2006. *Nieuwe rituelen en de natie: Nederland in de Spiegel van Vietnam* (inaugural lecture). Amsterdam: Vrije Universiteit/Free University Amsterdam.

Sennett, Richard. 1997. *The Corrosion of Character: The Personal Consequences of Work in the New Capitalism*. New York: Norton.

United Nations Development Programme. 1994. *Human Development Report 1994*, edited by Mahbub ul Haq. New York and Oxford: Oxford University Press.

Yelvington, Kelvin. 1991. Ethnicity as Practice? A Comment on Bentley. *Comparative Studies in Society and History* 33: 158–68.

7

'I'd die without the Cybersouk': Local Experiences in a Dutch Digital Community Centre

Lenie Brouwer

The words quoted in the title are those of an Afghan refugee I met at the Cybersouk digital community centre in the Zeeburg district of Amsterdam. He told me that he had been a doctor in his home country, but as he had been unable to find a suitable job in the Netherlands, he was not allowed to bring his family over to join him. To ameliorate his solitude and feeling of uprootedness, he regularly frequented the Cybersouk. He said that he went there to meet his friends, most of whom are refugees, and to practise his Dutch. He also used the centre's computers to email or chat (via MSN) with his family and friends abroad, which helped him to keep informed about the latest developments and thus gave him a sense of belonging. This illustrates how the Cybersouk provides local residents from different ethnic backgrounds with the opportunity to unite the offline and the online world, which creates a form of security.

In many of today's societies, information and communication technology (ICT) is an important means of communicating and a powerful tool for tracking down information. It is generally considered necessary to acquire some basic computer skills in order to become a 'modern' citizen. However, not everybody has access to ICT or knows how to use it. Particularly senior citizens, ethnic minorities, the poorly educated and those with a low income have become the 'socially excluded' or the 'information-poor' (Green 2003: 46). They feel uncertain about the demands of the information society, in which people have to know how to use a computer and the internet. These groups face not only financial but also social barriers that prevent them from making active use of ICT. Although some people do not understand why they should use ICT – or simply do not miss it – the majority would like to but are afraid that they will not understand it (Wyatt et al. 2002: 28). As a consequence, ICT developments not only increase the existing traditional social inequalities between the sexes, between people with different levels of education, and between natives and immigrants, but also create new inequalities between young and old people (van Dijk 2003, 2007: 36).

Because national and local governments increasingly use their websites to keep citizens informed, they regard this uneven access as a social problem. One of the policy measures to solve this problem is to provide free access to computers in community centres, or 'e-gateways'. This fits with the finding that the key issue is not the ownership of a computer, but knowing how to use one and thus being able to become part of a social network (Liff et al. 2002: 85). It has led to a special government ICT policy to improve access to the internet for the socially excluded. In the period 2001–03, almost 450 digital centres were set up in community centres, libraries and schools in socially disadvantaged districts in 30 Dutch cities (Scheltens et al. 2003). The goals of these e-gateways are:

- To reduce the digital divide and improve the self-empower-ment of citizens.
- To improve the labour market position of citizens through the acquisition of specific computer skills.
- To strengthen social cohesion in districts and to forge a sense of community among people of different ethnic backgrounds (Scheltens et al. 2003).

The centres are thus intended to provide free access to ICT in order to empower the information-poor and to help tackle the social problems that are typical of big cities, such as the growing lack of social cohesion and the increasing segregation in old districts (Beckers 2004, Drewe et al. 2003: 30). However, as Green (2003) noted in her study in England, one of the problems implicit in such programmes is that they assume that people who have access to ICT automatically become part of the 'information revolution'. In addition, access does not solve the problem of bad housing and a lack of employment (2003: 46–7).

Access to ICT in Amsterdam is provided in public libraries and community centres, as well as in two specialised digital centres that have mediated access. The Cybersouk is in the eastern part of the city; the other centre (the Amsterdam Computer Clubhouse) is in the western part. The target group of the latter comprises youths aged between 10 and 18, while that of the Cybersouk comprises all local residents who do not own a computer and/or would like to learn (or learn more) about this technology (Ambtelijke Projectgroep Digitale Trapvelden 2000). Although I conducted my research at both centres (Brouwer 2004a), in this chapter I focus only on the Cybersouk.[1] During my participant observations, I spoke with visitors, staff and volunteers, as we know little about immigrants' use of ICT (Steyaert and de Haan 2001: 87). My research focused not only on online studies of Moroccan and Muslim websites, but also on the background of the users in an offline context (Brouwer 2004b, 2006a, 2006b).

In line with the research programme *Constructing Human Security in a Globalizing World* (Department of Social Anthropology 2004), I highlight the visitors' experiences and their reasons for using a computer and the internet. The existential dimension of human security fitted perfectly with my study, as it covers ambitions, projects and desires (Department of Social Anthropology 2004). In addition, as Thomas Hylland Eriksen (2005: 2) suggests, the concept of human security can be very fruitful in updating and rephrasing such issues as social cohesion and integration. The Cybersouk centre is located in an old urban district that has weak social cohesion: people of different cultural backgrounds live side by side and have to deal with great insecurities (Beckers 2004: 65).

I found the concept of social capital very useful in the context of my research on social cohesion. Such capital refers to the value of social networks to people, organisations or neighbourhoods (Beckers 2004: 66, Putnam 2000). Putnam (2000), influenced by Bourdieu and Coleman, elaborates this concept to describe the collapse and revival of the civic and social life in American communities. Social capital can take different forms: it can stimulate social support or cooperation between people, or it can lead to corruption or ethnocentrism (Putnam 2000: 22). Social cohesion is weak when citizens have mainly social or bonding ties with their own social group, and strong when they also have relationships with other groups, thus developing 'bridging social capital' (Klumper and de Haan 2004: 18, Putnam 2007: 143).

The Cybersouk digital community centre is part of the city's strategy to halt and, if possible, reverse the trend whereby the district is experiencing increasingly weak social cohesion. Although this is of course not the only initiative to enhance social cohesion, it is paradoxical that such an individualised technology as the internet is being used as a tool, while some studies consider the internet as one of the drivers of increasing individualisation (de Haan and Klumper 2004: 17). Here, I first explore the concept of human security; I then discuss the objectives of the Cybersouk, as well as the ambitions and projects of the centre's visitors and their quest for security.

HUMAN SECURITY

Zeeburg is one of the poorest districts in Amsterdam.[2] Although more than 80 nationalities live in this district (68 per cent of its population is 'foreign'), most of the residents originate from Morocco, Turkey or the former Dutch colonies of Suriname, Aruba and the Netherlands Antilles (Beckers 2004). The slow integration of immigrants, the social isolation and the feelings of insecurity, have put the social cohesion in the district under great pressure (Beckers 2004: 65). The various ethnic groups do not interact much with each other, but remain segregated in their own social groups.

Not only do the inhabitants live in a district that suffers from great uncertainty but, as immigrants, they are also less secure regarding their labour and housing situation. In 2004, for instance, 13.6 per cent of the immigrant population in this district were unemployed (website of the City of Amsterdam). Some of them are not even sure about their residence permits. These insecurities are compounded by the current national integration policy, which seeks to prevent new immigrants from entering the country (by imposing strict marriage rules for example). The policy also requires both old and new arrivals to follow an integration programme: all immigrants must take Dutch language lessons and undergo vocational training in order to improve their chances on the labour market and to enhance their social integration. Although an anti-discrimination policy is an integral part of the programme, most complaints about discrimination concern the neighbourhood and the labour market (LBR 2004).

In general, rather idealised terms, our era seems to be more insecure than past periods, when people identified strongly with the community to which they belonged (Eriksen 2005: 6). Eriksen introduced two forms of sociality: the secure and the insecure, or the closed and the open (2005: 10). Applying these forms to immigrant communities in big cities brings up issues of closeness and feelings of safety, while from the perspective of the immigrant the outside world represents both openness and insecurity. My assumption is that those immigrants who visit the Cybersouk in order to work at a computer, seek to attach meaning to these feelings and are looking for a form of social security.

The notion of social capital emphasises a wide variety of benefits that flow from the trust, reciprocity and cooperation that are associated with social networks. Social capital can create value or security for connected people, as well as for friendship networks, neighbourhoods, schools or civic associations. A focus on the difference between bonding and bridging social capital has become crucial in analyses of social cohesion. Bonding networks connect members of specific groups, while bridging networks unite individuals from diverse backgrounds. Venues where people have the opportunity to interact with their fellow citizens can be a first step towards feeling more involved in the community, and this can strengthen social networks (Klumper and de Haan 2004: 18, Putnam 2000: 411; 2007: 164).

One of the important factors that enhance social cohesion is the way a centre is socially embedded in its local community (Beckers 2004, Liff et al. 2002: 86). The Cybersouk has links with several local primary and secondary schools, whose pupils visit the centre for information and to take various courses: for example, the Children's Press Office project, in which children are taught how to produce their own online local newspaper. Older clients have links with the local home for the elderly and such organisations as the Senior Web (a website for seniors), and immigrants become associated through several immigrant organisations in the district. The Cybersouk also has structural relations with the local council and such social institutions as Job Centres (Stichting Zeeburg 2007: 22).

THE CYBERSOUK AND ITS VISITORS

The Cybersouk – a combination of 'cyberspace' and 'souk' (Arabic for market) – was set up in September 2001. The centre occupies a central place in the district, as it is located in a small square near a kindergarten and a vocational secondary school. The old building was renovated for this ICT project; the funding came from national and local governments, and several private sponsors. The fresh red colours on the walls give the space a modern look and make it a nice place to be.

The Cybersouk is divided into three parts. Just inside the entrance is a large, open room equipped with ten computers arranged in two rows along the left-hand side, each with a modern flat-screen monitor. At the front of the room is a long wooden table with benches on either side; this is intended to promote socialising. The third area is a partly closed-off room with 14 computers sitting on small tables that stand against the wall; this room is reserved for courses. The centre's modern decor and up-to-date equipment contrast with commercial internet cafes and old community centres, and create a site where people can 'feel comfortable and can come and go' (Oldenburg in Liff et al. 2002: 82–3). The Cybersouk is thus a 'third-place model of informal public locations' (2002: 89). It provides more than just internet access: it is a place where users feel connected with others.

The centre's coordinator regards this work with computers as a 'new form of community work'. She was very proud of the results the centre had achieved in such a short time: between September 2001 and the end of December 2003, the Cybersouk received 16,708 visitors (Stichting Zeeburg 2003: 17).[3] The coordinator told me: 'We want the site to be a safe place for every resident in this district. We hope to stimulate them to feel more self-confident in the use of computers.' The centre therefore has specific courses for specific target groups, and convenient opening hours that allow people to drop in when they wish or when it is convenient. Five paid staff members and around 20 volunteers teach the visitors digital skills. The coordinator continued:

> Our special 'women's hours' attract quite a lot of Moroccan women; entry is free and they can bring their children with them. In our introduction course for seniors, we adapt to their tempo – that is, make it slower – so that they can follow the lessons. Furthermore, computer classes are part of the integration course for 'old-comers', which we take care of.

During the afternoon 'internet cafe hours', youths mainly come to the centre to chat online, but during school hours they can learn how to build websites. I attended a whole range of courses, open hours and some joint gatherings during my participant observation, and had the chance to talk with the clients, both while they were working at the computers and during coffee breaks.

'Women's Hours'

Every Thursday morning the centre has a special open hour for women, who can drop in and use the computers for whatever purpose they want. During these sessions, a female staff member and several female volunteers walk around and help the women if they need assistance. Although this staff member told me that they never know how many women will come, on most of the days that I went there, all the computers were occupied. Virtually the same group of women turned up every week. Two of the most regular visitors were a pair of Moroccan women wearing headscarves. One was in her 20s and had lived with her parents in the Netherlands for eight years; the other was in her 40s and had been a Dutch resident for 15 years. She was married to a Dutch man, but they had divorced a couple of years previously. She had no children and was living on her own, which is quite unusual for a Moroccan woman. Her father used to be a 'guest worker' in the Netherlands, but had returned to Morocco some years earlier.

These women struck me as unusual because their only activity on the computer was to practise for the theory part of the driving test. They both had the same goal, namely to pass the test so that they could drive to Morocco during the summer holidays. When I sat near them and read the text, I realised that the complex sentences and difficult words are very baffling to non-native speakers. 'I've already failed the test seven times,' the oldest woman said, with an air of disappointment. These women had undertaken a daunting (and perhaps hopeless) project, but in their view it was a way to improve their social and physical mobility.

Another regular visitor to the special women's hours was a Kurdish woman from Iraq. She always performed the same ritual on the computer: she first looked at the online Iraqi newspapers, and then did her Dutch lessons. She, her husband and their child had arrived in the Netherlands 13 years earlier as asylum seekers, and had finally been recognised as political refugees. She said that she had sat at home for seven years, raising her children, and that now she wanted to learn Dutch. During the breaks she did not have much contact with the other women, and she was rather quiet. Only when another Iraqi woman was attending the centre did I see her talking and laughing. In her computer use, she managed to combine a need for information about her country of origin (to fulfil her notions of belonging) with a desire to fully participate in Dutch society (quest for a secure future).

The idea that a computer can further one's participation in society was supported by a young Moroccan woman who regularly attended the women's hours. One of her neighbours had told her about the Cybersouk, and she had gone to the centre by herself. She had lived in the Netherlands for 12 years, and was taking the language course provided by the integration programme. 'My husband works all day,' she said. 'I have to raise our four children. It is very important to learn to speak Dutch well.' She was practising her Dutch on the computer, and she wrote down on a piece of paper the difficult words she came across, such as 'work conditions' and 'artistic'. Another time, I saw her browsing a website about the upbringing of children. Two of her children were with her, and she was looking for advice on how to deal with children who quarrel all the time. This use of the computer is another example of looking for ways to improve social integration and social security.

Two of the other regular visitors were a pair of older Dutch women who used the Adobe Photoshop software to edit photographs. They had been motivated to learn to use a computer and felt 'proud' that they now understood messages in the media, such as 'visit our website for more information'. One of the women had passed by the Cybersouk by chance, and had decided to go in. Once inside, she had found out that it is free and that one can take computer courses there. This had been nine months earlier, and since then they had attended various lessons. She told me:

> I now know how to email, and how to look for information on the internet. My daughter lives abroad, so I can email her and send her photos as attachments. But it is not that easy to learn something new when you are old. Unless you use it constantly, you immediately forget.

There are now few native Dutch families living in Zeeburg, as most such families have moved to the modern suburbs on the outskirts of the city. However, I met a 60-year-old woman who had lived her whole life in the district, as had her children and aged father. 'Without the Cybersouk,' she said, 'I'd never use a computer.' She was writing the story of her childhood for a website that collects memories of the district from its older residents. She said she was 'too old to move', even though most people she knew had already left. She explained how the district had changed greatly over the years:

> I used to live in a small street, and I knew all the neighbours. Now I have no contact with my neighbours; I don't know them. I don't like the shops either; for instance, we have no longer shoe or bag shops.

Her neighbour agreed with her. 'Where can you buy a nice pastry these days?' she asked. 'And where are the confectioners? We have only one Dutch bakery. It's no longer cosy here; the nice atmosphere has disappeared.' This quote characterises the great insecurity felt by the older female inhabitants. For them, the special website with its collected stories of the district is a way to keep that lost past alive, and thus to maintain some sort of security in a very insecure district.

Another native Dutch woman told me that she lived next door and did not own a computer. 'It's so easy to go to the Cybersouk, and they always help you if you have a question. I like to come here.' She was unemployed and therefore had plenty of time to learn about computers. One of the goals of the centre – namely to enhance the labour position of its visitors – was reflected in the kind of activities this woman engaged in, such using a computer to compile her CV and write job application letters. A volunteer told me that she had helped a client to write such a letter, and that the client had finally been invited to a job interview. The volunteer felt very satisfied about this.

Another of the goals of the centre is to contribute to social cohesion in the district. The staff members therefore do their best to stimulate social contacts between the visitors. This is not an easy task, because working at a computer is mostly an isolated activity. Nevertheless, I often observed visitors asking their neighbours for help or sitting together searching for information on the internet. Although everybody is free to choose which computer they work on, I noted that that the immigrant women tended to sit together in the large, open room, while the indigenous Dutch women preferred to work in the smaller room. When I commented on this to one of the staff, she nodded ruefully and said 'Yes – but that shouldn't be the case.'

Coffee breaks are one of the ways in which the centre stimulates mutual contacts between the visitors. 'Coffee breaks are a must,' one of the volunteers told me. Needless to say, although coffee breaks provide an opportunity for informal social talk, such talk does not arise automatically. If a volunteer did not ask all the visitors to get together for coffee and then start a general chat, I noticed that people of the same ethnicity would talk among themselves during the breaks. This segregation continued after closing time: around midday, most of the immigrant women left the centre, as some of them had to fetch their children from school, while most of the Dutch women stayed longer and would stand around in front of the centre while they continued their animated discussions.

Open Access Hours

During the open access hours, the centre is attended by an extremely diverse mix of users – men and women of very different ages and cultural backgrounds. Each visitor has his or her own particular reason to visit the centre and to learn to use a computer or surf the internet. For instance, an older Dutch woman who had had a stroke some time previously visited the Cybersouk almost every day to do her rehabilitation exercises. Another older woman, who had recently become a widow, visited the centre to meet other people and to play computer games. A Surinamese teacher in her 50s felt very insecure about her knowledge of computers, especially when compared with her pupils, and was looking for professional advice. And another visitor – a young woman from India who had just arrived in the Netherlands to join her husband – was so eager to learn Dutch that she could not wait for the lessons provided by the integration programme. She tried to study Dutch as much as possible by using a computerised language course.

The more skilled users come to the Cybersouk for various reasons. For example, one Surinamese man in his late 40s was writing his CV and an application letter, and was seeking help to make his documents look neat and professional. A young Afghan couple, the woman wearing a headscarf, would sit side by side and read an online Afghan newspaper. They were always so engrossed with it that they isolated themselves from their surroundings, although I once saw the man helping an Afghan friend to complete an application form for a rent subsidy.

One day, I observed a young man from Trinidad talking with a student who was using a website-building program. The Trinidadian – a professional photographer – had heard about the Cybersouk in a local bar, and had been told about a special course for artists that teaches them to present their products on a website. He wanted to learn to do this by himself, as he lacked the money to get somebody else to do it for him. Although he was anxious to get started, he was afraid that he would make mistakes. The student explained a few things to him about the program, and offered him a copy of the software he needed. The photographer was very pleased with the offer.

Other visitors searched the web for information. For instance, I saw a young Moroccan man visiting a housing-exchange website. He said that he liked the district very much but his house was too small, as he had a wife and two young children. He had placed an ad for his own house on the website, and was looking for interesting exchange offers.

I once spoke with an Egyptian man I had met the week before during a course. Mr Atum (not his real name) had just learnt how to use email and he asked me to help him to send an email with an attachment; he had found an article in an Arabic newspaper that he thought would interest one of his friends. Mr Atum had lived in the Netherlands for 15 years. He is a trained bookkeeper, but worked mainly in restaurants and the catering industry, although at the time he was unemployed. It was sometimes difficult to understand him, as he did not speak Dutch very clearly. Apart from learning digital skills, practising the language is another common reason to visit the Cybersouk, which is an attractive place and one at which it is possible to meet Dutch people in a relaxed atmosphere. Mr Atum's wife and three young children had left the Netherlands to take care of his mother-in-law, who was ill and living in Egypt. They were due to return in the summer. 'I hope they come back soon,' he said. 'I miss my children very much.'

Mr Atum told me that he wanted to chat online with a friend in Egypt, as his wife did not have access to the internet. His friend had recently returned to Egypt with his Dutch wife, and he owned a computer. After we had logged in to MSN, a short message appeared on the screen: his friend in Egypt had noticed that he was online and asked in English after his health. Mr Atum was both surprised and enthusiastic, and he started to answer his friend's question in phonetic Dutch words. As there was no Arabic keyboard, he used a combination of Dutch and English words to chat, which he did rather slowly as he lacked typing skills. Nevertheless, he had managed to start an online conversation about the situation of his friend's family, as well as about his own wife and children: his friend had just visited Mr Atum's family and he wrote that the visit had been 'rather dull' because of Mr Atum's absence. This online interaction with his friend in Egypt gave Mr Atum a feeling of belonging, a sense of security, albeit only a temporary one.

Sitting next to the Egyptian was a refugee from Iran. He was working at a computer, practising his Dutch by sending emails to Dutch friends. He was 37, married and has a daughter. He told me in almost perfect Dutch:

I was somebody in Iran. I had an important job, a house and a car. I'm nobody here. I have to make a new start. I'm different from the migrants who came to work here. I had no choice; they chose this country for me. I'm a foreigner – I feel it every day, when I watch television or walk in the street. If you don't speak Dutch well, people think you're stupid. They don't differentiate between foreigners and they think you're a peasant, but I used to work at a university.

The Iranian man said that he wanted to fully integrate himself into Dutch society, and that he therefore no longer followed the news from his home country as other refugees do. His daughter now spoke better Dutch than Iranian: 'She *is* more Dutch than Iranian,' he said with a smile. His diploma had not been recognised, but he hoped that he would soon be admitted to a new technical school.

These examples show how visitors to the Cybersouk are eager to use the digital facilities for their individual projects and to further their ambitions, in order to extend their social networks, or to improve their social position or to participate in the information society. As Putnam (2007: 164) states, 'most immigrants want to acculturate', in particular at sites where they can meet native Dutch people. While most of the users I met lived in a rather insecure situation, they told me that they believed that computer skills and internet access would help them to achieve more security in their social existence.

CONCLUSION

The Cybersouk has created a central place where the offline meets the online in a poor district that is characterised by human insecurity and social segregation. The centre provides internet access to a mixture of local immigrant women and men, senior citizens, persons with a low level of education and young people who do not have internet access at home and/or lack specific digital skills. The centre's variety of opening hours and its trained staff members and volunteers have created a pleasant and safe place – a 'third place' – in the district for civic participation and e-learning. While the district is becoming more socially segregated and its residents are living increasingly parallel lives, the Cybersouk is encouraging the different social groups to participate in the centre's activities and to meet their fellow residents. The Cybersouk is facilitating its visitors' growing social networks, or social capital, and thus can be characterised, in Putnam's terms, as one of those important places 'to become comfortable with diversity' (2007: 164).

This e-gateway has managed to attract increasing numbers of visitors and has therefore made a modest contribution towards narrowing the digital divide in the district. To begin with, most visitors feel insecure and anxious about using computers, but after they have received some training they feel proud of their new skills. The centre thus achieves the intended goal of empowering the 'information-poor'. Recent research emphasises that a special approach is needed in order to reach certain target groups and to enhance the users' digital skills (van Dijk 2007: 46–7). This finding is supported by the success of the Cybersouk, which specialises in teaching and assisting these particular groups.

The Cybersouk staff and volunteers teach people the computer skills they need in order to become modern citizens in the information society. The visitors' individual strategies and ambitions are related to such issues as social cohesion, empowerment and the quest for social security. However, the visitors are very diverse and individual in their desires and motivations. Some of them – for example, the senior citizens, the immigrants and the refugees – have such a marginalised and insecure position in contemporary society that attending a digital centre can be a first step towards building social capital, and thus achieving a form of social security. Having seen each other at the Cybersouk, when they meet in the street or at the market, they are no longer complete strangers and so find it easier to make contact with each other. Some of the visitors have more practical ambitions and search the web for jobs or for a new place to live. Computer literacy and social networks comprising other local residents help them to improve their position on the labour market and to increase their social capital, although this of course does not solve their problems in the labour or the housing market.

In terms of social cohesion and social capital, the centre is an open site that provides access to residents of different backgrounds, ages and cultures, and that can bring these heterogeneous people together. This is a special achievement from the perspective of urban segregation, but from the angle of social cohesion it is only a start. We need to find out more about the significance of these meetings for the users, for example, about the kinds of ties they establish with other residents who are different from them.

While at the Cybersouk, I observed more examples of bonding than of bridging social capital. Although the centre is an open communal space that attracts diverse target groups, the visitors – who are living in a situation of human insecurity – still feel more connected to their own communities, both online and offline, and therefore construct more bonding than bridging social capital.

NOTES

1. This research was part of the international project 'Netculture and the Politics of Ethnic Identity: A Comparative Research on Transnational eGovernment Projects in Four National Contexts' (see Dracklé 2002).
2. Zeeburg comprises the Oostelijk Haven (14,652 inhabitants), the 'old' Indische Buurt (23,500 inhabitants) and the new IJburg, which is home to mainly highly educated Dutch inhabitants (Beckers 2004: 72). The Cybersouk is located in the Indische Buurt, the poorer district.
3. Two years later, these numbers had increased: between 1 September 2001 and 31 December 2005, 44,409 people visited the centre (Stichting Zeeburg Interplein 2007: 27).

REFERENCES

Ambtelijke Projectgroep Digitale Trapvelden. 2000. *Beleidsnota laagdrempelige ICT-voorzieningen op wijkniveau*. Amsterdam.

Beckers, D. 2004. Effecten van ICT op sociale cohesie in Cyburg, Amsterdam. In J. de Haan and O. Klumper (eds) *Jaarboek ICT en samenleving. Beleid in praktijk*. Amsterdam: Boom, 65–89.

Brouwer, L. 2004a. Creatief met computers. In J. de Haan and O. Klumper (eds) *Jaarboek ICT en samenleving. Beleid in praktik*. Amsterdam: Boom, 141–59.

Brouwer, L. 2004b. Dutch Muslims on the Internet: A New Discussion Platform. *Journal of Muslim Minority Affairs* 24(1): 47–55.

Brouwer, L. 2006a. Dutch Moroccan Websites: A Transnational Imagery? *Journal of Ethnic and Migration Studies* 32(7): 1153–69.

Brouwer, L. 2006b. Giving Voice to Dutch Moroccan Girls on the Internet. *Global Media Journal* (Special Issue on Women and the Media) fall.

Department of Social Anthropology (2004). 2004. *Constructing Human Security in a Globalizing World* (research proposal). Amsterdam: Vrije Universiteit/Free University Amsterdam.

Dijk, J.A.G.M. van. 2003. *De digitale kloof wordt dieper. Van ongelijkheid in bezit naar ongelijkheid in vaardigheden en gebruik van ICT*. Den Haag: Kenniscentrum Grote Steden.

Dijk, J.A.G.M. van, 2007. De *e*-surfende burger: is de digitale kloof gedicht? In J. Steyaert and J. de Haan (eds) *Jaarboek ICT en samenleving. Gewoon digitaal*. Amsterdam: Boom, 31–51.

Drewe, P., A. Fernandez-Maldonado and E. Hulsbergen. 2003. Battling Urban Deprivation: ICT Strategies in the Netherlands and Europe. *Journal of Urban Technology* 10(1): 23–37.

Eriksen, T.H. 2005. *Risking Security: Paradoxes of Social Cohesion* (inaugural lecture). Amsterdam: Vrije Universiteit/Free University Amsterdam.

Green, S. 2003. Digital Ditches: Working in the Virtual Grass Roots. In C. Garsten and H. Wulff (eds) *New Technologies at Work: People, Screens and Social Virtuality*. Oxford: Berg, 45–69.

Klumper, O. and J. de Haan. 2004. Beleid in praktijk. In J. de Haan and O. Klumper (eds) *Jaarboek ICT en samenleving. Beleid in praktijk*. Amsterdam: Boom, 11–29.

LBR. 2004. *Racisme in Nederland. Stand van zaken*. Rotterdam. URL: http://www.art1.nl/?node=1231 (accessed on 10 March 2008).

Liff, S., F. Stewart and P. Watts. 2002. New Public Places for Internet Access: Networks for Practice-based Learning and Social Inclusion. In S. Woolgar (ed.) *Virtual Society? Technology, Cyberbole, Reality*. Oxford: University Press, 78–115.

Putnam, R.D. 2000. *Bowling Alone: The Collapse and Revival of Civic America*. New York: Simon and Schuster.

Putnam, R.D. 2007. *E Pluribus Unum*: Diversity and Community in the Twenty-first Century. The 2006 Johan Skytte Prize Lecture. *Scandinavian Political Studies*, 30(2): 137–75.

Scheltens, J.S., S. Lenos and J. van Steenhoven. 2003. *Monitor digitale trapvelden 2003, stand van zaken*. Amsterdam: Netwerk Digitale Trapvelden.

Steyaert, J. and J. de Haan, 2001. *Geleidelijk digitaal. Een nuchtere kijk op de sociale gevolgen van ict*. Den Haag: Sociaal Cultureel Planbureau.

Stichting Zeeburg Interplein. 2007. *Cybersoek. Jaarverslag 2007*. Amsterdam. URL: www.cybersoek.nl (accessed on 10 March 2008).

Wyatt, S., G. Thomas and T. Terranova. 2002. They Came, They Surfed, They Went Back to the Beach: Conceptualizing Use and Non-use of the Internet. In S. Woolgar (ed.) *Virtual Society? Technology, Cyberbole, Reality*. Oxford: University Press, 23–41.

8
Religion, Identity and Security among Pomeranian Lutheran Migrants in Espírito Santo, Brazil (1880–2005): A Schema Repertoire Approach

André Droogers

A SCHEMA REPERTOIRE APPROACH TO SECURITY AND INSECURITY

Religion has been both a source of security and of insecurity. In this chapter the role of religion in constructing existential or ontological security (Giddens 1990: 92) in a situation of insecurity is explored through a case study of the Pomeranian immigrants who in the nineteenth century came to the region of what is now the municipality of Santa Maria de Jetibá, in the interior of the state of Espírito Santo (Brazil). This long-term study includes their descendants. The focus is on the relation in the course of time between religion, ethnic origin and ontological security, with a special interest in the identity construction of these migrants and in the role the Lutheran Church played in it. Identity is understood as a stronghold of security, even though the search for identity is often marked by insecurity and uncertainty.

To describe and analyse the case of Santa Maria de Jetibá, I will take the concept of schema repertoire as starting-point for my theoretical framework. Schema is a concept coined in cognitive anthropology, especially connectionism (Bloch 1998, D'Andrade 1995: 136, Strauss and Quinn 1997). This approach is called connectionism because it emphasises the role of physical connections between neurons in the brain, connections that form schemas. Strauss and Quinn (1997: 6) have defined schemas as 'networks of strongly connected cognitive elements that represent the generic concepts stored in memory'. Schemas can be viewed as culturally accepted minimal scripts (or scenarios or prototypes or models) for and of a certain act, thought, emotion or sensation. They make life predictable and thus secure. Yet, in case of increasing insecurity they also allow for flexibility and adaptation in the interaction between people, helping to overcome a social or personal experience of crisis. At the actor level they steer the actor's behaviour, and also offer modes for the interpretation of events lived by the person. At the social level they provide accepted scripts and codes for behaviour and offer adaptation possibilities in changing contexts. In short: though guaranteeing a certain degree of continuity, schemas may be transformed over time and in their use. Being composed of a minimal number of elements, the substitution of just one element in a schema or a minor change in its pattern will already produce a different schema. This may occur on purpose and explicitly but may also be unintended and imperceptible. Schemas are important tools to cope with experiences and feelings of both security and insecurity. At the same time, unexpected outcomes and new, unfamiliar schemas may cause insecurity, calling for response.

One concrete example from Santa Maria de Jetibá is the schema of the *Kirchweihfest*, the feast that marks the anniversary of the dedication of the church building (Droogers 2001). The basic elements are a church service, followed by a common meal, and a bazaar that includes a bingo game and is meant to boost the parish income. The feast, especially the bazaar, attracts virtually everybody living in the region, and there are even visitors from other regions. Local politicians maintain their network while circulating at the bazaar. Annually this basic minimal schema is made into a real fully fledged social event that reproduces the parish and local society and thus confirms their dominant schemas. In its details the feast differs from year to year, just as all people, men and women, young and old, Lutherans and Catholics, experience this feast in their own way.

Another example of a schema – actually a sub-schema of the church dedication feast – regards the church service. All church services follow a liturgical and ritual schema, with weekly variations, depending on the pastor and influenced by the liturgical and parish calendar, also reflecting current events and issues. Thus all church services are similar, but none is identical to the others.

The concept of schema is combined here with that of repertoire, a schema repertoire being a collection of schemas and sub-schemas, proper to a particular field. 'Field' is meant as in the sense that Bourdieu gives to the term as 'the world of' e.g. religion, education, politics, economics. * The metaphor of repertoire has the advantage that it combines continuity and change; it contains latent and manifest elements; there usually is room for inconsistency and contradiction; and it is used and constructed at both the actor and the group level. 'Repertoire' mirrors a number of insights prominent in current ways of viewing culture and theorising about it. This is especially the case in its way of combining poles such as actor and structure, continuity and change, rule and deviation, the social and the cultural – in short the dichotomies that, in their one-sided forms, have plagued social science theorising. The notion of repertoire helps to avoid one-sided thinking about these dichotomous terms. It also accommodates the delicate relationship between experiences of security and insecurity.

Schema repertoires can be organised in a number of ways. There may be key schemas that come with a number of sub-schemas, possibly organised in a tree structure or a dual structure of opposites. Schemas may also be organised in a linear sequence through time, possibly forming a causal chain. They may also take a parallel correlative or a cyclical repetitive form. Their use in a particular field will influence and change the way in which they are organised.

All over the world the processes of migration, transnationalisation, globalisation, mass communication and hybridisation have introduced schema repertoires from beyond the familiar local or national cultural limits. They bring people into contact with schema repertoires other than those that they are familiar with by primary socialisation in their own culture – culture understood here in the localised sense, as a set of schema repertoires, knowledge of which is necessary within a particular society to participate in its different fields and thereby to find economic, political, social and ontological security. The above-mentioned processes, however, concern all of humanity and thus appeal to culture in the general, universal and singular sense, as the typical human ability to produce schemas and repertoires that make sense of lives and contexts, both old and new, establishing feelings of security and reducing insecurity. This more general concept of culture depends on the human capacity to handle and manage the supply and demand sides of the schemas and repertoires that are or become available, either from cultures in the localised sense, or surpassing cultural boundaries, borrowing from other cultures or from supra-cultural settings. Nevertheless this process of making sense usually takes place in the local context, in which cultures, in the restricted, bounded and plural sense, may still predominate, despite the fact that the above-mentioned processes have perforated their boundaries. One criterion for the ultimate selection of plausible schemas by the actor is their contribution to a condition or feeling of security, whether economic, political, social or ontological, either traditional or innovative. If the need is to reinforce identity and to diminish insecurity, any schema that serves these needs is welcomed. The unfamiliar thus may be turned into the familiar, gradually or in a more rapid dramatic way.

In this context ethnicity represents a particular schema repertoire, favouring the localised cultural assets pertaining to the construction of identities and boundaries of a group of people with similar culture and origins who wish to distinguish themselves from groups with different cultures and origins. Such a repertoire contains a number of markers that serve to underline the ethnic identity that is being maintained.

One other aspect that is important in the theoretical framework proposed here is the role of power, already implicit in the Bourdieusian sense of 'field'. The use of schema repertoires depends on the power relations that prevail at a certain moment in specific fields, at the micro, meso and macro levels. The content of the repertoires is to a large degree established by those in power. They will seek to determine the choice and use of schemas. It is thus important not only to search for schemas and the corresponding repertoires, but also to be aware of the power relations that mark their production.

THE CASE STUDY

The rather abstract schema repertoire approach needs to be complemented by concrete fieldwork. The case of a group of migrants serves as a good test case, because the process of moving and settling demands the redefinition of old schemas and the adoption of new schemas, including their organisation in a constellation of repertoires. In the case of the Pomeranian migrants, for quite some time after their arrival in Brazil this constellation included the homeland, its language and its church organisation, but also, for example, its common law. Besides, however, they had become citizens of Brazil, the nation that had recruited them for migration and had facilitated their transfer. The Brazilian authorities had submitted them, at least formally, to the nation's power and laws. In the new context, within this tension between two sets of repertoires, new compromise patterns of economic, political and religious power slowly emerged, marking the migrants' identity. To the Lutheran Pomeranians of Santa Maria de Jetibá, religion was among the primal markers, together with racial, cultural, linguistic, geographical and economic characteristics. What interests us here is in which way the Pomeranian migrants and their descendants have, since their settlement in Brazil, used religion, in a constellation with other repertoires, to create a feeling of being at home in the new context and experiencing some degree of security. The dynamics of the situation will show how people are able to combine continuity and change. Therefore the fieldworker must discover which schemas – in which fields and from which repertoires – play a role in the migrants' transfer from one setting to the other. The historical dimension must receive due attention, especially identifying schemas that disappear, are transformed, are rejected or are embraced. These schemas may be linked to one particular field, but may also be connected across field limits. Thus the focus of this chapter is on the religious field, studying the schemas that have played a role in the migrants' quest for ontological security, without ignoring the connectedness of schemas from different fields. Since migrants' motives were primarily economic, religious schemas must be considered within that context. Besides these, the ethnic and political schemas are important.

The case study focuses on the Pomeranian migrants and their descendants in the region and Lutheran parish of Santa Maria de Jetibá, a small but booming town at 700 metres above sea level, 80 kilometres west of the Espírito Santo state capital Vitória. According to the 2000 Census, the municipality of Santa Maria de Jetibá has 19,315 inhabitants. The size of the municipality is 736.3 square kilometres. Agriculture is the primary source of income, with vegetables, coffee, poultry and eggs being the main products.

Research began when, from 1980 to 1985, I worked as professor of social science of religion at the theological school of the Brazilian Lutheran Church in São Leopoldo. Between 1982 and 2006 I spent seven short periods of fieldwork in Santa Maria de Jetibá, varying from one to six weeks. Apart from open interviews and participant observation, my data come from the available literature. I also used archival data, both from Brazil and Germany.[1]

In this case study, several aspects need consideration. Thus the question is how the Pomeranians who came to the region of Santa Maria de Jetibá constructed, reproduced, deconstructed and reconstructed their identity – and thereby security – from their arrival up until now. More particularly the role of religion must be studied. Second, the schema repertoires that played a role in their gradual move from an almost exclusive focus on the country of origin to the predominant perspective on Brazilian society must be studied. A third aspect regards the power mechanisms and processes that were characteristic for the process of identity and security construction. Fourth, the processes of migration, globalisation, hybridisation, state formation and transnationalism must be considered in their relationship with the dominant repertoires and mechanisms. Finally, the question is what role was played by ethnicity, as a particular form of identity and security construction, in connection with religious identity, i.e. the membership of a Lutheran Church with a German background.

The chapter will follow a more or less historical sequence, since in each period people developed their own way of using available repertoires and markers and of defining new ones. I will distinguish between three periods. The first is that of migration and settlement. The second is characterised by consolidation, Germany still being the main point of reference, especially when Hitler was in power there. The third period is that of increasing integration into Brazilian society, beginning roughly after the Second World War and gaining a strong impulse in the 1980s with the coming of liberationist theology to the region. In the conclusion I will return to the five questions that were just mentioned, thus summarising what this exercise, with this case and this theoretical approach, has taught us about the relationship between religion, identity and ontological security. This leads us to a redefinition of the concepts of transnationalism, globalisation, hybridisation and diaspora. The case also contains a lesson about the concept of ontological security.

MIGRATION AND SETTLEMENT

The first substantial migration of Germans to Brazil dates from 1824. Migrants came to the region of São Leopoldo in the southern state of Rio Grande do Sul. The name of the city refers indirectly to Empress Leopoldina, daughter of the Austrian Emperor Franz I and married to the Portuguese Emperor of Brazil Dom Pedro I. The Portuguese imperial family had fled to Brazil when Napoleon's army approached Portugal. In 1822, Dom Pedro I had declared Brazil independent from Portugal. The name São Leopoldo was given in accordance with the Brazilian practice of using saints' names for towns and villages, but in fact it refers to the empress, who is supposed to have played a crucial role in recruiting German-speaking Europeans as migrants to Brazil (Dreher 1984: 29). German peasants were selected to occupy and develop the still relatively empty spaces of Brazil. For some decades, recruiting agents visited several German-speaking regions on behalf of the

Brazilian imperial government. The majority of the thus recruited migrants were settled in the south of Brazil, especially in the three southern states of Paraná, Santa Catarina and Rio Grande do Sul. A significant number, however, came to the state of Espírito Santo, many of them Pomeranians.

An initial group of Pomeranians arrived between 1829 and 1833 from what is now north-eastern Germany and north-west Poland. They were recruited to work on the construction of a road between Vitória and Ouro Preto. When that job was finished, they were settled in the region west of Vitória (Schwarz 1952a). In 1831 they were joined by German mercenaries who had served in the army of Dom Pedro I. Upon being released, they came to live in the same region (Schwarz 1952a). Around the same time, a village was established in the region that was called Santa Leopoldina, again in honour of the empress. Between 1856 and 1859 a second wave, of German (including Pomeranian), Austrian, Luxembourgian, Dutch and Swiss migrants came to the region, occupying land that was specially demarcated for them (Schwarz 1952a). The region was visited in 1860 by the then Emperor Dom Pedro II (Schwarz 1952b).

In 1873 two shiploads of altogether nearly 800 Pomeranians from Hinter-Pommern (now north-west Poland) arrived in the region, forming the start of a third migration wave (Schwarz 1952b). More were to follow in 1877. Around 1878 some 7000 persons were living in the region of Santa Leopoldina (Schwarz 1952b). In 1884 the village was formally established as a *município* (municipality) (Schwarz 1952b).

In East Pomerania most of them used to work as tenants on the lands of *Junker* landowners. Although in 1807 a Prussian land law had temporarily favoured small farmers, within a decade the old law was reapplied (Roelke 1996: 23). The promise of land of their own had pulled many of them to Brazil (and also to North America), at the same time as the beginning mechanisation pushed them off the land that many of them lived and worked on, because the landowners now preferred to work with large plots and to hire seasonal workers.

Some migrants may have had religious motives, belonging to a movement that opposed the unification of the Prussian Church in the Unierte Kirche (Roelke 1996: 31, 32). In 1839 a group of 570 Pomeranians had migrated to the United States for religious reasons, setting an example (Roelke 1996: 33).

As to the presence of the Church among the migrants, already in 1857 a Lutheran pastor, who had come at the initiative of the

Prussian consulate in Rio de Janeiro and who was actually paid by the Brazilian state, had been active in the Santa Leopoldina region, but after a few months he died from yellow fever. A year later his successor met a similar fate. The third pastor however succeeded in staying for six years (Urban 1907: 13). From 1864 on, the Basel Mission sent two pastors (Urban 1907: 15). In view of the difficulty in travelling and the distances to be bridged, pastoral care was most probably minimal during this period. Religious life depended to a very large degree on the initiatives of lay believers, who were self-supporting. Personal piety, focused on bibles, hymnals and devotional books brought from Germany, must have been the main religious focus in this pioneer period. This helped people to accept the afflictions of hunger, disease and death that they were confronted with as pioneer settlers in a frontier region that still had to be opened up to agriculture (Urban 1907: 9, 10). *Deutschtum* or 'Germanity', as the ethnic component of the immigrants' identity, was not a relevant issue at that time. Only when the parishes started to employ German pastors did the ethnic horizon of the Pomeranian immigrants widen to that of the newly unified German nation-state.

With the growth of the population, including the second- and third-generation descendants of the first two migration waves, and reinforced by new arrivals, settlement proceeded westward from Santa Leopoldina. The village of Jequetibá was founded. From here in turn Santa Maria de Jetibá was established, having its own cemetery demarcated in 1889 (Roelke 1928, 1955: 173). Local traders (*vendistas*) established themselves in the region at the same time. Their shops (*vendas*) usually included a bar, serving as a meeting-point. A school was built in 1891, serving on Sundays as a church. Later on a chapel was added. The majority of farmers in the region were Protestant and Pomeranian, though there was a minority of Italian Catholic migrants, who had come from the north, from the region of Colatina, where many Italian immigrants had come to live, just as the Pomeranians had been given land in the region of Santa Leopoldina.

The migrants had a natural – or, better, cultural – tendency to stick to the identity they came with, if only as a way to survive in the unfamiliar country where they had been brought, often on a one-way ticket and passport. Those who had survived the sea journey were treated as a group and were settled together. Thereby they became a majority in the region where they were given land lots. Mutual help between neighbours, as fellow Lutheran Pomeranians, was the rule. Though they were expected to become Brazilian citizens and formally obtained that status, under the dire conditions of settlement they opted for the secure continuation of their ethnic, linguistic and religious identity. The *vendistas*, who bought their commodities outside the area, served as intermediaries for inevitable external contacts, so the need to learn and speak Portuguese was minimal. Although Portuguese was on the curriculum in the schools that were founded, High German served as the common formal language, not only in school but also in church, the Pomeranian language being spoken on all other occasions.

In the village and region of Santa Maria de Jetibá, new religious and economic schemas and repertoires were gradually developed as a way of facilitating a secure life. Geographically speaking the region of Santa Maria de Jetibá was a mountainous area, rising to over 1000 metres. The climate was much cooler, in a way more European, therefore, than in the lower parts of the state of Espírito Santo. The first decades were marked by the struggle to gain a living on the newly owned land and to survive the initial difficulties. Support from the Brazilian government stopped after the first years. Some settlers succeeded where others saw their dream turn into a nightmare. Initial efforts to reproduce the agriculture of the homeland failed, and it took some time before the knowledge necessary for the cultivation of local crops became common. Earlier settlers in the region were helpful in the process of acclimatisation. The majority of the people lived spread out through the region, in farmhouses built on their land lot. The wooden houses of the Pomeranian farmers were constructed after the model used in Pomerania. They were painted blue, as was the custom there, probably a survival of Swedish influence. The people continued other regional customs from Pomerania, such as elaborate wedding feasts. They were generally endogamous within their Pomeranian group, though there was occasional intermarriage with people from other German-speaking groups in the region. Thus they kept reproducing schemas brought from Pomerania in the new context. This included church life. From 1892, two annual church services were held by the pastor of Jequetibá in the school building of Santa Maria de Jetibá, for which he rode on horseback the 15 kilometres to the new settlement. Returning the same day, he just had the time to lead the church service. Any other pastoral care was impossible under the circumstances (Droogers 1984: 22).

The church council of Jequetibá, defending its pioneer position, had only consented to allowing its German pastor hold a church service in Santa Maria de Jetibá under the condition that an independent parish would never be established. Weddings could only be held in the church of Jequetibá. The Jequetibá church council was not willing to lose members paying church tax.

About ten years before, church members in Jequetibá had gone through the same process as the people of Santa Maria de Jetibá were now experiencing, of establishing their own school and church, and of finding – and funding – their first pastor (Burger 1955: 222). The Prussian Evangelische Oberkirchenrat (EOK, Evangelical Upper Church Council) of the Unierte Kirche (Unified Church) in Berlin had sent the first pastor at the request of the church council of Jequetibá. The EOK was one of the German organisations that supported pastoral work among German Protestants in the diaspora, wherever they lived in the world.

In 1902, the 40 Lutheran families that then lived in Santa Maria de Jetibá built a chapel near the school. Despite promises of assistance, they did so without any help from Jequetibá ('Brasilien' 1904). In wanting to have their own church community and their own pastor, these families were simply following the traditional Pomeranian village model or schema. In August 1903, the conflict with Jequetibá led to a complete break in relations, when the pastor of Jequetibá refused to hold the wedding service for a couple from Santa Maria de Jetibá who, with relatives and friends, had ridden to the church of Jequetibá (Roelke 1928: 84).

In neighbouring Santa Joana, the German pastor had not come from the EOK but from the competing *Gotteskasten*, an organisation founded in Bavaria in 1860. Whereas the EOK sent pastors who were trained academically and usually took liberal theological positions, the pastors of the *Gotteskasten* were educated at mission seminaries such as that of Neuendettelsau or Hermannsburg, and took theological positions that were more exclusively Lutheran and confessional, giving more emphasis to strict morality and being more missionary and revival-minded. There may have been a difference of class as well, with EOK pastors having an urban upper-class background. Generally speaking, the EOK pastors came for determined periods, whereas those from the *Gotteskasten* remained for an indefinite period. The EOK pastors, who were the first to arrive in Espírito Santo, viewed those from the *Gotteskasten* as intruders in their parishes and regions, an accusation the *Gotteskasten* pastors consistently denied. As a consequence, deep and personal conflicts were fought out for years (Rie 1907–08: 67–8). In Brazil, both organisations ended up having their own synods, gathering different groups of pastors, both seeking to widen their influence (Fischer 1922: 38).

Making a strategic use of the prevailing power relations and conflicts, the families in Santa Maria de Jetibá asked the pastor of Santa Joana for help. Those who had come to Brazil for religious reasons, out of protest against the unification of the Prussian Church, may well have suggested this solution. Already in the Prussian context, before migration, Pomeranians were known to be staunch defenders of the Lutheran confession, who disliked the Calvinist influence in the Unified Church. The pastor of Santa Joana arranged for the *Gotteskasten* to send a pastor to Santa Maria de Jetibá, who happened to be his brother-in-law. Thus, the first pastor for the parish in Santa Maria de Jetibá, *Pfarrer* (pastor) Heinrich Wrede, arrived in 1904 and was to stay till 1923.

It took some time after Wrede's arrival to fully establish the parish. To complete the external signs of an independent parish, following a familiar schema from the German church repertoire, in 1906 church bells were brought from Germany. In 1917 and 1918 the chapel was enlarged into a real church building. In regions that were too far from the church, now and then services were held locally. Pastor Wrede once calculated that, in the course of a year, he had spent 280 hours on horseback (letter Wrede to *Gotteskasten* chairman Stirner, 15 February 1909).

Before leaving, Wrede succeeded in continuing the parish's affiliation with the *Gotteskasten*, asking that organisation to send a successor. Pastor Hermann Roelke was selected, who had been trained in Neuendettelsau and was 29 years old when he arrived in 1924 (Roelke 1955: 174, 175). He was to be the pastor of Santa Maria de Jetibá parish for almost 40 years.

The relationship with Jequetibá remained strained. After initial efforts in 1906 to reach an agreement (letter Peter to Stirner, 16 May 1906), it was only in 1925 that the conflict was officially ended, Pastor Roelke being the architect of the agreement. Till then members who had a conflict with the pastor of their own parish, e.g. about disciplinary measures in moral matters, or who found the annual contribution too high, went for better conditions to the competing parish (Roelke 1955: 176). The repertoires of the two parishes differed. Sometimes theological differences played a role. When a member had underlined the importance of the Lutheran confession, a pastor who sympathised with the EOK replied: 'Do you want to go to a Lutheran heaven?' (letter Wrede to Stirner, 29 June 1910).

In the traditional church repertoire the pastor was an authority. Yet in the new migrant parishes he had to negotiate his influence with the local traders. These were usually also German by origin, rarely Pomeranian. Where the pastor was the central religious figure, the trader played a central economic role. In the local society pastor and trader met all the time, because both acted as managers of the schema repertoire of their respective fields as well. Just as the pastors had to establish their formal church repertoire, putting an end to informal practices from the pioneer time when there was no pastor, the *vendistas* had gradually defined and developed the new economic repertoire for the region and established themselves as the leaders in this field. Thus they bought the agricultural products from the farmers and at the same time sold to these farmers what they needed for their homes and their farms. The prices the traders paid for the farmers' products were kept low, whereas the price of the commodities they sold reflected the monopoly the *vendistas* usually had.

These traders gradually came to occupy a higher position that was reinforced by their role as interpreters and intermediaries in the contacts of the farmers with the authorities and the world outside the 'colony', as the region was called. They developed their own sphere of influence and network, often serving as godfathers to newborn children. Their shop – especially the bar – served as the meeting place for the region. When a farmer became indebted to the *vendista*, as happened after crop failure or disease, the latter in the long run became the owner of the land. He thus turned himself into a landowner, often leaving the peasant on the land as a tenant, usually claiming half of the harvest as annual payment. In terms of security, the migrant was then back to where he had been before the migration from Pomerania, or in an even worse position. Also in church matters, these *nouveaux riches* often held power positions, being elected again and again by their clientele to the church council. Their power extended from the economic field into other fields. They often took care of the financial affairs of the parish and through their material help were crucial to the survival of the parish (letter Zijlman to Stirner, 25.7.1910; letter Wrede to Stirner, 7 July 1914). Even the pastor could become indebted to the *vendista* when support from Germany failed to materialise, as often happened in the first months after arrival (letter Roelke to Schmidt, 26 June 1927). At the civil political level, the new economic elite also shared and alternated the jobs between themselves when representatives had to be chosen in the municipality. The pastor, though a big man in his own field, had to reckon with these local big men.

A GERMAN CHURCH

Though initially the settling of the new migrants and the founding of villages and parishes seemed a local affair, the events surrounding the coming of the first pastor to Santa Maria de Jetibá have shown that the migrants' world was much larger than their farms, village and parish. In constructing and reproducing their identity in the new country, they were directed by repertoires from the country of origin and, through the church, they maintained transnational relations. Though in a way buried in the Brazilian hinterland, in self-imposed isolation from Brazilian society, they also felt German, or at least Pomeranian, and thereby were part of a global framework, even more than the ordinary Brazilian was. They formed an obvious bridgehead for the expansive ambitions of the young German nation-state. The German organisations that sent pastors were instrumental in this policy and explicitly subscribed to it. The events of the two world wars linked the fate of the Teuto-Brazilians even more firmly to global affairs, because their German identity had been maintained, or even reinvented and reinforced, through their ecclesiastical contact with German church organisations for Germans abroad such as the *Gotteskasten*. This was even more the case since, long before Hitler came to power, representatives of these German organisations, among them some of the pastors, propagated *Deutsches Volkstum* or *Deutschtum* (Germanity) as an ideal. However, once Brazil was involved in the war on the anti-German side, the German-speaking Brazilians and their German pastors had to face the fact that they were in a vulnerable and insecure position.

It was not just a matter of using High German as a language, or sustaining a form of Protestantism that had its origin in Germany. The pastors, and also the teachers in the schools (sometimes the pastor was the teacher), promoted and served the Germanity of the migrant community. Some did this because they were not able to speak Portuguese, especially in the beginning, but usually they saw themselves as defenders of not only German Christianity but also of the German civilisation. The latter position also coloured their views on Brazilian society. As one of the German pastors wrote in the periodical of the Institute for Germans Abroad (Deutsche Aus-land-Institut) in Stuttgart, Brazil was *sittlich minderwertig* (morally inferior) (Fischer 1922: 37). The role of the church was to maintain

Deutschtum (Fischer 1922: 36, 37). As Fischer put it: the church and the faith served as:

> ... eine Kraftquelle zur Bewahrung deutscher Sitte und Zucht im Kampf mit den mancherlei Versuchungen, die Land und Leute der neuen Heimat in sich tragen. [... a source of strength to keep German customs and discipline in the battle with manifold temptations that the country and the people of the new homeland carry within them.] (Fischer 1922: 36)

The pastors had their own definition of a secure life. One of the periodicals at the beginning of the twentieth century is called *Gut Deutsch und Evangelisch Allewege* [Good German and Evangelical Anywhere].

Using their contacts with German banks, some of the pastors played an economic role in serving as a personal savings bank, thus preventing their members from using Brazilian banks (Fischer 1922: 38). They also kept a small library of their own books (in German) that were lent out to their church members (Fischer 1922: 37). Already in 1905 Santa Maria de Jetibá had its own library and readers' association, with 100 German books (Roelke 1928: 84). Fischer suggested that only pastors should be sent who would defend *Deutschtum*, but added that they should have a course in Portuguese before leaving for Brazil (1922: 38). Thus Hermann Roelke, pastor in Santa Maria de Jetibá between 1924 and 1962, was so tired of waiting for permission to go to Brazil that, still in Germany, he suggested to the *Gotteskasten* chairman of that time that he could go to Brazil without an invitation from the parish, to do any work he could find and at the same time learn Portuguese (letter Roelke to Schmidt, 1 December 1923). In 1924 there was an effort by Lutherans in the United States to help parishes in Espírito Santo, but this was interpreted by the German organisations as anti-German (Dreher 1984: 192). Another threat came from missionary Adventists who, already in 1906, were mentioned in a letter that Pastor Wrede sent to his superior in Germany (letter Wrede to Stirner, 3 September 1906).

The pastor's grip on the ethnic identity of his parishioners was partly founded on the authority his office carried, especially when vested in his gown as in church services, but often also on the natural authority of his personality. Pastors enjoyed a certain reputation among the ordinary members. 'People today do not respect God in the same way as formerly they respected the pastor,' one of my informants told me. And another summarised the pastor's position as follows: 'When we saw the pastor's dog coming, we already removed our hats' (Droogers 1984: 23). In a way, the members used to accept the pastor's authority and approved of the order he represented in the community. Pastors served as judges in conflicts, often bypassing the Brazilian tribunals and basing themselves on German juridical notions. Some of the pastors tried to improve the level of agriculture. Pastor Roelke introduced the tomato as a new crop, having obtained seed from Germany. Nowadays tomatoes form a major product of the region (Granzow 1972: 20).

In sum: whereas the migrants in the pioneer phase organised their church life as laymen, they subsequently asked for German pastors as religious specialists, who in a relatively short time came to behave as the proprietor of the church and the religious repertoire, rather than as the employee of the parish, which in fact they were. Of course the pastor had his own schema of vocation and sacramental theology to define and defend his position. This position of command made it possible to make Germanity an essential part of the life of the migrants, despite the fact that, to begin with, it was not a strong element in their identity, 'Pomerty' – if that is the right word – being much stronger. Germanity probably was much more resistant to Brazilian influences than Pomerty could have been, mainly because it was backed transnationally by a religious and nationalist justification.

Paradoxically, from the point of view of the Brazilian society and its authorities, the migrants were considered backward, maladapted and isolated, certainly not the farmers Empress Leopoldina had once set her hopes on. Shopkeepers and civil servants in Vitória considered the Pomeranians' maladroitness in dealing with society outside their region an invitation for exploitation and discrimination. Only going to Vitória when it was inescapable, they could not say in Portuguese what they wanted, let alone negotiate about the price to be paid. Health care was a problem because of the lack of fluency in Portuguese. Still in the 1980s the Lutheran Church employed a social worker whose task it was to accompany elderly people to the hospital in Vitória, serving as an interpreter. When the second and third generation began to seek possibilities for education in Portuguese outside the region, the church in Espírito Santo created a protected environment by founding its own professional training centre, directed by an influential German pastor, where for a long time German was the main language.

It should be added that, besides the official German (*Hochdeutsch*) spoken by the pastors and the teachers, and also by the *vendistas*, the Pomeranian farmers had maintained their own language (a form of *Platt*) and often were not able to speak the pastor's language correctly. Here too the *vendista* served as interpreter, for example when the pastor's ritual services were needed for a baptism, wedding or burial. It was normal that the church council or parish meeting worked with an interpreter, often the *vendista*, who translated the pastor's comments into the Pomeranian language, and vice versa (Soboll 1934: 236). Soboll adds that the interpreter often let his own preference influence his translation (Soboll 1934: 236). Sometimes the position of the pastor as a foreigner to his parish was recognised at the synod level and expressed in official reports (Dreher 1984: 212, note 140). *Hochdeutsch* was said to sound like a foreign language to Pomeranian children when they first went to school. As a consequence the teacher had to serve as an interpreter (letter Wrede to Stirner, 18.7.1905, interview with Gerda Roelke, former headmistress of primary school). Whereas the first generation of migrants brought the education they had received in their country of origin with them, the following generations had to do without this schooling, until schools were able to offer education. Up to that point, farmers sometimes served as teachers without being able to teach very well. Often they were not able to write faultless German.

While the pastor was the intermediary with Germany and Germanity, the *vendista* served as a broker for the economic, political and civil contacts with Brazilian society, but also with the pastor. In the church council there was an in-built tension between the authority of the pastor and that of the *vendista* as the local big man. *Vendista* and pastor ran the two places where people could meet, the bar and the church. In view of the relative isolation of many farmers, the social function of these two places, the *venda* during the week, the church on Sundays, was strong. In fact, people used to arrive long before the church service started and to stay on afterwards, socialising and even doing business. Normally the pastor's house, next to the church, would have a meadow for his own horse or mule where, on Sundays, the churchgoers parked their horses, mules and carriages (Volkert 1929: 11).

If a pastor had sufficient strategic insight, he would maintain good relations with the *vendistas*, because they contributed more than the average member to the church's finances. Fischer (1922: 37) complained that the church council often saw the pastor as its employee (he uses the word *Knecht*, servant), a schema from an economic repertoire in which the *vendistas* were experts. Annually the church council had to fix the parish's budget, establishing both the members' contribution and the pastor's salary. One of Pastor Roelke's children told me that her father experienced that annual parish assembly as the most difficult meeting of the year. Pastor Roelke also mentions the trouble he met with having his house repaired (Roelke 1954). Apparently the house was in a terrible state, due to neglect by the church council. Roelke reported that if somebody dropped a coin in the kitchen, that person was sure to have lost it to – as he put it – the nether earth. He added, with some humour, that only when complete persons had disappeared through the wooden floor was a new kitchen built (Roelke 1954). In an annual report on his parish, Roelke explicitly mentions the financial help of the local *vendistas* for the annual bazaar, reporting names and amounts given (Roelke 1954). The pastor also depended on the church council for his means of transport, horse or mule. In Santa Maria de Jetibá, it was only in 1963 that a jeep was bought, a year after Roelke had retired.

This repertoire of schemas for local church life had been established in the decades after the arrival of the first German pastor in Santa Maria de Jetibá. During the two world wars the geopolitical circumstances influenced local church life and introduced new schemas. In the first years of the First World War the Lutherans in Brazil even organised *Missionskriegsfeste*, mission war feasts. In both wars, Brazil joined the anti-German allies in a later stage of the war. In the First World War this happened in 1917, when German torpedoes hit a Brazilian naval vessel. Links with Germany were severed and financial and personal help no longer reached the parishes (Dreher 1984: 17). Those German schools in Brazil where Portuguese was not the school's main language were closed (Dreher 1984: 47). After the war this policy was first softened and then abandoned.

The Second World War was preceded by years of German Nazi propaganda in the church communities of German descendants in Brazil. Films from Germany were shown to the members. Swastika banners were hoisted during church feasts. Some of the pastors joined the Hitler movement, while others (including Roelke) took a neutral stand, without actively opposing it. The regional and national church periodicals (published in German) contained articles in which Hitler, Luther and Germanity were presented to the Brazilian flock as a God-given trinity. In 1935, Pastor Roelke became the editor of the newly founded *Heimatbote*, a periodical for the Lutheran communities in Espírito Santo.

Nazi ideology was thus a new impulse for *Deutschtum* and reinforced the focus on Germany. The Kingdom of God and *das dritte Reich* became associated with each other. It is clear that members were influenced by ideas that were common in Germany at the time, though there are also signs that their isolation kept these influences at a relative distance as well. The negative attitude towards Brazilian society was reinforced by the racist views of Nazi Germany. In my interviews with older local farmers I sometimes still heard the echoes of that period, including a denial of the Holocaust. Feelings of superiority had been stimulated. The Brazilian Germans were supposed to be part of a process of global German expansion and civilisation. Mixed marriages were frowned upon. The basic idea was that, by sticking to their German identity, the people of German descent could make their best contribution to Brazilian society. The isolated position of the parishes was viewed as an advantage, and as a way of keeping Brazilian (read: negative) influences away. The church was called the German Lutheran Church in Brazil. The Nazi ideology even stimulated efforts to create more unity among the Lutherans of German descent, including the synods that governed them.

Initially, the Nazi propaganda seemed to confer with the integralist trend in Brazilian politics during the 1930s. The government of Getúlio Vargas adopted a policy of integralism. Vargas wanted to mix the different migrant communities that had populated Brazil and he used education, with Portuguese as the official language, as one of his instruments. The integralist party (Ação Integralista Brasileira, AIB) supported his policy. This approach was influenced by German and Italian fascism, but did not copy its racism. It met with sympathy among members of the German (and Italian) communities who became active in the AIB. Yet, in November 1937, when Vargas established his personal dictatorship and took measures against schools where Portuguese was not the language, he lost their sympathy. In 1938 the AIB was prohibited after an unsuccessful coup. Schools were nationalised and all lessons, including religion classes, in school and in church, were to be in Portuguese. In an indirect manner Vargas succeeded in silencing the pro-German and pro-Nazi propaganda of the previous years. Once Brazil was drawn into the war, German was forbidden. As a periodical fully written in German, the *Heimatbote* came under suspicion. Meetings, including synods, became almost impossible because many people were not able to speak Portuguese. In 1942 the German pastors, including Pastor Roelke, were interned for a year. After the pastors were released, they were not allowed to preach for another year. In a way, the parishes were back where they were before the German pastors arrived. Many of them felt abandoned.

In short, whereas in the early phase of the migration the identity of the farmers of Pomeranian descent was primarily Pomeranian, reproducing the way of life in the region of origin, the work of the German pastors added a more German and nationalistic dimension to this reproduced regional ethnicity. The Lutheran Church in Germany strongly identified with the German nation and the majority of its pastors in the Brazilian context served the nation's overseas interests. In the end the parishes' members had to discover that Germanity represented a failing experience of security, and ultimately contributed to strong feelings of insecurity. They were confronted with the high price they had to pay for the use of German repertoires. The global German ambition had failed and the people of German descent had, for the most part, learned their lesson. This experience prepared the way for a turn to Brazilian society that started after the Second World War. The descendants of the Pomeranian migrants had to find other sources of ontological and religious security.

A BRAZILIAN CHURCH

The experience of two world wars, in which the church had suffered setbacks because of the German origin of its pastors and members, had consequences when after the Second World War things returned to normal. The normal was no longer natural, and at the national church level there was much discussion about the role of the Lutherans of German origin in Brazilian society. After having used the German repertoire for more than a century, living within and yet outside Brazilian society, always looking to Germany for pastors, assistance and theological orientation, the church gradually turned around and chose to follow a Brazilian schema and to become a Brazilian church. *Heimat* gradually became *pátria*.

After the war a first generation of Brazilian pastors went to work in the parishes, usually being fluent in both German and Portuguese – and sometimes also in one of the German dialects, commonly known as *Platt*. Already in 1921 a pre-theological school had been established by the synod of Rio Grande do Sul, the southernmost state of Brazil (Dreher 1984: 17). Yet, after finishing this school, the future pastors were sent to Germany to complete their theological training. After the Second World War the pre-theological school in São Leopoldo was transformed into a theological school that was to train Brazilian pastors for Brazilian parishes. They had no need to go to Germany, unless they were to receive advanced academic training such as doctorates or specialised courses. Though the school depended for some time on German scholars as professors, in the 1970s the staff became predominantly Brazilian, many of the professors being alumni of the same school but having obtained doctorates in Germany or the USA. Nowadays the school offers its own doctorate programme.

After the Second World War a form of regular contact was established between the different regional synods, notwithstanding diverse theological and historical roots, as for example those already mentioned within Espírito Santo in the controversy between the pastors of the EOK and the *Gotteskasten*. In 1950 a first council of synods was held in São Leopoldo. This had symbolic and historical significance, the town being the oldest destination of German migrants to Brazil. In 1954 a federation of synods was founded and a new and Portuguese name for the Lutheran Church was adopted, the name that is in use till today: Igreja Evangélica de Confissão Luterana no Brasil (IECLB): Evangelical Church of Lutheran Confession in Brazil (Dreher 1984: 18). Significantly this name expressed both the Evangelical (EOK) and the Lutheran confessional identity (*Gotteskasten*), but also the intention to be a Brazilian church, and no longer a German church in Brazil. The theological school in São Leopoldo became the church's official training school for pastors. Yet, for decades to come the number of pastors trained in the country was too low to make the employment of German pastors superfluous. Thus Santa Maria de Jetibá had two more German pastors after Pastor Roelke retired in 1962. Towards the end of the 1970s the first Brazilian pastor began his work there.

The IECLB is nowadays the main Lutheran Church in Brazil, with an estimated 715,000 members who find a religious home in almost 1800 communities (www.ieclb.org.br). A second, smaller and more orthodox confessional Lutheran Church is the Igreja Evangélica Luterana do Brasil (IELB), the Evangelical Lutheran Church of Brazil, which finds its origins in the influence, from the beginning of the twentieth century, of Lutheran churches and organisations from the United States, especially the Missouri Synod, formally known as 'The German Evangelical Lutheran Synod of Missouri, Ohio and Other States', Brazil being one of the other states. In Brazil the

IELB is commonly known as 'Missouri'. In Santa Maria de Jetibá the IELB has a small parish as well. Relationships between the two local parishes and pastors have not always been friendly, mainly because members, when in conflict with their parish or pastor, easily moved to the other community, as had happened in the past between Santa Maria de Jetibá and Jequetibá. With regard to the question of Germanity, the history of the IELB differs radically from that of the IECLB and its earlier synods, German influence coming indirectly and having passed through an American reinterpretation.

The intention to view the IECLB as a Brazilian church was not only motivated by the experiences during the war, but was also nourished by new theological insights, partly coming from Karl Barth's theology, that stressed the mission of the church in the society where it existed. Though still German in origin, these ideas were implemented in the Brazilian context. The process of turning the church into a Brazilian church was slow, because many members still followed German customs, in which school and church had for decades socialised them, and still spoke German or *Platt* among themselves. In many places, church services were still held in German, though Portuguese more and more took its place. Already before the Second World War, with Vargas' integralism, debates about the role of German language and culture had been held, the war experience adding to the arguments in favour of a Brazilian orientation (Dreher 1984: 212). As a consequence the German pastors who still came had to have sufficient command of the Portuguese language. Yet they were preferentially sent to parishes where the majority of the members had German (or in many cases *Platt*) as their primary language. Some of these pastors, as had happened before in a few cases, e.g. in that of Pastor Roelke in Santa Maria de Jetibá, in fact ended up migrating to Brazil and never returned to Germany.

In the 1960s an important new motive for the mission of the church in Brazilian society came up when theology of liberation was developed, first of all in Catholic theological circles in Latin America, but soon reaching the IECLB as well. A leftist view of an ideal, classless society was combined with a reading of the Bible that focused on the poor and the weak. The biblical Exodus and exile stories of liberation from slavery and of the migration to the Promised Land were considered paradigmatic. In theological education this approach became an important element that, in the 1970s and 1980s, was predominant among the staff of the theological school in São Leopoldo and in the training of pastors.

In due course the church had its own liberationist theologians. Simultaneously, a more evangelical tendency was promoted, having been introduced by an American pastor who had worked in one of the parishes. Next to the liberationist and the evangelical wing in the church there was also a confessional Lutheran modality, stressing the Lutheran roots, theology and confessional texts. Thus, the number of theological repertoires had augmented.

In the case of Santa Maria de Jetibá, the liberationist repertoire became influential at the beginning of the 1980s. The pastors and church workers of several parishes in the region, almost all of them trained in São Leopoldo, joined forces. They formed a pastoral team that was called '01' (Zéro Um, i.e. Zero One), after the first item on their list of priorities that was inspired by liberationist theological formulations of pastoral tasks. Interestingly, several of these pastors were of Pomeranian origin and were not only fluent in the dialect (which they used in sermons, introducing an innovation) but also in German and Portuguese. Yet their mission, as they saw it, was fully Brazilian. Germanity was an absolute non-issue to them. If the church was to be a real Brazilian church, it should do all it could to promote a fair society, starting from the direct context of the parish. Thus, their vocation was to improve the position of the small farmers, especially the tenants and agricultural workers among them. The general liberating message that was central to their theology was translated to the concrete economic and political situation of the poor among their church members. They thus addressed the causes of economic insecurity that prevailed in the lives of many of their church members, justifying their approach with biblical paradigms.

Inevitably this meant that they entered into full collision with the local *vendistas*-landowners, who dominated economic and political life. The traditionally delicate tension between pastor and *vendista* thus gained a new dimension. The pastors of 01 used the pulpit to legitimate their economic and political message with religious reasons, much to the shock of the local traders who dominated life in the region, including the church councils. The *vendistas* were sometimes directly mentioned in sermons when wrongs and abuses of power were openly condemned in the application of the biblical text to daily reality. Indebted tenants were helped in their struggle with their *vendista*-landowner. Assistance of tenants in conflicts over landownership became a regular part of pastoral work when a law was passed that gave tenants the right to ownership after having worked on the land for a period of five years. Though a significant number of the members subscribed to the pastors' approach, not a few others were too dependent on the *vendistas* and opposed the pastors. The *vendistas* sometimes used their network, including their role as godfathers (in the literal sense), to maintain their power.

As a consequence of their approach, the pastors sought to influence not only the elections of members for the church councils, but also those for mayors and municipal councils in the region. They moved into local politics, a task that would have been unthinkable at the time of the German pastors, especially when, as a consequence of the political situation, these foreigners were interned during the world wars. The Brazilian pastors acted as responsible citizens. They also made an effort to change the local agricultural trade union, which they saw as an instrument in the hands of the big landowners.

The main pastoral method adopted by 01 was the formation of cell groups, after the model of the Catholic 'church base communities' (*comunidades eclesiais de base*, CEBs), bringing the farmers of a particular area together for Bible study and training for *conscientização* ('conscientisation' – or 'awareness raising'). These groups were organised in a horizontal manner, as a mini-society of equality. Correspondingly, the pastor stepped down from his historically given and divinely legitimated pedestal and tried to treat members without the authority that had been characteristic of many of the German pastors. In a way this was an important farewell to Germanity, not only because the pastoral style changed radically, but also because of the turn to Brazilian society, first of all the local situation. In Vertovec's (2000: 34) terms – borrowed from Jacques Waardenburg – with regard to a religion's position, the pastors of 01 gave a strong incentive to a move from the 'ethnic-religious' and the 'cultural option' to the 'cooperative option', with aspects of the 'behavioural' and the 'ideological' options. Whereas religion had for a long time been a reason to avoid contact with Brazilian society, it now supplied the motives to take a very active part in it. A schema that was characteristic of CEBs is the three-steps model, known as '*ver, julgar, agir*' (see, judge, act). A concrete – usually local – situation was described and analysed, almost always in terms of rich and poor, of exploitation and submission, of tenancy and landownership, in short of class membership. A biblical text that contained a lesson for that situation was reflected upon. As a consequence action was defined, and taken.

The new pastors preferred to be called by their first name, not their surname, though they were still addressed as pastor ('Pastor Pedro' etc.). Those who had a Pomeranian background used Pomeranian in their contacts with members, especially the elderly among them. In the meetings of the cell groups, they also used Pomeranian. The new pastors took an almost humble position as facilitators, or servants of the community. This was a direct application of one of the basic schemas of theologies of liberation, i.e. that the common member, from his or her context and life experience, was as good an exegete as the theologian, and was perfectly able to discover new meanings in the biblical text. The direction of who-taught-whom was reversed. In practice this did not always work, because the members were often too shy to talk, and the pastor sometimes had difficulty in abandoning his authority and putting his expertise between brackets. In other words, both member and pastor had difficulty in deviating from traditional roles. One of the pastors, though, made a radical choice and with his wife began to live and work as a farmer, having obtained a cottage and a small piece of land, thus sharing the farmers' problems in a direct way. Later on two couples of young pastors, recently having finished theological school in São Leopoldo, joined this couple.

In consequently applying this method to their pastoral work, the pastors of 01 succeeded in creating a majority for their position, not only in church, but also in the municipality of Santa Maria de Jetibá. Interestingly the young mayor who was elected with the explicit help of 01 – albeit with a rather narrow margin – was on the maternal side the grandson of Pastor Roelke who had served the parish for almost four decades. Even more interesting was that his father had come from one of the *vendista* families in the region. For some time the church council of Santa Maria de Jetibá continued with a minority representation from the most important of the *vendista* families in town, which was the cause of much strife and conflict, until they also left the council. This *vendista*'s wife subsequently put her energy and influence at the service of the local IELB (Missouri) parish that – with US Lutheran funding – founded a hospital in Santa Maria de Jetibá.

In the beginning of the 1990s ideological differences and a number of personal conflicts put an end to the work of 01. Yet, their work of *conscientização* had converted an influential number of church members into partisans of liberationist causes. These members also had developed ecological consciousness. They had assimilated the pastors' discourse, were able to apply it without their help and had become more vocal, especially the women. The seed had been sown and was producing fruit. Though in a more moderate version, the ideas of 01 thereby continued to influence church life and also remained a factor in local politics. The mayor chosen with the help of 01 remained a strong player in that context and succeeded in being re-elected. Yet, at the time of writing the local elites have in fact regained the strength they had before 01 succeeded in upsetting the power constellation that these elites had been able to sustain for decades. Presently the pastors focus on pastoral rather than political action, as well as reinforcing the Lutheran confessional identity, to prevent members from leaving for one of the Pentecostal churches that have recently entered town.

There is one interesting recent development that needs to be mentioned. The turn to Brazilian society was accompanied by an economic opening of the region to the rest of the state of Espírito Santo and beyond. After the road to the state capital had been asphalted in 1990, it became much easier to sell local agricultural products to the markets in the capital and also as far away as Rio de Janeiro and São Paulo. Santa Maria de Jetibá attracted new economic initiatives. Another development was the promotion of tourism by the local authorities. The regional scenery was a potential asset. The mayor elected with the help of the 01 pastoral team opened a small museum, with objects from the early years of the migration. Several shops included some reference to Pomerania in their name, written in German Gothic font, like the municipal logo (www.pmsmj.es.gov.br). They restyled their front in German timber framing style or painted it blue. The local internet provider is called Pomernet. Besides, some annual festivals were introduced that were meant to attract people from nearby Vitória. One of the markers of the tourist version of Pomeranian ethnicity is the brass band that finds its origin in church where the *Posaunenchor* accompanies the community's hymn singing. During festivals this band, clad in khaki uniforms, plays secular music, especially German *Heimat* music, as it has done for decades during the bazaar of the church dedication anniversary.

Another instance was the formation, again supported by the mayor elected with the help of the 01 team, of local dance and music groups that performed during festivals and on other occasions. There are now seven of these groups, showing dances that are viewed as Pomeranian or are more generally German in origin, because – as one of the leaders told me – the Pomeranian dances are not considered very interesting. Yet almost all of these groups use the adjective Pomeranian in their names. In most cases the dance repertoire and the costumes can be characterised as invented tradition, but the interesting aspect is that Germanity still plays a role, albeit in folklore version and as tourist attraction. Thus the turn to Brazilian society is accompanied by a compromised new version of the turn to Germany that for such a long time determined local life in Santa Maria de Jetibá. In 2004 the members of the national synod of the IECLB met in Santa Maria de Jetibá, to debate the church's current position and policies. During an interval one of the dance groups presented itself to the synod members, thus bringing together several of the elements that were discussed in this chapter.

CONCLUSION

In the introduction to this chapter a number of questions were raised. Each of these questions can now be summarily answered. The first question was how the Pomeranian migrants who came to the region of Santa Maria de Jetibá constructed, reproduced, deconstructed and reconstructed their identity – and thereby security – from their arrival and up until now. More particularly the question was what role religion played in this. It was suggested that the first generation of migrants to the region of Santa Maria de Jetibá came for economic and perhaps also religious reasons. They were looking for economic and existential security, hoping to find a better life in Brazil. Whereas to the Brazilian empire they were Germans, and were recruited for that reason, they themselves felt primarily Pomeranian, by origin and language. Religion, in its popular form, was an asset that helped them survive, both socially and existentially. When German pastors arrived to work among these Germans in the diaspora, religion obtained new connotations. The type of religion these pastors brought was closely linked to their being German citizens, coming from all over Germany. In the new Brazilian context, they represented a clear and explicit ethnic and religious identity from the migrants' country of origin. This identity was reinforced and at the same time made problematic by the two world wars. In particular, the Nazi propaganda brought a strong impulse and a new feeling of security and strength to the German identity. In the church, religion and ethnicity were linked with the ambitions of the Third Reich. Vargas' policies, as well as the fact that Germany ultimately lost the war, were a significant blow to the promotion of this German identity. In fact, after the war the lesson learned from it was a first impulse to review the transnational bonds with Germany, even though dependence on German financial and personal help remained. The influence of theology of liberation, addressing experiences of especially political and economic insecurity in the local context, reinforced the argument for becoming a fully Brazilian church, and moreover assuming responsibility for the improvement of Brazilian society. Though its strength has diminished, the attitude is still there. The move from a transnational to a national church is not yet completed, but it has been realised to a large degree.

Second, the schema repertoires that played a role in the gradual move of the immigrants and their descendants from an almost exclusive focus on the country of origin to the emphasis on Brazilian society were studied. An overview of the history of the Pomeranian migrants shows that – alongside continued schemas, such as the ritual liturgical schemas or wedding schemas – schema repertoires have come and gone, sometimes reinforcing each other, sometimes substituting one another. The initial urge to migrate came from Empress Leopoldina's schema of migration that attributed a decisive role to German migrants. The economic situation of the migrants contained schemas that pushed them from Pomerania and attracted them to Brazil. In terms of identity they were primarily farmers looking for more security. The German pastors applied new schemas to them, making them into Lutheran migrants and diaspora Germans. Each of the two world wars brought schemas that justified this position but in due time also revealed the risks involved. After 1945 the turn to Brazilian schemas set in. There were theological reasons for this, especially when the schema repertoire of theologies of liberation was introduced in the 1980s. At the same time, the economic development of the region opened it to new economic schemas that increased participation in Brazilian society. At the political level, the foundation of a municipality contributed to this process.

The third question regards the power mechanisms and processes that were characteristic of the construction process of identity and security. In the course of the decades described here, the Pomeranian migrants and their descendants were confronted with a series of power mechanisms and tensions. Having escaped from the power of the landlord in Pomerania, some migrants soon were as dependent on this figure as before. The power of the Brazilian Empire brought the migrants to Brazil and facilitated their settlement, but then turned into a power above them that they did not know how to deal with, unless they accepted another dependency, on the *vendistas*. Once the German pastors had established themselves, the migrants and their descendants were confronted with the pastor's power as a specialist, especially in rites of transition. The world wars brought global power mechanisms into the region. The pastor himself often had to face the *vendista*'s local influence, and vice versa. This tension became considerably more delicate in the 1980s, when the pastors were following the principles of theologies of liberation. All these different forms of the exercise of power had their impact on the construction of identity of the church members. Sometimes the latter manipulated power conflicts between different religious groups, either within the church or outside it. In general, depending on the players and the ideologies, power relationships created situations of both insecurity and security.

Fourth, the processes of migration, globalisation, hybridisation, state formation and transnationalism were considered in their relationship with the dominant repertoires and mechanisms. The case studied in this chapter shows that a schema repertoire approach helps to make sense of these currently fashionable concepts. The move of the Pomeranian Brazilians from a transnational to a national perspective has been both hampered and facilitated by the adoption of schemas from these two repertoires. When they are identified, it becomes visible what exactly is at stake in the processes just mentioned. This should be considered in relation to the previous question, i.e. it should be clear who is introducing, defending and imposing certain schema repertoires. The anthropological approach of looking for the way the economic, political, religious and social levels are connected can be given more content when the schema repertoires are identified.

Some of the central concepts can now be redefined in terms of schema repertoires and security. *Transnationalism* can thus be understood as the process – activated by migration and insecurity – by which relations across state and nation boundaries, and in reaction to their dominance, are maintained by the use of common schema repertoires, in order to stimulate feelings of togetherness and thereby security. *Globalisation* is the process by which more and more schema repertoires become available for common use, the influence of time and place being reinterpreted through the way this new stock of schema repertoires is made available and applicable to the local situation and its demands for security. *Hybridisation* is the process by which schema repertoires from different sources are used, deconstructed and reconstructed, to serve strategic purposes in the users' context, especially offering a fresh security – till events bring new insecurity and demand better repertoires and schemas. *Diaspora* is the supralocal community of people who, despite the fact that they are not living together, share schema repertoires, usually of a religious type but complemented by schema repertoires from the economic, political and social levels.

The last issue was what role ethnicity played, as a particular form of identity and security construction, especially in connection with religious identity, i.e. the membership of a Lutheran Church with a German background. The case of the Pomeranian migrants to Santa Maria de Jetibá shows how two different schema repertoires, one ethnic German and one religious Lutheran, can be brought together to strengthen each other. The role of Pomeranian ethnicity is certainly not finished yet, although it may be that the dance groups that perform for tourist audiences (and synod members) represent its last vestige. Depending on the contexts in which they find themselves and with whom, people will choose from their repertoires of identity schemas. It is significant that, at the national level, the website of the IECLB contains only one reference to 'ethnic', drawing attention to the work the church has been doing – for several decades already – among Indian tribes in Brazil, rather than any connection with Germany.

Finally the case and the schema repertoire framework can be said to have relevance for the study of security and insecurity. The case study served as a test case. A common schema repertoire is usually a source of security in a particular field, guaranteeing continuity. Yet new conditions, such as increased insecurity in the region of origin but also the move to a new habitat, contain a challenge, since not all old schemas prove effective in establishing new security. Besides, the new environment calls for new schemas, especially because of the inherent economic insecurity of the frontier situation. Continuity and change are thus inevitably linked in a strategy to manage available schema repertoires. New scripts must be adopted, while old scripts may need adaptation or reactivation. This is done to bring security, but will also create further feelings of insecurity. The constant struggle for security may become part of the migrants' mindset, especially when the move to the new homeland does not produce the security that was hoped for. Culture, as the knowledge of schema repertoires that guarantee security, is then under constant pressure to be reconsidered, either because the conditions oblige people to do so, or because people take the initiative to experiment with schema repertoires. Religious schemas are usually meant to promote security but, as was clear from the case we studied, may provoke insecurity as well. In sum: a schema repertoire approach is a useful tool in describing and analysing, in detail and from a historical perspective, the delicate relationship between security and insecurity.

NOTE

1. I am indebted to Henrique Krause for valuable help in this respect.

Other versions of this chapter were read at the conference of the Society for the Anthropology of Religion, Vancouver, 8–10 April 2005, during the session on 'Religion, Migration and Conversion: The Morality of Adapting Beliefs to New Contexts', organised by Mara Leichtman, and during the conference on 'Religion and Dislocations: Comparative Studies', organised by the Paulo Freire Programme at the Universidade Estadual de Rio de Janeiro, 4–6 Sept. 2006. A Portuguese version of this article is published by *Religião e Sociedade*.

REFERENCES

Bloch, Maurice. 1998. *How We Think They Think: Anthropological Approaches to Cognition, Memory and Literacy*. Boulder, CO: Westview Press.

Brasilien. 1904. Brasilien. *Der Lutherische Gotteskasten* 3: 43–7.

Burger, Georg. 1955. Die Pommern-Gemeinde Jequetibá (Espírito Santo). In *Lutherische Kirche in Brasilien, Festschrift zum 50-jährigen Bestehen der lutherischen Synode am 9. Okotober 1955*. Joinville: Lutherische Kirche in Brasilien, 222–38.

D'Andrade, Roy. 1995. *The Development of Cognitive Anthropology*. Cambridge: Cambridge University Press.

Dreher, Martin N. 1984. *Igreja e Germanidade: Estudo crítico da história da Igreja Evangélica de Confissão Luterana no Brasil*. São Leopoldo: Editora Sinodal.

Droogers, André. 1984. *Religiosidade Popular Luterana*. São Leopoldo: Sinodal.

Droogers, André. 2001. Feasts: A View from Cultural Anthropology. In Paul Post, Gerard Rouwenhorst, Louis van Tongeren and Ton Scheer (eds) *Christian Feast and Festival: The Dynamics of Western Liturgy and Culture*. Leuven: Peeters, 79–96.

Fischer, H. 1922. Das Deutschtum in Espírito Santo (Brasilien): I. Die Bedeutung der Kirche für das Deutschtum. *Der Auslanddeutsche* 5(2): 36–9.

Giddens, Anthony. 1990. *The Consequences of Modernity*. Cambridge: Polity Press.

Granzow, Klaus. 1972. Blau-weisz ist auch die Farbe der Urwald-Pommern. *Globus* 4(2): 20–21.

Rie, Pfarrer. 1907–08. 10 Jahre Gotteskastenarbeit in Brasilien. *Evangelisch-Lutherisches Gemeindeblatt* 3(9): 67–9.

Roelke, Hermann. 1928. 25-jähriges Jubiläum der ev.-luth. Gemeinde Sta. Maria, Esp. Santo. *Evangelisch-Lutherisches Gemeindeblatt* 22e*?*(11): 83–5.

Roelke, Hermann. 1954. Sta. Maria. *Heimatbote/Folha de Notícias* 4(7).

Roelke, Hermann. 1955. Sta. Maria – Espírito Santo. In *Lutherische Kirche in Brasilien, Festschrift zum 50-jährigen Bestehen der lutherischen Synode am 9. Okotober 1955*. Joinville: Lutherische Kirche in Brasilien, 172–7.

Roelke, Helmar Reinhard. 1996. *Descobrindo Raízes: Aspectos Geográficos, Históricos e Culturais da Pomerania*. Vitória: UFES.

Schwarz, Francisco. 1952a. Die Einwanderung in Santa Leopoldina (I). *Deutsches Wochenblatt* 6(24), 14 June.

Schwarz, Francisco. 1952b. Die Einwanderung in Santa Leopoldina (II). *Deutsches Wochenblatt* 6(25), 21 June.

Soboll, Pfarrer. 1934. Deutsches Volkstum im Staate Espírito Santo, Brasilien. *Der Deutsche Auswanderer* 30(11): 235–9.

Strauss, Claudia and Naomi Quinn. 1997. *A Cognitive Theory of Cultural Meaning*. Cambridge: Cambridge University Press.

Urban, Pfarrer. 1907. Santa Izabel, die erste deutsch-evangelische Gemeinde im Staate Espírito Santo (Brasilien). *Gut Deutsch und Evangelisch Allewege* 16(1): 1–16.

Vertovec, Steven. 2000. Religion and Diaspora. Paper presented at the conference on 'New Landscapes of Religion in the West', School of Geography and the Environment, University of Oxford, 27–29 September 2000, URL: http: //www. transcomm.ox.ac.uk/working%20papers/Vertovec01.PDF (accessed 8 Sept. 2008).

Volkert, Pfarrer. 1929. Die Synode zu Santa Maria (Brasilien) 1928. *Gotteskasen Bote aus Bayern* 1(1): 11–12.

Part III

States of (In)security

9
Changing Notions of Belonging: Migrants and Natives in an Amsterdam Multicultural Neighbourhood

Marion den Uyl

The Bijlmer, also known as the Bijlmermeer, is a multicultural neighbourhood located in the south-east of Amsterdam.[1] In 2007, there were around 43,000 people of more than 100 different nationalities living in the Bijlmer. The neighbourhood, which started during the 1970s as a newly built 'white' Dutch suburb that had been constructed on a former polder on the outskirts of Amsterdam, attracted an increasing flow of migrants, particularly from non-Western countries. Within the course of 30 years, it was transformed from being a district with a relatively homogeneous population to one with a highly culturally and ethnically diverse population. Migrants from a variety of non-Western countries, particularly from Latin America and Africa, currently make up three-quarters of the population; migrants from Western countries constitute 7 per cent, and the remaining 18 per cent of the population are of native Dutch origin (Onderzoek en Statistiek 2007).[2]

The percentage of migrants has continued to increase. Indeed, such growth is characteristic of many modern urban neighbourhoods. In a recent article, the US sociologist Robert Putnam remarked that: 'the most certain prediction that we can make about almost any modern society is that it will be more diverse a generation from now than it is today' (2007: 137). Moreover, he contends that this increase in ethnic and social heterogeneity will be one of the most important challenges faced by modern societies. This chapter focuses on one of the places where both the increase and the challenge are currently taking place. It explores the history of the Bijlmer, the development of various different ethnic groups, their changing relations and the new notions of belonging that have subsequently emerged, especially among the youth.

SOCIAL COHESION AND NOTIONS OF BELONGING IN
MULTICULTURAL NEIGHBOURHOODS

In Western societies, multicultural neighbourhoods, which have come into existence as a result of the continuing processes of globalisation and migration, are often populated by poor and disadvantaged migrant groups. Their emancipation and integration can be conceptualised in terms of the challenges faced by modern societies that were outlined above (Putnam 2007).

Various social scientists (Bauman 2001, Fukuyama 1995) have argued that it is important for disadvantaged groups to increase their social capital, for this will potentially allow them to become socially and economically emancipated both as individuals and as a group. Social capital, which is vested in human relations and capacities, and in ethnic traditions and cultural ethics, refers to 'the ability of people to work together for common purposes in groups and organizations' (Coleman in Fukuyama 1995: 10). Fukuyama argues that groups of people need shared values, shared ethical habits, to be able to develop themselves economically.

The tensions associated with belonging to one's own group (and remaining in a recognisable homogeneous social environment) and the need to create ties with other groups are discussed by Zygmunt Bauman (2001) in relation to the concept of community. Communities, in line with Tönnies' concept of *Gemeinschaft*, refer to smaller and more recognisable groups, which are characterised by homogeneity, by sameness. They are different from larger social entities, such as society, *Gesellschaft*, which are more heterogeneous (Tönnies in Bauman 2001: 11–13). This sameness, and the notions of belonging that go with it, possess qualities that are comparable with Putnam's[3] bonding social capital: it enables people to feel secure within their own social setting. However, the sameness of community has also another more restricting quality: it can lead to a fear of strangers and consequently to increasing feelings of insecurity.[4] Community is thus able to generate ambivalent social (and spatial) boundaries. On the one hand, community can function as a source of security, but, on the other, it can also contribute to an increasing distance between different social groups, and thus become a source of insecurity.

Some social scientists are more positive than others with respect to the outcome of the process of increasing diversity in multicultural societies, certainly when it comes to the question of whether this will lead to a growing distance between natives and migrants or new forms of citizenship. Using Berlin as an example, the German anthropologist Werner Schiffauer (2004) has challenged Jonathan Friedman's (1999: 1) notion that migrants have increasingly greater difficulty and less interest in identifying with the places to which they have migrated. Indeed, Schiffauer argues that people generally overlook the fact that immigrants develop strong emotional ties to their place of residence under the surface of transnational identifications. After all, for the migrant, the new city is 'the place where he lives his life, where he goes to school, falls in love, marries, where his children grew up' (Schiffauer 2004: 100). While Friedman warns against a growing gap that is based on increasing differences in cultural and emotional identification, Schiffhauer is rather more positive for he identifies possibilities for new forms of citizenship; he points to changing notions of belonging, which can enable migrants to actually feel part of their new neighbourhood – although this does not mean that he also develops a positive identification with his new country.

The discussion on the problems of disadvantaged multicultural neighbourhoods in the Netherlands has largely focused on liveability and social cohesion. Policy measures aim to stimulate the middle class, create a mixed population and to keep neighbourhoods safe and clean. However, it has become apparent that the present policy measures have not led to the desired rise of a stable middle class in disadvantaged multicultural neighbourhoods (Veldboer et al. 2007). A recent government report, which proposes measures to encourage the socially mobile to remain in disadvantaged neighbourhoods, observes that declining social cohesion has led to the departure of residents. Nonetheless, this declining social cohesion should not be attributed to an increase in individualism and social atomisation, as it has been in the past, but instead to an increasing lack of trust, recognition, and the feeling of being at home and accepted in the neighbourhood (VROM-Raad 2006: 57–8). This raises the issue of whether the rapidly increasing diversity of a neighbourhood will also lead to changing notions of belonging, which in turn will also lead to a decrease in social cohesion.

This chapter is based on my experiences as both a resident and a researcher. During the mid 1990s, I moved to the Bijlmer.[5] Ten years later, in 2004, I started researching effects of urban restructuring in my own neighbourhood. Together with Lenie Brouwer, I began a research and educational project in the Bijlmer. From 2006 onwards, the main focus of this project was on teenagers.[6] When looking at the history of the Bijlmermeer for this chapter, I have considered the following questions: is sameness a necessary quality for notions of belonging to contribute to social cohesion in a neighbourhood, or are feelings of being accepted and being at home more important for developing social cohesion? What kind of feelings of belonging do people in the multicultural Bijlmer actually experience?

FROM A HOMOGENEOUS TO A – PROBLEMATIC – HETEROGENEOUS NEIGHBOURHOOD

At the time the plans to build on the reclaimed Bijlmermeer near Amsterdam were drawn up, the architect Siegfried Nassuth was in charge of city planning in Amsterdam.[7] Nassuth was strongly inspired by the Swiss architect and city planner Le Corbusier, especially with respect to his plans for a 'City of the Future'.[8] His idea was to create a vast green space with large honeycomb-shaped high-rise buildings – ten storeys high – in its midst. Traffic would travel along raised highways, while, at ground level, a network of winding walkways and bicycle paths would connect all locations. This would be a quiet, green and safe place without traffic, where one could enjoy, as one advertisement promised, the sound of the nightingale singing in the heart of the city.

The construction work began at the end of the 1960s. Within just a few years, 13,000 virtually identical apartments were created in 30 almost identical high-rise buildings. The apartments were spacious, light and well-built. The emerging white middle class, which had grown steadily during the prosperous years following the Second World War, could now leave the overcrowded and noisy inner city and start to raise a new generation in this so-called City of the Future.

The first inhabitants received the keys to their new houses in 1968. Six years later, more than 30,000 people had already moved to the district.[9] Many of the early Bijlmer residents cherish the memories of these early years. Gerda, a native Dutch woman of almost 70, recalls that it felt like being on a holiday:

We loved it, even when the shopping centre had not yet been finished and only a few buses could be taken to the city centre. We made friends; our neighbours had young children the same age as ours. In the summer, we sunbathed on the little beaches in the park, just near our flats. It was green and quiet. As if you were always on a holiday!

One of the first residents, Pierre Heijboer, a journalist, recently published a colourful history of the Bijlmermeer in which he describes the adventurous and pioneering spirit of the first residents. In this book, entitled *Waiting for the Nightingale: The Story of the Bijlmermeer* (my translation), he describes how the first public house, school and football club started (Heijboer 2006). Nonetheless, despite the growing feelings of togetherness and solidarity, there were also major setbacks. The first residents had to wait for more than ten years for the metro system to connect the former polder to the city centre, and even longer for the construction of the local shopping centre, which meant that they remained rather isolated in this new district. Moreover, when the high-rise flats had been completed, there was no money left for the planned infrastructure of crèches, cafes, pubs, community centres and small theatres, which had been intended for the ground floor of these buildings. Consequently, many rather uncontrolled activities began in the Kasbah-like structure under the flats, which eventually developed into a breeding ground for criminal activities.

In the meantime, several overspill cities near Amsterdam had started to build single family dwellings, which the (native) middle-class families seemed to prefer. Indeed, they even started to leave the Bijlmer before all the high-rises had actually been completed. New residents arrived: thousands of migrants found a place to live in the empty apartments that the middle classes had left behind, particularly those from the former Dutch colony Surinam, which had gained its independence in 1975. They were followed by many other migrants from the Dutch Antilles and other Latin American and Asian countries. More recent waves of migrants have come from various African countries, especially Ghana.[10]

Due to the continuing exodus of native Dutch residents and the influx of new migrants, the Bijlmer became a so-called 'black' neighbourhood, which was mainly populated by non-Western migrants. Furthermore, it also became the area with the highest rates of unemployment and school drop-out, and the highest percentage of single-parent households in Amsterdam. Heijboer (2006: 195) remarks that, in the eyes of policy-makers, the Bijlmer became: too poor, too black and too criminal.

The new migrants created an informal urban economy, with a great number of illegal taxis, black hairdresser salons and beauty parlours, illegal nurseries, bakeries, restaurants and brothels (Maurer 2005). An international drug scene became increasingly evident, especially in the dark Kasbah-like structure of the shopping centres and the largely unused parking garages. The area was – and still is – a relatively unsafe place. Crime rates are among the highest in Amsterdam, as are the numbers of school drop-outs and unemployed people, although it should be noted that these rates are declining and are still low in comparison to other countries (Van Heerwaarden et al. 2004: 66, 67).[11] Near the Bijlmer a new business centre was built, with many offices of international firms, banks and large shops. Besides the office buildings a cinema, a soccer stadium and a large music hall also appeared. More than 60,000 people were working there in 2007 (Bicknese and Slot 2007). However, because the new business area mainly offers jobs for higher educated people, the migrants who work in the new business centre are mainly from industrialised countries such as Japan, Germany, the USA or Canada. The local Bijlmer migrants, who work in the offices, have low-skilled jobs, like cleaner or security guard. Their work often starts when the business people leave their offices. One Ghanaian respondent remarked: 'After the white people leave the offices in the evening, you can see the black people enter.'

Unemployment figures were very high (up to 30 per cent) in the 1980s. In recent years this rate declined, just as it declined in other parts of the Netherlands. At present the local unemployment rate is 8.9 per cent, which is only slightly higher than the unemployment rate of Amsterdam as a whole, which is 6.7 per cent (Onderzoek en Statistiek 2008).

Heijboer (2006) describes how he looked for a school for his 12-year-old daughter during the early years of the Bijlmer. Cycling all the way to the city centre, where there were plenty of secondary schools, and back to the Bijlmer would have cost his daughter a lot of time and energy. However, there was little choice in the neighbourhood. Fortunately, during the mid 1970s, the Augustinus College, a Roman Catholic school with an excellent reputation decided to start a new offshoot school in the Bijlmer. His daughter was able to receive six years of a decent and good secondary education close to home. The school grew rapidly and acquired a good reputation. Around 1500 pupils attended this secondary school.

The story of the Augustinus College is illustrative of the Bijlmer's decline. During the 1990s, the number of non-Western pupils at the school increased. Many of these pupils were streamed into the school's lower secondary vocational educational programme, while the numbers of pupils following the more advanced pre-university education programme fell significantly. The school's reputation also sadly declined. It became increasingly difficult to find good teachers, and especially the higher secondary and pre-university programmes ran into problems. By the end of the 1990s, the Augustinus College decided that it would no longer offer these programmes and would now only offer a lower secondary vocational education to its pupils.

By 2007, there were less than 500 pupils attending the school. Almost every pupil comes from a non-Western background: their parents originate from countries such as Surinam, the Antilles, Dominican Republic, Turkey, Morocco, Ghana, Nigeria, Pakistan, and India. The majority are also from underprivileged single-parent households. They either walk to school or take public transport; the hundreds of bicycle racks now remain empty. They are the rusting remnants of bygone age when children from a very different segment of society attended the school.

The anthropologist Bowen Paulle (2005) carried out an in-depth qualitative research study at two 'black' secondary schools in both the Amsterdam Bijlmer and the New York Bronx. He taught at the Augustinus College for a period of three years. During his research, he observed that many schoolchildren between the ages of 12 and 16 in this deprived area were vulnerable and often felt anxious and insecure. According to Paulle, the emotional balance of these children is often unstable. Moreover, he noted that there were frequently sudden eruptions of violent behaviour in class. He both observed and experienced the fact that it is difficult to teach them, because most of the time the teachers are not actually teaching, but instead having to maintain order in the classroom.

The picture of the Augustinus, which one of my postgraduate students sketched, is rather different. Mary Lou Goossens, a good-natured young woman with an optimistic outlook, worked at the school as a homework assistant for several months. She enjoyed working with the young pupils. The 13- and 14-year-olds told her that they enjoyed school and planned to become hairdressers, ground stewardesses, sportsmen or musicians. Nearly all of them could name something that they were good at: rapping, singing, athletics, football, street dance, salsa or even, in a few cases, mathematics. The boys and girls did not want to be any different from what they already were: they claimed to like their clothes, hairstyles and skin colour. For instance, when asked whether there was anything in particular he liked about his own looks, body or appearance, a 14-year-old boy replied: 'Actually, everything' (Goossens 2007).

These different portrayals of pupils and school not only reflect different research situations, but also reveal the ambiguous nature of identity formation in this deprived multicultural urban neighbourhood. On the one hand, these pupils are viewed as 'the waste bin of the waste bin',[12] and some of them display a corresponding degree of low self-esteem. Yet, on the other, they also identify themselves with black heroes, such as black movie stars, musicians, models and sportsmen. Moreover, they are proud to live in the Bijlmer and enjoy speaking the local street language (Den Uyl and Brouwer 2007). Another postgraduate student I supervised participated in a local community centre for three months. Here she worked with black teenage girls from a disadvantaged background who experienced problems, such as teenage pregnancy, school drop-out or being arrested for shoplifting. It appeared that these girls were also fun-loving, outgoing teens, who were involved in several strong friendships across ethnic lines. Louise Hartman (2007) found that locality was a very important source of identification for these teenagers. Indeed, in the local street language, they called the neighbourhood their home: *Bimre mi osso*, Bijlmer, my home.

URBAN RESTRUCTURING: BUILDING FOR THE NEW BLACK MIDDLE CLASS

During the 1980s, the housing corporation, which owned and managed the high-rise buildings, was confronted with increasing problems of vacancy, high resident turnover and rental arrears. The corporation faced consequently potential bankruptcy. They concluded that it was impossible to find enough tenants to occupy the numerous identical high-rise apartments. The proposed solution was to demolish a number of the high-rise buildings and replace them with a greater variety of low-rise flats and single-family dwellings. Policy-makers and architects blamed the built environment and the architectural concepts for the Bijlmer's failure. There was too much of the same thing: the large identical buildings led to anonymity. In particular, the abundance of trees and greenery was blamed.[13] It was also argued that there were too many dark and dangerous areas under the bridges and buildings. The area was declared unsafe and uncontrollable.

It was decided that 50 per cent of the apartments would be demolished and the remaining buildings thoroughly renovated.[14] The planners' buzzwords were: differentiation, accessibility and safety. The architects took care to construct a safe environment and to design houses with large windows, which looked out over the streets; they avoided creating hidden angles and corners. Public space was minimised, trees were felled, bushes were trimmed and tunnels removed (Kwekkeboom 2002).

These plans demonstrate how, during the 1960s when the Bijlmer was built, trust was apparently taken for granted, while by the 1990s safety and security had become the overt focus of the planners, who emphasised visibility and control. Moreover, during the 1960s, when all people were supposed to live in identical apartments, sameness was seen as the basis for communal living. However, in the 1990s, differentiation became the keyword. Diversity was conceived as a solution and the multicultural identity of the different groups of residents should be respected. The architects who drew up the plans rebuilding the Bijlmer took up the challenge of building for a relatively new target group: the new migrant middle class. In accordance with the wishes of Surinamese and Ghanaian residents, they designed so-called 'compounds'; houses grouped around an enclosed garden (De Haan and Keesom 2004: 127). The planners hoped to transform the Bijlmer into a neighbourhood which would be more like other Dutch neighbourhoods; more average with respect to age, income, household composition and employment (Frieling 2004: 7).

Frieling, an architect and one of the planners, proudly writes:

What is happening and seems to continue and become sustainable is that the Bijlmer is becoming more and more a predominantly coloured society with more or less the same socio-economic characteristics as elsewhere in Holland. This of course is a huge and very important change. (2004: 8)

One of the goals of the urban restructuring is to discourage people from leaving the neighbourhood as soon as they become more socially and economically mobile. The planners have repeatedly stressed that one of the goals of this renewal project must be to keep the black middle class living within the boundaries of the neighbourhood. It aims to 'retain "climbers" and "advanced" residents, because the Bijlmermeer, a neighbourhood with a population of 40,000, cannot do without its own middle class (albeit of racial or ethnic minorities) ...' (Kwekkeboom 2002: 79).

When a significant amount of European funding became available for the regeneration of deprived urban areas during the mid 1990s, the Bijlmermeer migrants also wanted a say in the district council's plans for the spending these EU subsidies. A number of residents, mainly Surinamese men, united in the Zwart Beraad

(Black Consideration) and demanded that their voice be heard in the district council and with respect to the restructuring of the Bijlmer (Braam 1996). They were especially successful in gaining seats and influence in the Dutch Labour Party (PvdA), which in turn received an increasing number of migrant votes and eventually led to their gaining an absolute majority in the district council in 2006. European Union funds were used to build a sports centre and a cultural and educational community centre. The latter was also used to give a home to several Surinamese ethnic organisations and a Ghanaian church.

Nonetheless, the Labour Party, which claims to have taken the lead in the restructuring, only really focused on a handful of the more than 100 nationalities that can be found in the neighbourhood. It was only Surinamese (Creoles as well as Hindustanis), Antillean and Ghanaian representatives who found themselves on the candidate lists and received the votes of their respective supporters. However, the majority of neighbourhood's residents tend to show little interest in either local or national politics and the turnout at elections was – and still is – among the lowest in the Netherlands.[15]

The Bijlmer multicultural society has developed along ethnic lines. In his history of the Bijlmermeer, Heijboer characterises this as living next to, but not with each other (2006: 134, 135). He vividly describes how he and his native Bijlmer friends received new neighbours from Surinam, the Antilles and Africa. Although they were friendly towards each other, they stayed apart. In some of the pubs and local football teams people from different ethnic backgrounds mixed, or played together. However, the main tradition in the Bijlmer was to be friendly and tolerate differences, but to still maintain a distance from the other (Heijboer 2006: 131–6).

It has been my experience that, to a large extent, the different ethnic groups in the neighbourhood tend to live to so-called 'parallel lives'. This is a term that is often used to refer to ethnic segregation in the United Kingdom (Burgess et al. 2005). These parallel lives are expressed in the different networks in which residents in the neighbourhood find themselves. Dutch residents tend to be secularised, while many migrants still visit churches, mosques or Hindu temples. Many of the more than 80 Bijlmer churches are centred round a particular pastor or priest and attract specific ethnic groups. The churches also developed along with the process of urban renewal. Many church congregations originally held their services in the empty parking garages, and later, when the restructuring continued, in new buildings. The local Muslims built a beautiful large new mosque and the Hindus also worship in a newly built small temple close to a metro station.

Expressions of parallel lives can be found in many fields of social life, not only in the sphere of religion, but also in sports, community centres and shops. Although some sports activities, like fitness training, attract an ethnically mixed public, other sports tend to be favoured by specific groups; for example, Hindus play cricket, while the Dutch prefer chess. Local community centres focus their activities on the most socially and economically deprived residents, who are often the lower educated and underprivileged Surinamese and Antilleans.[16]

In this multicultural neighbourhood, where people generally tend to lead parallel lives, I found exceptions: one of these exceptions was my youngest daughter's primary school, which was also attended by many of the neighbourhood children. In almost every class, which have between 20 and 25 pupils, there are children from 10 to 15 different nationalities. Indeed, most of the children spoke two or even three languages. Friendships developed between these children of different nationalities, ethnicities and religions; birthday parties were almost always mixed. On the days I collected my daughter from school, while waiting for the bell, I talked (chatted, joked and gossiped) mostly with Dutch, but also with Surinamese, Antillean, Ghanaian, Polish and Indian parents. We shared our interest in the daily school routine, the teachers and the development of our children. I experienced this primary school as an enjoyable and relaxed multicultural setting. Here I found support for Schiffauer's view, which I quoted earlier, that for the migrant the new city is after all 'the place where he lives his life, where he goes to school, falls in love, marries, where his children grew up' (2004: 100).

In the eyes of the district council and the urban planners, the Bijlmer still struggles with two major problems: image and safety. The 'Bijlmer monitor', which evaluates the progress of the restructuring bi-annually, has observed a number of positive developments. Unemployment, vandalism and squalor have decreased and fewer people are reporting that they want to leave the neighbourhood. (Van Heerwaarden et al. 2004: 16). Nonetheless, although the neighbourhood seems to have become a safer place, unemployment rates have decreased, and the drug and dealer problems are now better under control, the image of the Bijlmer has still not improved and the sale of the newly built houses has stagnated. The planners note that it is particularly difficult to attract buyers from outside: it is only the people who are already living in the area, especially those with a Surinamese background, who are actually buying the new houses (Shared Spaces 2005). However, even part of the emergent black middle-class population of the Bijlmer is not staying put: a modest, but increasing number of these rising migrants have recently followed in the footsteps the native residents and started an exodus out of the neighbourhood. In particular, the city of Almere, built on newly reclaimed land near Amsterdam, has become increasingly popular among the Surinamese and Antillean populations. Their motives for moving are much the same as those of the native-born residents: they want to raise their children in a single-family dwelling in a safe and quiet neighbourhood with mixed schools that have a good reputation (De Groot 2004).

The Bijlmer monitor also notes that some problems continue to persist: school results have not improved and remain among the lowest in Amsterdam and, moreover, youth criminality has increased (Van Heerwaarden et al. 2004). Another problem concerns the population decline. Since 50 per cent of the high-rise social housing has been demolished, a large part of the poor migrant population has been relocated to other areas. Between 1995 and 2005, this contributed to a population decrease of nearly 20 per cent in the restructured area (De Kleuver and Nauta 2006).[17] As a result, many local shopkeepers and retail traders have run into trouble and have had to close down, which also does little to improve the image of the neighbourhood.

STAYING OR LEAVING

During the past 25 years, there has been a continuous exodus of native Dutch people out of the Bijlmer. Indeed, the most recent Bijlmer monitor concluded that the proportion of Dutch residents in the restructuring area was now less than 15 per cent (De Kleuver and Nauta 2006). Interviews with people who leave reveal that one of the reasons for their departure relates to a declining sense of identification with the neighbourhood. Some native residents are experiencing an increasing sense of insecurity, as expressed by Ella, a 55-year-old single female professional, who left the Bijlmer several years ago:

There was a point that it simply was not nice here any more, too much noise, and I did not feel safe anymore. I felt scared to take the lift when I came home late. My friends urged me to return to the city, which I did. But, oh my God, I miss the beautiful view from my window, so green, so nice.

As one of the native Dutch inhabitants, it has not escaped my notice that the familiar Dutch shops, such as the cycle repair shop, the cheese specialist and the bookshop, have been supplanted by black hairdressers, international phone houses and overseas shipping companies. These kind of commercial enterprises, which have been tailored to the needs of new residents, hardly attract any Dutch customers. The rapid transformation of the Bijlmer has also found expression in the changing composition of the population that uses the metro system. The old black-and-white film footage of the Bijlmer metro shows white middle-class people sitting on the shiny seats while travelling past the high-rises outside. Today, five or ten different languages can often be heard in the same metro carriage. People often wear colourful African prints, or the latest fashions. The carriages are no longer new and clean, but worn-out, damaged and full of graffiti. Sometimes, on Saturday evenings, I will often find that I am the only white person in the compartment, and often also the only passenger above the age of 30. Although, as an anthropologist and enthusiastic user of public transport, it can seem like an adventure to feel like a stranger in the city where one's own mother and grandmother were born, I can also imagine that such estrangement could create a feeling of being lost.

In my research, I also discovered that some native people had decided to move because they wanted their children to live in an ethnically mixed setting, instead having to grow up in a nearly entirely non-Western context. Anna, a neighbouring teacher, mother of a small son and daughter, explains why she and her husband decided to leave. In the first place, she says, their new house and garden in Almere are larger; moreover, she expects that her children will benefit from growing up in the new social surroundings:

You see, my 5-year-old daughter only has two other Western girls to play with in her class, one girl from Bosnia and one from Scotland. All the other girls are from Surinam, Africa and the Antilles and so on. Well that is all right, of course, but, well, I am not sure if it is nice to be the only white child in the class, when she grows up. So, it is also because of the children that we are moving.

Native people, who stay in the neighbourhood, do not always remain there because they participate in multicultural networks, or enjoy living in such a multicultural setting. Some people stay because they manage to live parallel lives with native friends and networks. As Jacob, a violin player, with two young sons explained:

> People sometimes ask me: you really live there, in the Bijlmer? With small children? Then I tell them that I live on a kind of white island, that all my neighbours are white, and that we do our shopping with our car, outside the neighbourhood. So actually I do not see much of the neighbourhood, or of its problems. I simply live with my family in a nice house with a wonderful garden.

The aforementioned government report (VROM-Raad 2006), which seeks to explain what influences the socially mobile to continue living in a neighbourhood, reveals that trust, recognition and feeling at home are crucial for creating a social tie to a neighbourhood. The report argues that people need space for their own way of living, they must have the feeling that the environment is controllable, they need to live with 'intimate strangers', and must be able to identify with their environment (2006: 58). Following this point of view, and looking at the Bijlmer, it is clear that in a process of rapid change, natives appear to have lost many of their points of identification and recognition; this is clearly expressed in Ella's fears, Anna's desire to relocate and Jacob's withdrawal to his white enclave.[18]

In a recent article on increasing diversity and social cohesion in America, Putnam contends that people react by 'hunkering down'. By this he means that increasing diversity leads to a decrease in communal involvement, less solidarity and an inward-looking attitude (Putnam 2007). Comparable feelings of growing insecurity and a hunkering down response are evident in some of the native Bijlmer residents' responses. Not surprisingly, the experiences of many migrants differ from those of natives. One of the first interviews I carried out when I decided to conduct research in my own neighbourhood was with Charmilla, a 32-year-old care assistant in an old people's home. At the time, she was the mother of two daughters aged 12 and 2. Her mother had migrated to the Bijlmer from Surinam with her seven children, but without a husband, when Charmilla was a young girl. Charmilla feels very much at ease in the neighbourhood and she also approves of the urban restructuring:

To me the Bijlmer is just like home. It is just like Surinam. All my brothers and sisters live here. Soon, I will have to leave the apartment, because of the restructuring. Then they will have to offer me a new one, won't they? They gave my sister and her children a better house, so why not? They make such beautiful new houses.

For Charmilla, the neighbourhood is 'just like home', with friends and family and discos to go out dancing nearby:

I like going out. With my friends and my sister. I like dancing, I love music. We go out dancing often. You ask me what language I speak with my family and friends? Well, I will sometimes speak Dutch, sometimes Sranang or we mix. At school, we had to speak Dutch. The teachers were always angry with me, because I would play truant so often. They were Dutch. They call us '*allochtones*' [(im)migrants or aliens], I hate that word. I simply hate it being called by that name. They should stop it, we are no longer living in the days of slavery!

Like the majority of mothers in the Bijlmer, Charmilla also raises her children alone without the help of a partner:

The father of my boy is from this neighbourhood, he is from Surinam, but I do not see him often. With the second child I wanted a Dutch man, because Dutch men will stay with you, they are not *players*, like the Surinamese. They are different, at least that is what they say. But when my daughter was only a few months old, he left. Now he is living with an African woman, she is pregnant. But I still love him, I pray to God every day for him to send him back to me.

Most children in the Bijlmer grow up in single-parent households.[19] During the restructuring operation, there was an increase in the number of single-parent households, which are sometimes considered to be a sign of a weak socialisation structure.[20] Single-parent families, almost always female-headed households, are among the most underprivileged households in the district (Onderzoek en Statistiek 2004).[21]

Sara is a divorced 50-year-old woman from Ethiopia. She came to the Bijlmer with her husband when her children, a son and a daughter, were still very small. She is a Christian and visits a church outside the Bijlmer, where people from different nationalities gather. Her husband has left her and now lives in Sweden with a new family. She works as a cleaning lady and lives together with her daughter:

> I was a special child, I could not go to school in our village, but I always tried to learn whatever I could. I learned some reading and writing. I tried so very hard. My daughter is just like me, she wants to work and she wants to learn things. She has passed all of her exams, primary school, secondary school, and now she is studying business at the university. She is such a good girl. She brings me so much joy. I am happy that we can live here in Holland, in the Bijlmer, but I find it difficult to speak Dutch. I do not see many people. But that is all right, I am lucky that we can live here. I can work, so we can live with that, so we do not have to ask anybody for anything.'

Not all migrants feel as accepted and at home in the Bijlmer as Charmilla and Sara do; some residents appear to be rather lonely. One day a refugee from Somalia started to talk to me in the metro. He told me that he lived alone in one of the apartments in the high-rises, which was due to be demolished: 'I came here. You people have given me a house. You let me learn your language. You give me money to live. You talk about me. But you do not talk to me. Only about me. So I live alone.' It appears that the Bijlmer migrants' feelings of belonging, of being accepted and being recognised vary significantly. They can be expressed just as much in the loneliness of the Somali refugee, as the contentedness of Sara and Charmilla's positive feelings of being completely at home in the neighbourhood.

In a multicultural neighbourhood, such as the Bijlmer, having family members and an elaborate network like many Surinamese, Antillean and Ghanaian residents, or belonging to a small group of refugees from countries like Iraq, Somalia, Sri Lanka or Sudan, does seem to matter. Migrants who belong to a larger ethnic group often have larger networks, and migrants who have been in the Netherlands for a longer period of time often speak better Dutch. Moreover, some groups – especially the Surinamese and Ghanaians – have a well-organised political representation.

I also found that many migrants expressed feelings of being caught between two different worlds. On International Women's Day, 8 March 2006, I visited a meeting in a local cultural centre called Kwakoe. There were around 40 women and a few men present, almost all of them with a Surinamese or Antillean background. The evening started with presentations from several Surinamese and Antillean female writers, followed by a lively discussion. Women talked about love and single motherhood, about slavery in the past and about living between two worlds. In the heat of the discussion, one tall elderly Creole woman stood up and spoke loudly with great passion: 'Each of us, we know that each of us has a fully packed suitcase in her attic.' The audience responded with recognition, sad smiles and confirming nods. At that moment, I not only felt awkward, obviously not being included in the 'we', but was also puzzled. I knew for certain that none of the women had an attic (there are no attics in the high-rises and modern architects do not like them in single-family houses either), and I doubted if any of them would keep their clothes in a closed suitcase for 30 years or more. I then realised that the suitcase was a metaphor, a symbol of being ready to leave at any moment, a symbol of not being here, while still staying here, a symbol of living in two worlds and experiencing different ways of belonging.

A NEW GENERATION, NEW NOTIONS OF BELONGING

Throughout the course of time, the Bijlmer has become the kind of place that the anthropologist Stephen Vertovec (2006) would label 'super-diverse'. With this term he refers to the increased multitude of ethnic, cultural, and religious diversity, which one can encounter in modern urban neighbourhoods.[22] He suggests that one can find processes of new and more inclusive identity formation in these super-diverse areas, which are the result of increasing and continuing globalisation and migration. He argues that it is the younger people in particular in these settings who are involved in shifts between different cultural codes and contexts, and in changing from one language to the next.

The notions of belonging among the Bijlmer youth differ from those of their parents. Research into ethnic segregation and parallel lives tends to devote attention to the fact that 'the peer groups that children play with, talk to and work with are important factors moulding their view on society' (Burgess et al. 2005: 1027). Growing up in increasingly diversified surroundings makes a difference. Research among Bijlmer youngsters in 2006 and 2007 shed new light on their current notions of belonging. Unlike their parents, the majority of youngsters have been born and raised in the neighbourhood. Their networks and friendships are more diverse and cross more ethnic and religious boundaries than those of their parents. They also speak Dutch fluently. Moreover, the Bijlmer is the place where they have grown up, where many of their friends live, where they date and fall in love.

Franklin (18) was born in the Dutch Antilles.[23] His family lives in the Bijlmer, but he was not living with them at the time. Franklin wants to be a musician, just like his father, who is a reggae singer:

> With my friends we rap, we are rappers, we have a band, it has been serious for two years. The other boys of the band are from the Dominican Republic, and from the Antilles. You know, I can rap in Dutch, but also in Papiamento, Spanish or English.

His heroes are Tupac Shakur, Nelson Mandela, Martin Luther King and Pater Tula from Curacao:

> Because he fought for the freedom of our little island. Well, I think you have to be proud on your roots and your colour. Black is black. I am glad that I am black. Nothing against white people. But I am glad I am black. It is pure nature. Face it.

Franklin sometimes hangs out with his friends at the sports centre and playground, which were built at the beginning of the century with European money. He thinks that the Bijlmer is a cool place:

> I love the Bijlmer. Here I really feel good, I really feel good here. You know, the Bijlmer is really multicultural. There are different cultures here, and you learn from each other. There are Surinamese, Hindustanis, Africans, Dominicans, Dutch, even Moroccans, all of them are here. All different cultures. So that is what is cool about the Bijlmer.

This feeling of being at ease in the Bijlmer was expressed by almost all of the youngsters, both boys and girls, who were interviewed at schools, in churches, in community centres or at other places where they hang out. These young people are proud of the multicultural character of their neighbourhood and repeatedly stress that they have friends from different ethnic backgrounds. In contrast to many of their parents, who might have 'a fully packed suitcase in their attic', the youngsters feel much more at home in the multicultural Bijlmer. Belonging to different cultural contexts does not seem to be difficult or painful for them, but instead an enriching source of identity formation (den Uyl and Brouwer 2007).

Franklin points out that there is a difference between generations with respect to inter-ethnic mixing:

> You know, the older people, they just isolate themselves. No, I do not mean that they do it on purpose, but I mean they just live their lives, and with the young people it is different, then it becomes one culture. Just one culture, we learn from each other.

These processes of identification and inter-ethnic interaction among the Bijlmer's youth indicate that sameness should not be viewed as a static concept, which draws lines between 'we' and 'them'. Instead, it should be viewed as a dynamic and negotiable concept. The Bijlmer youngsters find a sense of community not only in shared age and shared locality, but also in the mixed nature of their neighbourhood, in shared diversity.

While their parents' generation, who were often migrants who made the step from one country and culture to the next, largely live parallel lives in the neighbourhood, this is much less the case as far as the youth, their children, are concerned. Youngsters mix much more, and more frequently, with different ethnic groups, including native Dutch people. The Bijlmer youth creates its own expressions: rappers, hip-hoppers and the local street language have an influence outside the area (Appel 1999). Franklin:

> If you apply for a job or something, then you better not tell them you are from the Bijlmer, but if it has to do with music, it is all right, then it is cool you are from the Bijlmer.

Emmanuel is a 20-year-old sportsman and student, who moved to the Netherlands from Ghana when he was a boy: 'My mother was already in the Netherlands, she wanted me to come, for a better future, and so on.' He loves athletics and trains every day. He went to a primary school in the Bijlmer and then to the Augustinus College. After this, he studied at a sports education institute. At present, he is studying marketing communication: 'If I do not make it as a sportsman, I can work with that, organising sport events or something like that.' Emmanuel has many friends in as well as outside of the neighbourhood. He jokes about the international character of the Bijlmer:

> My girlfriend is from the Antilles. Well, it is the Bijlmer here, isn't it? But I dated a girl from Ghana once and for a while I was

seeing a girl from French Guyana. But I feel fine with the girl I am seeing now.

Emmanuel says that he can see a difference between his own and his parents' identification with both Ghana and the Netherlands. He speaks Dutch fluently and sees his future in the Netherlands:

> My parents often speak Twi, I do it less. They have a better bond with Ghana than I do. That is absolutely true. If you ask me who I am? Well, I am a Ghanaian, that is what I feel, but I also feel, how should I put it, well I feel 'Bijlmerian', or should I say Dutch? Yes, that too. I mean I go to school here, I speak Dutch, I speak better Dutch than Twi, I have a closer bond with the Netherlands than with Ghana, but you know, you will always feel love for the place where you come from.

He says that he plans to visit Ghana with a group of Dutch, Ghanaian, Antillean and Surinamese people. This visit to Ghana will be the first since he left as a child:

> We are going to visit the place where our roots lie. Yes, the Dutch have a history there too; they traded slaves, in the fort El Mina. So it is our shared history. What do I expect to find? Well, I will probably cry a few times, and I will get angry a few times, because of what has happened to Ghana. It has gone through a lot, it still has to conquer poverty, and I want to see how they do it, what I can do to help.

It is apparent that many children of migrant families feel at ease in different cultural contexts. They feel Dutch, but also Bijlmerian, and also Hindustani, Surinamese, Ghanaian, African, Antillean or Dominican. They speak different languages and switch from one language or cultural code to the next easily. Many friendships in the Bijlmer cross ethnic and religious boundaries. According to Emmanuel it is not sameness in people's background that is important in friendship, but character and personality that counts:

> You know, if you can get along with someone it has nothing to do with his or her origins, no, it does not have anything to do with nationality. It has to do with the person, with the human being. It is not the stereotype; it is the person that counts. You

like someone or you don't, and after some time you discover that. That's all.

While the generational differences between parents and their children became manifest in the research, I also experienced them in my personal life as a resident. Most of my friends are middle-aged, white, left-wing intellectuals, and they live outside the Bijlmer. The friendships of my youngest daughter, who grew up in the Bijlmer, show a much more diverse picture: her friends are from Afghani, Israeli, Filipino, Surinamese, Moroccan and Dutch backgrounds. She has visited the synagogue, read the Koran and enjoys singing in an African Pentecostal church on Sundays; she also loves to salsa.

CONCLUSION

The vision which lay behind the construction of the Bijlmer, the City of the Future, in the 1960s, shows optimism and trust in people's capacity to live together peacefully. It assumed that all human beings are equal, that they need to be in touch with nature, and that they are capable of filling the collective space both inside and outside their buildings with useful and creative activities.

The vision behind the rebuilding of the Bijlmer demonstrates much less trust in the reliability and stability of human nature. Residents are supposed to be in need of control: they need more windows that look out over the streets, more security cameras and more police. The public space has been minimised; trees and bushes have been cut down, tunnels removed, any niches or hidden angles must be avoided at all costs. In some respects, the story of the Bijlmer is as much a story of vanishing trust as it is a story of natives and migrants in a globalising world.

In the earlier plans for the neighbourhood, sameness (all people were supposed to live in identical apartments) was emphasised, while in the plans for the restructuring the accent was placed on differentiation. Neither the building nor the rebuilding of the neighbourhood has had the anticipated results. The rebuilding aimed to create a neighbourhood which would be more average – more like other Amsterdam neighbourhoods. However, during the process of urban restructuring, in some respects the Bijlmer became more *unlike* other neighbourhoods: the percentage of non-Western migrants increased, as did the percentage of single-parent households. This was due to the fact that, although thousands of poor non-Western migrants were silently – albeit with a financial incentive and their

own consent – relocated to social housing in other neighbourhoods, there was also a significant influx of new poor non-Western
migrants. Moreover, the restructuring operation could not put a stop
to the slow, but continuing exodus of native residents. Nor could
it reverse the negative image of the neighbourhood: the Bijlmer
remained 'too poor, too black, too criminal'.

When one looks at the motives of those leaving the neighbourhood,
it becomes clear that many native residents lost the feelings of
recognition and trust in the process of rapid change. They left
because it was no longer a nice place to live, and because it felt as
if they did not belong there any more. Others chose to stay, but
hunkered down or focused on their parallel lives, including their
contacts with native people outside of the neighbourhood.

The Bijlmer is still an area with relatively high rates of
unemployment, welfare dependency, criminality and school
drop-out. It might be concluded that thus far the Bijlmer planners
have not been able to attract a considerable number of higher
educated middle-class residents – as desired and planned for –
nor did they succeed in stopping the exodus of the original white
residents. However, if we look at the developing notions of belonging
in the Bijlmer, the fact that many of the plans for the area were not
successful, does not have to be seen as an insurmountable problem.
Despite the failure of many interventions, there are also positive
elements with respect to the development of the area.

First, the responses of many migrants to the urban restructuring
are far more positive than those of many native residents, who,
although they value the decreased crime level and the increased
safety of the area, lament the loss of greenery and the disappearance
of familiar points of reference. In contrast, many migrants argue
that the area has not only become far safer, but also more beautiful.
Moreover, they have found new points of reference, such as new
churches, shops and cultural activities, like gospel choirs and brass
bands, which have contributed to their feelings of being at ease and
at home in the Bijlmer.

However, more importantly with respect to changing notions of
belonging, the younger generation seem to tell a quite different and
new story. This is a consequence of the fact that their inter-ethnic
contacts and friendships started when they were schoolchildren
and continued into adolescence. Youngsters are very proud of the
multicultural character of their neighbourhood. Young people's
identities in the Bijlmer seem to be developing into more inclusive
identities, in which neighbourhood, youth culture, country of

origin and country of arrival are included and expressed as new notions of belonging. This latter development can be characterised as an unintended, but certainly positive outcome of the increased migration to the neighbourhood by people from a variety of countries of origin. It means that, despite the failure of many plans and interventions, the story of a neighbourhood like the Bijlmer can continue and is more than just a continuation of negative pages and disappointments: there will also be unexpected and promising new tales to be told in the future.

NOTES

1. An earlier version of this chapter was presented at the Human Security panel at the EASA in Bristol in 2006. I would like to thank the participants for their useful remarks. Furthermore, I must also give my special thanks to Thomas Eriksen, Lenie Brouwer and Peer Smets for their comments and discussion.

2. On 1 January 2007, the Bijlmer (East and Centre) numbered 32,374 non-Western migrants, 3059 Western migrants and 7943 native born Dutch people. The non-Western migrants included 15,999 Surinamese and 3133 Antilleans (www.os.amsterdam.nl, visited 10/01/2008).

3. Putnam remarks that social capital 'simply refers to the social norms and networks that enhance people's ability to collaborate on common endeavors' (2001: 135). He distinguishes between different kinds of social capital: on the one hand, bonding social capital, which is located in one's own social group, and on the other, bridging social capital, which one can use to create ties with people outside one's own social group. These various kinds of network are related to different kinds of identities. Bonding social relationships reinforce exclusive identities of homogeneous groups, while bridging relationships are outward looking, encompassing people across different social cleavages, and involve more exclusive social identities (Putnam 2000, 2007).

4. Bauman argues that in the case of (rich) ghettos, where people try to create a safe place, sameness means the absence of the Other: 'In the figure of the stranger (not just the "unfamiliar", but the *alien*, the "out of place"), the fears of uncertainty, founded in the totality of life experience, find their eagerly sought, and so welcomed, embodiment' (2001: 115).

5. I chose the Bijlmer because the house prices were the lowest in Amsterdam and it was the only place that I could afford a small single family house with a garden, for my children and myself.

6. Together with Lenie Brouwer, four Master's students, and several groups of undergraduate students I conducted research among the Bijlmer youth in 2006 and 2007 as part of the 'Amsterdam Global Village' project.

7. The Bijlmer was to become his only major work, for which he was eventually awarded an *oeuvre* prize in 1998. Ironically, he received this prize when the demolition of his work was already in full swing.

8. For Le Corbusier architecture was the spatial translation of a specific social structure. The architect must be socially engaged and should use modern materials, such as concrete, steel and glass, and elementary geometrical forms. Le Corbusier was inspired by the possibilities of the new technology of the

twentieth century: technology could be a source of freedom. In 1935, he developed a plan for Manhattan, *La Ville Radieuse*, also called the City of the Future. In Le Corbusier's dreams, Utopia could be found in a vertical city, with towering skyscrapers set amongst a vast sea of open green space. The city would be connected by various highways built above the ground. Walkways were planned at ground level in a vast green space. This would be a world in which modern man could breathe and experience light, space and nature.

9. The highest number of inhabitants of the south-east district was in 1990, when the district, including the Bijlmer and adjacent new low-rise neighbourhoods, had nearly 90,000 people (Tamboer 2004: 73).

10. Ghanaian residents now constitute around 10 per cent of the population. However, there are also other African migrants from, for example, Nigeria, Cameroon, Somalia and Sudan. Migrants also arrived from Asia, in particular from Pakistan, Indonesia and China, and from eastern European countries.

11. The Bijlmer does not have the severe problems of poverty, unemployment and segregation that one can find in the ghettos of America's inner cities; see, for example, Wilson (1987).

12. One of the teachers of the Augustinus said that she was teaching 'the waste bin of the waste bin'. By this, she was referring to the pupils with the lowest educational ability in the most deprived district, the Bijlmer. However, most other teachers displayed a rather more positive attitude towards their pupils (Goossens 2007).

13. To carry out the building plans, the built and asphalted area had to be transformed from 25 per cent to 75 per cent, which meant no more abundance of green. Already, 17,000 trees have been cut down, and, to complete the plans, many thousands more will follow (Stadsdeel Zuidoost 2005).

14. The renewal project, one of the largest Dutch restructuring projects, has been going on since 1992, and is intended to be completed in 2009. The total investment is over €1.6 billion, which has been contributed by local, national and European sources (Kwekkeboom 2002: 79).

15. During the district council elections in 2006, the turnout in Bijlmer Centre was 39.4 per cent and 46.5 per cent in Bijlmer East (www.os.amsterdam.nl, visited 10/01/2008).

16. Many of the activities offered by the community centres, such as playing in a brass band, Surinamese headscarf folding, and courses in the languages of countries of origin, such as Sranang and Papiamento, are of interest only to Surinamese and Antillean residents.

17. More than 5000 social housing units have been demolished and nearly 8000 residents of the high-rises have been relocated to other parts of south-east and other districts of Amsterdam. As of March 2007, only 2009 new houses had actually been completed, of which only one-third were intended as social housing. (Rochdale 2007: 23). This restructuring strategy basically comes down to simply relocating people and their problems, instead of actually solving them. There is an ambivalence in the restructuring strategy: on the one hand, the renewal policy welcomes difference, especially middle-class migrants, but, on the other, there is a certain urge to relocate poor migrants (Leeming and Shakur 2004).

18. Because of the long-term nature of the process of gradual departure of the original white residents and their complicated and diverse motives (illustrated by Ella, Anna and Jacob) I prefer the term 'white withdrawal' or 'white

departure' over the often-used term 'white flight' (see also Smets and den Uyl 2008).

19. The single-parent families in the Bijlmer have different backgrounds. The Surinamese and Antillean family structure, often labelled matrifocal, has its roots in a history of poverty and slavery, which led to a central role of mothers as caretakers and income-earners (Wekker 2006). The West African family structure is vested in changing matrilineal traditions, while the gendered process of migration enforces different responsibilities on males and females (Kraan 2001).

20. Fukuyama considers the family structure of the Afro-American inner-city population to be weak (1995: 10). He thinks that strong and stable families are better instruments to socialise people in their culture and provide them with skills that allow them to successfully participate in the broader society (1995: 4–5).

21. During the restructuring process, the number of single-parent households increased from 14 per cent to 20 per cent, while the percentage of households with two parents decreased from 12 per cent to 9 per cent of all households (Van Heerwaarden et al. 2004: 18).

22. Super-diversity not only refers to differences in ethnic background, but also in legal status, migration history, gender, work experience, age, religion, networks and so on (Vertovec 2006).

23. Ten groups of undergraduate students interviewed 5–10 respondents in the framework of the project Amsterdam Global Village. The interviews with Franklin and Emmanuel were conducted by the 'Kraaiennest group' (Mieke van Dijk, Marlieke van Eerden and Fleur Hoffman). Any mistakes in translation and interpretation are entirely my responsibility.

REFERENCES

Appel, Rene. 1999. Straattaal. De mengtaal van jongeren in Amsterdam. *Toegepaste taalwetenschap in artikelen* 62(2): 39–56.

Bauman, Zygmunt. 2001. *Community: Seeking Safety in an Insecure World.* Cambridge: Polity Press.

Bicknese, Liselotte and Jeroen Slot. 2007. *De staat van de aandachtswijken: Zuidoost.* Amsterdam: Dienst Onderzoek en Statistiek.

Braam, S. 1996. Zwart-zijn is ons wapen. *De Groene Amsterdammer* 30 Nov.

Burgess, Simon, Deborah Wilson and Ruth Lupton (2005) Parallel Lives? Ethnic Segregation in Schools and Neighbourhoods. *Urban Studies* 42(7): 1027–56.

Friedman, Jonathan. 1999. *Concept for the Conference: Globalization and Cultural Security – Migration and Negotiations of Identity.* House of World Cultures Berlin and the Toda Institute for Global Peace and Policy Research, 14–17 October.

Frieling, Dirk. 2004. Bijlmermeer/Compressed Urbanism. Lecture at the Delft School for Design, 23 April.

Fukuyama, Francis. 1995. *Trust: The Social Virtues and the Creation of Prosperity.* New York: The Free Press.

Goossens, Mary Lou. 2007. VMBO students at Delta School and the Meanings They Attach to School. Master's thesis, Department of Social and Cultural Anthropology. VU University Amsterdam.

De Groot, Carola. 2004. 'Zwarte Vlucht' De (sub)urbane locatiekeuze van klassieke allochtonen in Amsterdam. Den Haag: Ministerie van VROM.

De Haan, Hilde and Jolanda Keesom. 2004. Terug naar de straat. De vernieuwing van de F-buurt, Amsterdam Zuidoost. Haarlem: Architext.

Hartman, Louise. 2007. Bimre mi Osso. Experiences of Socio-cultural Background and Expressions of Identity among Young Girls in South-east Amsterdam. Master's thesis, Department of Social and Cultural Anthropology, VU University Amsterdam.

Heijboer, Pierre. 2006. Wachten op de nachtegaal. Het verhaal van de Bijlmermeer. Amsterdam: Van Gennep.

De Kleuver, Justin and Oberon Nauta. 2006. Bijlmermonitor 2005. Amsterdam: DSP-groep.

Kraan, Marloes. 2001. Blijven of teruggaan? Een sociologische analyse van potenties en problemen van Ghanezen in Amsterdam Zuidoost. Amsterdam: Wetenschapswinkel Vrije Universiteit.

Kwekkeboom, Willem. 2002. Rebuilding the Bijlmermeer 1992–2002. In Dirk Bruijne, Dorine van Hoogstraten, Willem Kwekkeboom and Anne Luijten, Amsterdam Southeast. Centre Area Southeast and urban renewal in the Bijlmermeer 1992–2010. Bussem: Thoth, 75–113.

Leeming, Karen and Tasleem Shakur. 2004. Welcoming Difference or Wily Dispersal? Emerging Problems of Urban Regeneration in the Multiply Deprived Area of Bijlmermeer (Amsterdam). Global Built Environment Review 3(3): 61–72.

Maurer United Architects. 2005. Bijlmerscope. Amsterdam: Centrum Beeldende Kunst Zuidoost.

Onderzoek en Statistiek. 2004. Armoede Fact Sheet Zuidoost. URL (consulted 17 December 2005): www.os.amsterdam.nl

Onderzoek en Statistiek. 2007. Amsterdam in cijfers. URL (consulted 8 September 2007): www.os.amsterdam.nl

Onderzoek en Statistiek. 2008. Statsdelen in cijfers 2008. URL (consulted September 2009): www.os.amsterdam

Paulle, Bowen. 2005. Anxiety and Intimidation in the Bronx and the Bijlmer: An Ethnographic Comparison of Two Schools. Amsterdam: Dutch University Press.

Putnam, Robert D. 2000. Bowling Alone: The Collapse and Revival of American Community. New York: Simon and Schuster.

Putnam, Robert D. 2007. E Pluribus Unum: Diversity and Community in the Twenty-first Century. Scandinavian Political Studies 30(2): 137–75.

Rochdale. 2007. Jaarverslag 2006. Amsterdam: Rochdale.

Schiffauer, Werner. 2004. Cosmopolitans are Cosmopolitans: On the Relevance of Local Identification in Globalizing Society. In Jonathan Friedman and Shalini Randeria (eds) World on the Move: Globalization, Migration and Cultural Security. London: I.B. Tauris, 91–103.

Shared Spaces. 2005. The Fall and Rise of the Bijlmermeer. URL (consulted 28 November 2005): www.sharedspaces.nl

Smets, Peer and Marion den Uyl. 2008. The Complex Role of Ethnicity in Urban Mixing. A Study of Two Deprived Neighbourhoods in Amsterdam. Urban Studies 45(7): 1439–60.

Stadsdeel Zuidoost. 2005. Zuidoost Open Huis. Ontwerp-Structuurvisie Zuidoost 2020. Amsterdam: Stadsdeel Zuidoost.

Tamboer, Kees. 2004. Amsterdam buiten de gordel. Amsterdam: Dienst O&S/Het Parool/TNO.

Den Uyl, Marion and Lenie Brouwer. 2007. De verlokkingen van de stad. Meiden als cultuurvernieuwers. *Lova. Tijdschrift voor Feministische Antropologie* 28(1): 69–76.

Van Heerwaarden, Yvonne, Oberon Nauta, Mark Rietveld and Paul van Someren. 2004. *De Bijlmermonitor 2003*. Amsterdam: DSP-groep.

Veldboer, Lex, Jan Willem Duyvendak and Carolien Bouw (eds). 2007. *De mixfactor. Integratie en segregatie in Nederland*. Amsterdam: Boom.

Vertovec, Steven. 2006. *The Emergency of Super-diversity in Britain*. Working Paper 25. Oxford: Centre on Migration, Policy and Society (COMPAS).

VROM-Raad. 2006. *Stad en stijging. Sociale stijging als leidraad voor stedelijke vernieuwing*. Den Haag: VROM-raad.

Wekker, Gloria. 2006. *The Politics of Passion: Women's Sexual Culture in the Afro-Surinamese Diaspora*. New York: Columbia University Press.

Wilson, William J. 1987. *The Truly Disadvantaged: The Inner City, the Underclass, and Public Policy*. Chicago: University of Chicago Press.

10
Tales from a Captive Audience: Dissident Narratives and the Official History of the Seychelles[1]

Sandra Evers

During the three-decade period from independence up until our arrival,[2] no foreign anthropologists were allowed to conduct independent research in the archipelago. Local publications remained limited to tourist brochures and propaganda documents on what was labelled by the government as 'Seychellois history and folklore'. These documents were generally published by the ruling political party, the Seychelles People's Progressive Front (SPPF), which has held power since the 1977 coup d'état orchestrated by its leader René Albert. To date, the official history remains virtually the only history of the Seychelles.

Publications on colonial and pre-colonial Seychelles (including studies on slavery in the archipelago) have been written principally by local historians (Adam 1999, Ducrotoy n.d., Lionnet 1972, 2001, McAteer 2000, 2002). There is little covering the post-independence era. The sole social history written and published during the post-coup period which purports to be comprehensive is authored by Derek Scarr (1999). The book traces the history of slavery and emancipation in the Seychelles, but contains only six pages covering the 'bloodless coup' which brought President Albert René to power.[3] However, the following phrase in the acknowledgements of the book, while not conclusive, raises the issue of the author's independence as a researcher:

> I am indebted to former President J.R.M. Mancham for an instructive interview, as well as to then Prime Minister and later revolutionary and in the end democratically-elected President F.A. René for a number of conversations as well as for hospitality at his home.[4]

The last anthropological fieldwork carried out by a non-Seychellois is the result of studies undertaken during the colonial period. In 1970, Burton Benedict of the University of California (Berkeley) published his first work on the Seychelles, titled *People of the Seychelles*. Fieldwork for this book was completed ten years earlier, in 1960. His final research was conducted during 1974 and 1975 in collaboration with his wife Marion and published in 1982 under the title: *Men, Women, and Money in the Seychelles*.

Benedict portrays the Seychellois as a people who lack well-entrenched social traditions, which he explains by the period of slavery ending in 1835. The islands were first settled by the French, who arrived with their slaves in 1770 (Benedict and Benedict 1982: 117). The slaves worked on small farm holdings run by their French masters. Sexual relations between early settlers and their slaves were common, such that, by the time of independence (29 June 1976), the population had become largely mixed (*métissage*).

Benedict and Benedict conclude that money was the chief arbiter of social relations at the time of independence. Men and women arranged their social and more intimate interactions on a commercial basis. Family links are described as tenuous. Many households were composed of single mothers: in 1976, 56 per cent of children were registered as 'illegitimate children' (Benedict and Benedict 1982: 221, quoting from Statistical Abstract 1977: Table 8:10). Benedict and Benedict consider alcoholism, next to the history of slavery, as a key factor undermining social cohesion. Alcohol was primarily a male problem, perceived as crucial to their lives. A study cited by Benedict and Benedict discloses that workers spent on average 42 per cent of the monthly family budget on alcohol (*Alcoholism in Seychelles* 1973: 6). Generally, Benedict and Benedict portray the Seychellois as a people adrift, a condition originating in the historical circumstance that both settlers and slaves had been severed from their historical and geographical ties.

Since the period of Benedict's research, the SPPF 'revolution' has come to the Seychelles, and with it pervasive censorship. Given the lack of free access to information and the ubiquitous role of government propaganda, the research focused on the narratives of ordinary Seychellois and how they dealt with the official government discourse that the Seychelles is a socialist paradise, characterised by equality, free education, affordable housing and free health care services.

RESEARCH METHODOLOGY

In 2003, the Department of Social and Cultural Anthropology of the Vrije Universiteit/Free University Amsterdam established a joint research programme on human security. The concept of 'human security' was first coined in the 1994 United Nations *Human Development Report*, which had the stated aim of expanding the concept of physical security to encompass both states and individuals. Security was reformulated as 'safety from chronic threats such as hunger, disease and repression' and 'protection from sudden and harmful disruptions in the patterns of daily life' (United Nations Development Programme [UNDP] 1994: 23). The concept of human security remains fluid. As of 2003, approximately 25 definitions of human security were in circulation (Alkire 2003: 15, cf. Eriksen 2005).

Two key elements of human security have been formulated: 'freedom from fear' and 'freedom from want'. Freedom from want is comprised of elements including economic security, food security, health security and environmental security.[5] Freedom from fear contains elements such as personal security, community security and political security (UNDP 1994: 24–33). Although the themes of 'freedom from fear' and 'freedom from want' certainly can be inferred from the life stories of the Seychellois, interviews more often than not turned to the practical issue of circumventing government constraints on their daily lives. Thus, in order to use human security as a useful analytical grid for the multi-dimensional study of society, any classical analysis of human security has to be expanded to include the existential (which brings individual cognitive, emotional, and symbolic dimensions within the ambit of the study):

> Existential security is the human attempt to make sense of this world and of the human being's place in it, in relation to family, community, society and the wider cosmos, through processes of signification in connection to belief, trust, belonging, and mental and spiritual fulfilment. (Department of Social and Cultural Anthropology 2006: 12)

Methodologies included participant observation, interviews using the life history method, consultation of quantitative studies and archival research in the Seychelles National Archives. Documentary source material includes IMF and World Bank reports, and the two opposition newspapers (*Regar* and the *Nouveau Seychellois*

Weekly). I attempted to interview people from all social strata, ranging from fervent SPPF loyalists to the opposition, and political and religious leaders[6] to people in the street. Men and women of all age categories were interviewed.

The official history of the Seychelles over the past 30 years was investigated and analysed by a review of SPPF documents, speeches of party leaders, radio broadcasts, national television, teaching material used in schools, the official newspapers *Nation* and *The People* and other publications that have appeared in the Seychelles over the past three decades. Public records contain quantitative data collected through their Management and Information Systems Division, which are reported in annual studies on Population and Vital Statistics, Migration and Tourism, External Trade, National Accounts and Finance, Production, Transport and Communication, Prices, Wages and Employment, and Health and Education.

The Seychellois national archives contain a wealth of information related to the pre-colonial and colonial periods, but documents on contemporary history are scarce with the notable exception of SPPF literature such as public speeches of past-president René.[7]

CONTEMPORARY POLITICAL DEVELOPMENTS

> One of the main purposes of my speeches has been to prevent a situation arising in the Seychelles where violence will come, because I believe that violence comes by itself as a result of conflicting forces where there is no way out. (Albert René, quoted in *The People*, 1972–3 and cited in Scarr 1999: 187)

When the Seychelles was granted independence from Britain on 29 June 1976, James Mancham, leader of the Democratic Party and chief minister under the British colonial regime, was appointed 'Executive President'. Albert René, by virtue of his position as leader of the Seychelles People's United Party (the forerunner of the current SPPF) was appointed Prime Minister (Benedict and Benedict 1982: 271). The story of the rivalry between Albert René and James Mancham is the tale of Cold War rhetoric put to work for highly personal political agendas.

Within a year of independence, Mancham was overthrown by forces loyal to Albert René in the coup d'état of 5 June 1977. Mancham was in London at the time, attending a Commonwealth conference in the company of several members of his cabinet. The Constitution and the Legislative Assembly were immediately suspended. René formed a new cabinet of seven ministers, all members of his own political party. A militia was organised, and elections were promised for 1979. The major powers quickly recognised the new government. René consolidated these gains by banning the Democratic Party (DP) and promulgating a new constitution. Elections were held on 5 June 1979, which confirmed the constitution. René was elected to a five-year term as president with a 98 per cent vote. He was also appointed commander-in-chief of the armed forces and leader of the Seychelles People's Progressive Front (SPPF), the only political party (Benedict and Benedict 1982: 272).

René remained president of the Seychelles until April 2004 when he transferred power to James Michel, who had held numerous portfolios in earlier governments. To this day, René remains the acting president of the SPPF. René and President Michel held regular Monday meetings throughout the research period. Among others, the opposition newspaper *Regar* frequently questioned whether René did not in fact continue as the directing mind behind legislation and government policy.

President René as the Father of the Nation

The path to freedom is not paved with gold. It is long, torturous [sic!] and muddy. Some will lack the courage to go on and will turn back. Some will fall by the wayside. But hand in hand, the rest will get to the end and will be crowned with the dignity that all men deserve. (Albert René, 1964, President of the Seychelles from 1977 to 2004 and still current president of the SPPF ruling party; quoted on SPPF website)[8]

France Albert René is a simple man of enormous personal charisma, incorruptible ideals, unfailing generosity, sympathy for others, intelligent, and honourable. In simple term, one brilliant man in our history. (Opening quote of *The People* article dedicated to Albert René in February 2004, just after René transferred the country's presidency to his protégé James Michel)

René has been portrayed in SPPF propaganda as a child that grew up in abject poverty, when in fact he had a relatively privileged upbringing. As manager of an outlying island, his father was not a slave labourer, as the SPPF propaganda would have you believe.... But the propaganda callously exploited the false perception of old poverty images of the 30s and 40s to justify the coup d'état after the event. (Chow, 2004)

René's public posture was to nominally embrace a form of socialism inspired by Castro's Cuba. This required a reinvention of his own past, as his father was a member of the managerial class, and René had followed an educational path exclusively reserved for the *grands blancs*,[9] obtaining a law degree in England, and subsequently joining the exclusive Seychelles Club, considered the principal bastion of *les grands blancs* long before his ascendance in politics.

Official SPPF histories describe how René introduced universal health care, improved housing for the poor, brought in a more equitable system of education and increased social security. The recurrent leitmotif in the president's speeches was party loyalty, also trumpeted in the columns of party newspapers *Nation* and *The People*. Many informants referred obliquely to the reality of this in their daily lives. On occasion informants would nevertheless be more forthcoming in their commentary, as a woman (aged 23) stated: 'You have to know that the Seychelles is about two things: fear and brainwashing.'

Multi-party System

Under international pressure, particularly exerted by former French President François Mitterrand, René allowed multi-party elections for the first time in 1991. The presidential elections were held in September 2001. René was elected with 54.2 per cent. His main rival was Wavel Ramkalawan of the Seychelles National Party (SNP), who scored 44.9 per cent. In December of the following year, elections to the national assembly were held. The national assembly had 34 sitting members, each of whom was elected for a five-year term. Twenty-five members were elected in single-seat constituencies, nine members by proportional representation. The SPPF won 23 seats and the SNP 11. The SPPF received 54.3 per cent of the popular vote, the SNP 42.6 per cent and the Democratic Party (DP) of former president James Mancham picked up the remaining 3.1 per cent (Elections in the Seychelles 2005). At the time of research, the SNP and the DP were the only opposition parties.

After living in exile in England following the 1977 coup d'état, James Mancham returned to the Seychelles on 12 April 1992. The story of Mancham's return is one of the great untold tales of the Seychelles, which dramatically exposed the ambivalence of the deposed president, or, as his campaigners and promoters currently refer to him, 'the apostle of national reconciliation'. Mancham returned to the Seychelles amidst massive expectations that democracy would finally return to the isles. Estimates vary, but between 10,000 and 20,000 people, almost one-third of the population, went to the airport to cheer the 'apostle's' triumphant return.

His return is described in the Library of Congress Country Studies (US Library of Congress 2005) section in the following terms:

> Since 1989, Mancham had mounted what he called a 'fax revolution' from London by sending facsimile messages designed to stir up opposition to the 200 fax machines in Seychelles. His program, entitled the Crusade for Democracy, was intended to restore democracy to Seychelles peacefully. Data transmitted by fax included accounts of human rights violations in Seychelles and charges of corruption of the René regime. René's government made it illegal to circulate a seditious fax in Seychelles, but fax owners eluded this regulation by photocopying the original before turning it in to the police. René then sought to counter the criticism through a Government media campaign, but in so doing he admitted the existence of an opposition in Seychelles. The end result was that he was obliged to give way and allow multi-party democracy to exist.

The same document cryptically refers to the outcome of this conflict in the following sentence: 'René recognized Mancham as official Leader of the Opposition, and Mancham received a salary as a government employee with various perquisites.'

In fact, as many Seychellois tell the story, the 'Crusade for Democracy' came to a grinding halt during one defining conversation between Mancham and René held behind closed doors. What actually occurred during this fateful *tête-à-tête* may never be known. Some speculate that Mancham's jet-set lifestyle and his earlier presiding over a world 'of colossal undercover commissions and underhand deals' (Scarr 1999:185), left him open to blackmail. An informant from his inner circle recounted that he had heard from Mancham himself on the outcome: 'They pay me too much to speak and if I do speak they will kill me.' His platform – not surprisingly – is 'national reconciliation'.

Over time, Wavel Ramkalawan of the SNP emerged as the most viable opposition leader. An Anglican priest, his popularity was largely based on his reputation for moral integrity. The SNP's claim to be the principal opposition party was justified by their electoral results, and the vigorous independence of the *Regar* newspaper. *Regar* is largely directed and written by individual SNP members.

Party membership rolls are not a fair reflection of their broad electoral appeal, a disparity the SNP leadership attribute to the fear ordinary Seychellois harbour of being publicly identified with the opposition. Throughout 2004, they nevertheless anticipated that their silent majority would push them to victory in the next presidential elections of 28 July 2006. As Ramkalawan reasoned during an interview with me: 'We have the moral obligation to win the next elections.' Indeed, both opposition parties were increasingly portraying these elections as a race against time, as stories multiplied of disappearing funds, SPPF party members selling off islands while buying secondary properties in other countries, and while international organisations such as the World Bank expressed their scepticism at the handling of the domestic economy.

On 30 July 2006, another long-awaited moment of change never materialised. James Michel of the SPPF won the Presidential elections with 53.73 per cent of votes (30,119 votes), Wavel Ramkalawan of the SNP supported by the Democratic Party, took 45.71 per cent of votes (25,626 votes) and independent candidate Philippe Boullé 0.56 per cent (314 votes). The SNP labelled the elections as 'Free but not Fair'. During the campaign, SNP militants and faithful were harassed by police. Political rallies were systematically disrupted. The governing party took full advantage of their monopoly of radio and television, and blocked SNP access to the electronic media (cf. SNP document of 16 August 2006, available on their website).

Regar journalists and members of the two opposition parties were disillusioned and exhausted by their uphill battle against government politicking. On the night of 8 December 2005, *Regar*'s presses were the target of an arson attack. Shortly thereafter, the courts ordered *Regar* to pay damages of €52,000 in a libel suit brought by a public official. Roger Mancienne, editor in chief, referred to this ruling and similar cases still pending in the courts as 'judicial harassment'.[10] By the end of October 2006, *Regar* was temporarily forced to suspend both hardcopy and online editions of the paper. The newspaper resumed publication in abbreviated form on 14 April 2007 and is now regularly circulated. However, the online version of the newspaper, which had constituted the gateway to the wider arena of an international public readership, has yet to resume.

COUNTER-NARRATIVES FROM A CAPTIVE AUDIENCE[11]

We resided on the central island of Mahé, seat of the national government, where 90 per cent (*Seychelles General Yearbook 2004*:

16) of all inhabitants (81,200) reside. Mahé is the largest island of the Seychelles, with a surface area of only 15,783.6 hectares. The government is almost literally camped in peoples' backyards. During early research, people displayed considerable reluctance to engage. Through daily interaction, more became amenable to being interviewed, although some preferred clandestine meetings.[12] In later stages of research, informants showed increasing eagerness to relate their own story and how they were affected by the constraints imposed by the government.

Before analysing how the government implemented its discourse in reality, we will give voice to six Seychellois who represented typical strategies employed by people in dealing with their government. These strategies range from compliance with party/government dictates, usually for personal gain, to outright resistance by taking an open stance against government policies, and the entire gamut of attitudes in between these two poles.

The Party Official: The Double-edged Sword

Thomas Leduc (aged 53) lives in a luxurious three-storey condominium development on the East Coast of Mahé with his wife and 23-year-old daughter. Mr Leduc is the owner of the development where he resides and leases or sells units to other occupiers. I entered via the electronic gate, walked around to seaside, where he awaited me. After a brief introduction, he informed me that the interview would be short as he had entered a windsurfing contest. His terrace looks out over two artificial islands. As I enjoyed the view he, unprompted, recounted some of his family history.

> My family came to the Seychelles a long time ago from Brittany, France, and has played a key role in the construction of the country. They arrived in the Seychelles as copra plantation owners and, were also involved in the African slave trade. My father went to school with the brothers, just like René. They were in the same class and good friends. He married my mother who is also from an important Seychellois family.
>
> I went to Seychelles College, finished my A levels in '75. In '76, I went to London, studied at Thames Polytechnic, now known as Greenwich University. I obtained a BSc. in Estate and Property Management. I went on a British Council scholarship. In '79, I returned to the Seychelles, and started my employment with the government as a Lands Officer, with EDPH: Economic Development Planning and Housing. We carried out property

valuations, and the buying and selling of government land. An Englishman ran the department. I succeeded him as Senior Lands Officer in 1984, in charge of the division.

Working for the government and thereby the SPPF became a reality he seemed no longer able to escape:

> In '86, I became the Principal Secretary of Land Planning and Management at the Ministry, which at the time was known as the Ministry of National Development. I was in charge of planning, development, surveying, environment, forestry and landscaping. It was a poisoned gift – no, I am joking, but at the time, in '86, I wanted to leave government, but they said, you must decide. The President announces your appointment tonight.

He places considerable stock in his own status as a public official in the Seychelles:

> Put it this way. If there's a land transaction of any kind in this country, I am notified about it. That's not in the law. I am the one who decides that. I deal with matters such as sale of land to non-Seychellois.

'Look out on the water', he said, pointing at the newly created islands in view. 'Look at this', he repeated, gesturing at the condominium development. 'I created this. God created land, but man, well, man can create it too. Excuse me, I have to leave for my windsurfing competition.'

Party loyalty has offered Thomas Leduc access to tertiary education and economic security. On the surface, his position is certainly privileged. The condition for that privilege is the demand for permanent party loyalty. Many party members related, or hinted at, their fear of expressing dissident opinions, as they knew this brought with it the risk of losing their status and wealth, and, in extreme cases, the risk of exile from the Seychelles. Tales of people who fell into disgrace with the party and were banished from the archipelago are numerous (see below, the ex-husband of Ms Joely). Once committed to the party, members would much rather follow prevailing winds, notwithstanding their privately held opinions, a view Thomas Leduc also shared.

The Dissident Journalist: Defying the Powers that Be

Jean Leduc is the brother of Thomas Leduc. He has followed a different path from his brother. Jean is a journalist with the opposition newspaper *Regar*. He is divorced and devotes his time to his work. I met him at a bistro in the docks area. During our interview, he detailed the range of challenges faced every day by *Regar* journalists due to lack of financing, and government and SPPF intimidation and lawsuits.

> We knew from the outset that we would have to push the limits and challenge the status quo to determine our freedom. The government constantly invades people's privacy. We nevertheless like to be as hard-hitting as possible on government policy. That is, we examine the behaviour of leaders but not their private lives.

Then he went on to explain:

> Lawsuits filed by the government, the ministers, have been very problematic for us. These people are very sensitive on the issue of transactions involving government property. Almost all the lawsuits concern articles we've written on land transactions implicating government officials and misappropriation of funds, dubious tender processes and the like. On political crimes, we're wiping the slate clean. But, we are careful about what we write. Our rule of thumb: anything controversial is vetted by our lawyer.

He related an anecdote on this type of problem:

> The government created a children's fund, but in fact were seeking a device to raise taxes. The children's fund allowed them to levy SR 1.50 per bottle of beer sold. But, the accounting is not clear, the money is commingled with general tax revenues. The question of double accounting was raised in an issue of *Regar*. Soon after we were sued for 3 million rupees.

Getting access to information is difficult, particularly where it concerns government documents:

> For sources, we rely on readers, government leaks we judge credible. A lot of people feed stuff. Our own people call a lot, the SNPers. We know them but they often do not like to be

identified as such, as this might be dangerous for them and hinder their personal and professional lives. Many people write letters to the editor: we have to know who the person is, but they can remain anonymous. It's the fear that is still there. On staff, we have myself, Jean-François, two journalists and a photographer. Both Jean- François and myself wrote for underground papers. Before liberalisation, we applied for a newspaper licence. It was initially refused, then granted subject to payment of a 1 million SR [Seychelles rupees]. Which amounts to the same thing. Finally, in 1991, we were granted a licence. We started out with a wish to be 'objective'. But, people wanted politics. So, we then hung out our shingle as an 'opposition' paper. The SNP has its own paper, the *Nouvelle Visyon*. When asked to describe ourselves, we say we are the only paper which is independent of State funds.

A deeply committed and private man, Jean Leduc preferred to steer the discussion towards public issues, particularly contemporary politics:

The SNP has a large youth support. So, the SPPF has transformed this into a political issue, and are doing top-down strategies, youth parliament, and other Government-sponsored initiatives. It's a form of manipulation. Many youngsters are unemployed. Yet, there are jobs that people refuse to take. Here's an example: the American Tuna plant, the Heinz factory. Two thousand jobs. But, half are held by foreigners. The basic problem is the wages they pay for tough factory work. Seychellois are not willing to do it. The government statistics only register the top of the iceberg where unemployment is concerned. There is no listing of people who are marginally employed. Attitudes are a problem here. The first thing you have to do in life is work, your responsibility is to yourself and your family. But too many Seychellois are dependent on soft jobs and welfare. They only think of themselves.

Towards the end of the interview, he addressed the issue of his personal security:

I was sent to prison during the one-party state for no reason at all. Told to leave the country, but I refused. I founded *Regar*. I was very bitter, but no more. I have told René everything I wanted through the paper. You might find a reticence of people to answer questions. It's a residue of fear from the time when things were used against people, and things can still happen. I am not afraid. I would like the luxury of writing the real history of this country. After all, journalism is the rough draft of history, isn't it?

Jean Leduc's narrative represents stories of Seychellois who have come out openly against the regime and have devoted their lives to unmasking the discourse of the government. They feel that they have no other choice than to take enormous personal risks. They have not wavered in their commitment, despite their limited material wealth and the ongoing physical intimidation by the state, which in some cases has meant serving time in prison. They are driven by a belief in their duty to critically monitor the government. This resolve and passion is crucial to their existential well-being. As many phrased it: 'I have no choice, I have the moral obligation to do this.'

A Grandmother Born into Poverty: The Currency of Exchange

Mrs Fanriry (aged 72) also wanted to talk about the history of the Seychelles, and she did so by describing her fate. The interview took place on a small veranda of her ramshackle house. She comes from a family of 13. Her mother had very little education and worked as a maid. She described her father as someone who always went with other women and someone who did not look after his children: 'The poverty of our family was enormous.' Finally, they were offered housing at a project initiated by the colonial British government of the time. Her mother worked as a maid for a British family and Mrs Fanriry also joined the workforce at a young age: 'I did whatever work came up.'

Mrs Fanriry was reluctant to discuss her family history in great detail:

I have heard about slavery and I know that some of my family members come from Madagascar. But President Albert René told us that we should forget about slavery, we are all the same here in the Seychelles. We are all Seychellois and I am proud to be Seychellois. Who cares what happened before? We live now. So I agree with that point of the president and probably not with many others. But let's go back to when I was a little girl.'

She explained that she was 15 when her mother and the children left the British family to go and live near the capital Victoria:

That was a ghetto area, meant for poor people like us. I married there, had two children. My husband left just like many other men after him. In total, I had ten children with I cannot remember how many different men. That was not my fault, as they decided to disappear. I was very poor but still I think that the colonial times were much better than how we live now. There were so many fruits and vegetables that you were never hungry and people always shared things with each other. For example meat was distributed, people helped each other. After the colonial period this changed dramatically, everything had a money value, exchange was no longer the case. Now you need money for everything. Friendly exchange made place for trading. Now all people can think about is *forex*.[13] I saw society changing and money affecting the minds of the youngsters. There is no respect, not for family, parents, elders or anybody for that matter. All people can think about is themselves. That makes me very sad. I blame politics for this but cannot speak about that. I have said enough. I think you get my point.

Elderly people commonly recounted their memories of 'a better time', and a subsequent period of hardship. Women like Mrs. Fanriry, have known extreme poverty and fear the loss of benefits provided by the socialist republic. Conscious that security comes at a price, she quickly reined in any casual criticism which emerged in the conversation. This caution was common among Seychellois, even more so the older generation. Silence, it would appear, was the exchange currency for the material and social benefits that were offered to them.

The Teacher: Trumpeting the Party Line

Mrs Trudy Bloty was born in 1941. I spoke to her at the primary school where she works. She had ten brothers and sisters, most of whom are teachers. Three of her sisters live abroad, just like her eldest daughter who married somebody from the US, while he was working at the US tracking station in the Seychelles: 'Many of those men married a Seychellois. She has a very good life there, very different from when I grew up. We were very, very poor. Maybe at the end of the month we would taste butter or cheese.' Her mother stayed at home with the children and her father was a sailor. 'My mother told me it was important to learn. But my parents did not have the money to send me to school. I was lucky that my uncle, who was a policeman, saw that I was bright and he financed my schooling.'

> After secondary school, I worked one year as a teacher's assistant and then went to the training college for one year so I could become a teacher. I was 20 when I finished all that and as I walked out of the school I literally fell in the arms of my future husband. He worked as a policeman.

They got married and she had her first child:

> It was a real ordeal for me when my daughter was born as I had to keep on working as a teacher. My husband did not help me at all. He considered it my job to take care of the baby. Sometimes I would spend the whole night with her and then go to work tired.

Eventually, her mother said that she should bring the baby to her during the week:

> I cried and cried as I missed my baby so much. It was the only solution though. Every Friday was a feast day as I could pick up my baby. In the six years that followed, I had two sons.

Her career as a teacher remained important to her:

> Teaching is very important. I want to help children to learn. President René made sure that all the children in the country can go to school for free. That is very important, I am all in favour of his aims and will always support him. I go on SPPF rallies almost every weekend. Well, I go off track. I wanted to tell you that he gave me the opportunity for further training in Russia. I was so happy about that and went. But after three weeks, I received a telegram from my husband saying: 'Accident, come home.' Well, I was so worried, I feared for the lives of my children. Needless to say I went home. At the airport, I found my husband and children in splendid health, smiling and happy to see me.

Her husband had sabotaged the trip as he could not manage with the children. 'Later Mr Michel, he is now the president said to me: "You were stupid not to finish your training. You could have been a person of importance."' She thought that she could have been a minister:

Yes, I think that could have been the case, I have done so much for the party. Now I do my work at the school where I teach the children about our beautiful country and everything our leaders do for us. I am proud to be Seychellois and to contribute to the future of our nation and the wonderful life president René has prepared for us.

Mrs Bloty's party loyalty has brought benefits, but is also anchored in her sincere belief in the 'good life' that government policies bring the Seychellois. She is one of the party faithful, committed to propagation of the party line. Teachers count among their ranks numerous party members and activists. It was implied during interviews that party membership was a prerequisite for employment in the education field.

The Emigrant: Paradise Lost

Ms Irene Joely was born in 1959. She viewed this 'wonderful life' quite differently. When I met her, she first related that her mother died soon after she was born: 'I cannot remember my mother's face but I do remember her beautiful long blonde hair.' Her father was in the army and had no time to take care of his daughter. She was lodged with her grandmother: 'My grandmother did not really want me either. I was a real burden to her. I had asthma and missed school all the time. I stopped going to school altogether when I was in grade three.' She regretted dropping out of school:

> I am stupid and never learned anything. Since I left school I have been making clothes and embroidery to make a living. This is quite hard as many women try to survive this way. I think that the fact that I did not learn anything got me into real trouble. My grandmother was very strict with me. I wanted to select my own husband but she refused all potential suitors. Then she came with somebody. I did not like him at all. She said he would be a good husband because he was a friend of Mr René. I was ignorant and felt I had to accept, as my grandmother was trying to get rid of me.

She married when she was 15, and gave birth the following year:

> By that time, I had learned to respect my husband and I liked him. That was also the time when I discovered that he had another girlfriend who also had a child with him. Life became very hard. I

could not leave him as at the time René had just become president. My husband was very close to him and therefore very powerful. I was so afraid something would happen to me if I would complain or, worse, leave. He made me very lonely and whereas before my grandmother could stay overnight at our house, he later refused this. I saw nobody and could only leave the house to go to market. I spent my time thinking about all those nice men I once wanted to marry, those that grandmother refused.

Ms Joely had four other children with her husband: 'Two of my children died of fever. A boy at two and a half and a girl at the age of five. And I also lost a baby when I was pregnant.'
Her face saddened as she continued:

The day of the coup d'état, I was in the garden of our house near Victoria. I found the sky above Victoria looking so dark. I asked our neighbour, who had also come out, whether she saw it as well. She said that the sun was shining brightly. I could not see that. I saw a sadness in the sky. The next day, my brother was arrested for no reason. I had no time to worry about that. I had to go to the hospital because I lost blood. A nurse told me about the coup d'état. That was the day that I lost my baby. The rest I cannot tell you, it is too secret.

Her life took another turn when she was almost 30:

I met this Spanish woman at the market and she asked whether I would be interested in working for her family in Spain. I quickly accepted, packed my bag that same night and went to her house here. The children I sent to my grandmother, I promised them that I would come back with lots of money. For a few weeks I stayed with her and then I left for Spain. I had written to my husband to say that I wanted a divorce. The funny thing was that he visited my grandmother right away to say that he accepted the divorce and could not care less about me. Why had I waited all those miserable years? Just because I was afraid.

Ms Joely remained in Spain for almost ten years and did not see her children all this time:

I was what they call a modern slave. I worked day and night with that family. They gave me very little money and treated me badly. You know, I did not even mind, I was used to that. When I developed a terrible back problem the people wanted to get rid of me. They paid for my return ticket and gave me some money. Now I am back and live in a small house, all by myself. I am fine with that. My goal now is to help my children to go to Spain. It is so much better there. There is no SPPF, lots of food, everybody can find a job there and be a happy person. Even my former husband found out about that. You see, he followed me to Spain when he had a fight with René. He met somebody there and had seven children with this lady. So you see, I was right after all. Leaving the Seychelles is the best choice one can make.

Most Seychellois entertained the dream of leaving the country, and part of that dream was conditioned by the desperate quest for *forex*. Ms Joely endured significant hardship abroad but considered this a petty price to pay for the material benefits and freedoms it brought her, and particularly for the broader opportunities it opened up for her children. Any prospect of long-term separation from loved ones was viewed as a necessary investment in their future.

The Young Single Mother: Making Ends Meet

Leaving the Seychelles is also Sylvia's (aged 28) ambition. When I spoke to her, we were both visiting the public beach at Beau Vallon. She discreetly approached me, as she had done during our earlier meetings:

> I am so upset. My brother was arrested on Friday. He is a taxi driver. He was held in custody until twelve the next morning. I went down to the police station to complain as they did not have an arrest warrant. The police mentioned that no warrant was required as he was on a list of criminals. But how ever did he get on the list? They said he drove a burglar to his job. My brother does not know anything about this. They released him but said they will revoke his taxi licence. It is crazy here. The police can pick you up at any time, over anything. They can do whatever they want.

Sylvia is a single mother, who lives with her two children, a girl of 12 and a boy of 9. Sylvia's biological mother lives in France where she remarried. When she left the Seychelles to join her husband, she brought the two elder children (a boy and a girl) with her, left her son with his father in the Seychelles and gave Sylvia up for adoption.

She was only one and a half at the time. The adoptive parents had no other children. Soon after she was adopted, her foster mother died. She recalls her childhood as miserable as her adopted father could not make ends meet.

She struggles under financial hardship. In her own words, Sylvia's own marriage failed miserably. Her former husband is unemployed and makes no support payments. This doesn't prevent him from having several girlfriends and fathering more children, a source of frustration:

> These children seem better dressed then mine. Well anyway, men are just hopeless. They spend their money on drink and expect their women to take care of them. Not for me. I am out of that deal now. I can manage much better by myself.

> The reality though is that many women work two to three jobs at once and are away from their children and are too tired to take care of them when they return. Do not think also that these are legal jobs; look at me, for example, I work in a bar from 4 p.m. to 4 a.m. I see a guy now and then, he complains about this job. Well too bad, he cannot tell me what to do. The little money I make there, I basically depend on the tips, is quickly spent. My kids go to the free government schools, which are not very good but offer food at noon. My son is sick all the time and the doctor told me that he should stop eating the canteen food but I simply do not have the money to do that. Big expenses for, for example, a washing machine or a cooking pan are out of the question. And you know what is most irritating? I still have contact with my real mother and she told me all these things are even cheaper in France. Import taxes are usually above 40 per cent. You wonder why food and everything else has to be so expensive here. But we are not supposed to ask questions about this. The government does not appreciate that. As you know, we live in paradise.

She smiled. 'My aim is to get out of this country. All young people want to leave the Seychelles and even the older ones. I hate it here. I want to go to France.'

Sylvia's story is typical of many single mothers. They are juggling numerous duties, with little support from the fathers of their children. Any income is quickly depleted by the exorbitant prices charged for staple foods and commodities that the government-controlled shops offer.

FREEDOM FROM FEAR

The above cases document strategies that Seychellois employ to carve out a life for themselves. Although these cases represent types of reactions Seychellois might employ, they nevertheless remain individual tales and experiences. Claiming voice is far from an established Seychellois custom. Self-censorship is notable in the stories. Most people who disagree with the institutions in power veil their dissent and express this in terms of joking, inversion and irony, a tactical arsenal which evokes the forms so eloquently described by James Scott (1985) in *Weapons of the Weak: Everyday Forms of Peasant Resistance.*

The government's presence is felt in virtually every aspect of the lives of the Seychellois since the 1977 coup d'état. This is justified by an overt policy of repressing 'conflicting forces' to 'prevent a situation where violence will come' (see above, p. 211), as party leader René put it during one of his early speeches. The above narratives demonstrate that some indeed gave lip service to the party line. Others display considerable courage in denouncing violations of fundamental human rights. Indeed, the government defines 'freedom from violence and disorder' as a situation where individual freedoms are conditional upon discursive and actual behaviour of a docile citizenry unquestioningly bending to the state's view of the nation. The military and police have a free hand in ensuring compliance with party dictates under the guise of the security discourse. Interviewees expressed openly at times, but more often by implication, a very real apprehension of the forces of order. Regular police are underfunded – and hence forced to work with the army on issues of internal security. The ad hoc implementation of law enforcement only serves to heighten the ordinary citizen's fear of the arbitrary (see the case of Sylvia's brother). A good example of this occurred during the crime wave which swept Mahé during May 2004 in the wake of James Michel's appointment as president. After a series of home invasions and random acts of violence, an infuriated President Michel made an impromptu national television address vowing that the perpetrators would be tracked down. The army was swiftly ordered to assume control over the police matters.

The Constitution prohibits torture, but reports of beatings by security forces are not uncommon. During 2004, the Supreme Court reported eight cases of police brutality, all of which were pending at year's end. *Habeas Corpus* is guaranteed by the Constitution, which in the normal course means that arrested persons must be brought before a magistrate within 24 hours, but police are rumoured to time their arrests to coincide with the weekend to maximise the time of detention (cf. U.S. Department of State Bureau of Democracy, Human rights and Labor 2004). Sylvia (see above), and other interviewees reported that the police and judiciary work in obscure ways which they found unpredictable and intimidating.

The Constitution guarantees an independent judiciary. The judiciary, however, is chronically inefficient and plagued by executive interference. The judicial system officially includes magistrates' courts (or small-claims court), the Supreme (or trial) Court, the Constitutional Court and the Court of Appeal, all of which are understaffed and underfunded. In 2004, the Chief Justice was a naturalised citizen. Only one other judge was a Seychelles native; the remaining members of the bench were recruited from other Commonwealth countries, including Mauritius, India, Sri Lanka, Nigeria and Zambia.

The separation between the legislative and judicial powers is often unclear. The lack of local expertise or access to laws (even by the police), arbitrary treatment of suspects, resentment of foreign judges, the use of the judiciary as a weapon to quell free speech, all undermine public trust in the judiciary and police as effective guarantors of civic freedom. The government-backed media, meanwhile, defend controls as the price for a 'safe' country, the *sine qua non* for a tourist paradise, crucial to the economic survival of the Seychellois, and ultimately guarantor of the food security of its citizens.

FREEDOM FROM WANT

> Ever since its formation in 1985, SMB's [Seychelles Marketing Board] role has been to ensure a steady flow of essential commodities at stable prices to the end customer. Today, as the single largest business in Seychelles and a major employer, SMB continues to play a significant role as a manufacturer, importer, exporter, retailer and employment generator in this small island economy. (Seychelles Marketing Board official website)

The reality, despite the SMB claim that it provides food security, is that life in the Seychelles is expensive for everyone, but particularly for the average Seychellois trying to get by on less than €400 per month. By African standards, an average income of €400 per month might appear luxurious, but spending power is quickly depleted by the high prices of staple goods. Food shortages, even of staple products, are a fact of life, because the bottleneck the SMB places on the import system through high tariffs and its monopoly all but eliminates healthy competition. The SMB enjoys vast monopoly powers, in addition to accessory privileges that go well beyond its statutory mandate. For example, prior to granting any licence to a person or company wishing to engage in trade, the Licensing Authority is required to refer licence applications to the Seychelles Marketing Board for pre-vetting and approval. In practice, after receiving an application for a business licence the SMB often elects to go into the proposed line of business itself.

In his former portfolio as Minister of Finance, President James Michel exempted the SMB from price control regulations. *Regar*, the opposition newspaper, described the effect of this decision as follows: 'The SMB exemption from price control regulations is the root cause of the high prices for basic goods, which have made the cost of living for ordinary Seychellois painfully high' (25 June 2004). Indeed, statistics (Seychelles Chamber of Commerce and Industry [SCCI] July 2000) bear out the extent to which overcharging by the SMB was practised on a large number of essential items: 257 per cent on potatoes, 193 per cent on onions, 114 per cent on rice, 263 per cent on apples and 322 per cent on beef.[14] Any customer entering the principal SMB outlet in Victoria would first be struck by the presence of armed guards, before noticing the rundown condition of the flagship supermarket, stacked floor to ceiling with Heinz baked beans, Heinz tuna, generic cereal boxes of indeterminate origin, and a drab inventory which conjures up images of consumer life in former Soviet satellite republics.

In order to create the conditions for the SMB to operate, the government virtually suffocates free trade.[15] Stringent legislation governing foreign exchange, negotiation of letters of credit or granting of import licences force the private sector virtually to abandon direct overseas trade. The impact is felt by the ordinary population (for example Sylvia, above, suffered directly from SMB policies of overpricing), and as a result, in the minds of the population the SMB is much more oppressive in their daily life than the army or militia.

Foreign Exchange

The government's recurrent theme that foreign tourists are crucial to achieving food security is not lost on the Seychellois. The scarcity of foreign exchange (*forex*), whatever its actual underlying causes, reinforces a reluctance to entertain ideas of upsetting the status quo. Many informants referred to the *forex* issue unprompted (see Mrs Fanriry). As a woman informant phrased it: 'Before we had very little but we felt we lived in paradise, now *forex* is paradise.'

Forex generally is obtained in three ways: through tourism, working abroad and/or the black-market. Economists speak of a critical threshold of government intervention and heavy-handedness beyond which a black market is created. Seychelles has a complex black market, and *forex* is at its nexus. During the research period, the offer to exchange for *forex* came daily, in the street, from drivers, and particularly in beach areas and access roads within proximity. However, the safest way to trade was through private contacts (or through merchants who performed the service as a 'favour'), or even directly through public officials who ran side operations from the relative safety of their offices. Not even the elite, it appears, can avoid this central *forex* problem. *Forex* is the portal to the outside world, not only in terms of acquiring material goods or gaining an advantage on local markets, but crucially, towards a freedom of movement and ideas denied to the average citizen.

How foreign exchange has become symptomatic of much of what afflicts the Seychelles, is a complex issue rooted in the history of the Republic, particularly the period when President James Michel was incumbent Finance Minister. A study conducted by staff of the World Bank-linked Foreign Investment Advisory Service (FIAS) in 2005 concluded that the arbitrary manner in which concessions are awarded, as well as foreign exchange deficiencies, are the principal barriers to attracting investment. FIAS leader Marc Reichel summarised the problem as follows: 'Foreign exchange constraints and the discretionary approach have a negative effect on the business environment.' The FIAS concluded: 'If you want to survive as a business you have to find your way around the laws.' FIAS team member Charles Krakoff was even more candid: 'if all laws and taxes were complied with very few businesses could survive' (World Bank Group 2005).

Tourism generated 60 per cent of *forex* in 1994, but by 2004 tourism had already moved into inexorable decline, as both tourists and operators discovered that neighbouring Mauritius and La Réunion gave far better value for money. The Seychelles had become tourism-dependent, but benign neglect and milking of their principal resource inevitably created a credibility deficit.[16] In 2004, the newspapers regularly reported downsizing of staff, or outright closures, ostensibly for renovations.

Security of employment is tenuous for inactive party members or non-members. The Ministry of Defence requires security clearances for employees seeking work in a broad range of fields, and exercises further control through defence reviews of licensing. The net effect of any defence veto is exclusion from the economic mainstream and arbitrary revocation of privilege in the case of licence holders (see the story of Sylvia's brother). Observers and informants commonly spoke of a 'black list' of those who dare criticise the government. During one family conversation, an aunt remarked to her niece: 'Oh, I know about the problems of your father. He will not find a job, he is on the black list.'

The Seychellois Nation – Where Comradeship Should Be the Guiding Principle

Man is a social animal and it is because of the natural tendency of everyone to live in a well-organised, well planned and equitable Society that the Party will strive to create that society, where our People will in common enjoy the necessities, if not luxuries, that human dignity demands – proper housing – adequate sanitation – sound education – good health and a decent standard of living. (Seychelles People's United Party Policy Statement prior to independence, on SPPF website)

Soon after he seized power from Mancham, René implemented his envisaged socialist system, and his reforms are offered to the public as proof of security. Currently, 91.8 per cent of all people above the age of 15 in the Seychelles are literate (World Bank 2005). By African or even European standards, this is an impressive statistic. For those who can afford it, children attend private schools which have been created over the last ten years, designed for pupils intending to pursue higher education abroad. The Seychelles has one polytechnic school and no university. The government offers grants to top students, principally to go to Cuba.

Education curricula during the research period were prepared by the SPPF. Teachers whom we interviewed were active SPPF members (see the case of Ms Trudy Bloty). Curricula include the 'official history of the Seychelles', which necessarily contains an official biography of Albert René. Until 1993, post-secondary students were forced to enrol in re-education camps (National Youth Service, NYS), and were often relocated to the outer islands. The two-year national service involved (para)military training and political indoc-trination. Youths were cut off from their families and indoctrinated in the teachings of Marx and Engels by Russian, Cuban and Angolan tutors. Pupils had to call each other comrade and were groomed to become loyal SPPF party members. In 1990, the NYS service was cut back to one year. In 1993, the NYS became voluntary and was finally abolished in 1998. Several informants mentioned that although the NYS was by then abolished, they still suffered trauma, stress and nightmares from the experience.

Health care in the Seychelles is nominally free, but public hospitals are sorely lacking in equipment and facilities. The privileged prefer private clinics for their medical and dental care, or leave the country altogether for treatment in Mauritius, South Africa and Europe.

Affordable housing remains beyond the reach of many Seychellois. The government experiences chronic difficulties in financing the building projects it has promised the population. Delays in governmental housing projects are the rule. These delays are frequently triggered by shortages of materials, which in turn is blamed on a lack of *forex*.

Thus, despite the dependence on tourists for foreign exchange, the government is relatively successful in securing minimal food sufficiency in the Seychelles. Individuals measure their relative privilege by comparing their condition favourably to that of the African continent. They nevertheless complain about the exorbitant prices for food staples, the high taxes and the lack of choice (see Sylvia's story). Seychellois value the government housing projects, free education and health care system, but claim that the demand for housing exceeds supply, or that public housing is of poor quality. Security of education and a professional life are compromised by the fact that mandatory obedience to socialist tenets of the party is the prerequisite for actually getting a job. Finally, on the issue of health security, people complain that doctors are poorly equipped to provide a decent standard of care. In the end, few trust the capacity of the public health system to deliver quality care.

CURTAILING DISCURSIVE EXPRESSION OF RESISTANCE

As Benedict observed over 30 years ago, Seychelles is indeed a fragmented society. When René carried out the coup d'état in 1977, he had a free hand to create a nation based on his socialist ideals. He has certainly been very successful in instilling the idea of the Seychellois nation, as informants frequently expressed their pride in being Seychellois. The socialist ideals are far from coincidental, having been imposed through the indoctrination camps that remained in existence until 1998. Nowadays, informants commonly utter the mantra that the Seychelles is paradise where everybody is equal and enjoys the benefits of its socialist leadership. Over time and with familiarity, however, criticism and a certain benign contempt crept into their discourse.

During the late 1970s and 1980s, then President René designated the nation as the primary societal reference. The historical narrative of René and the history of the Seychelles were tools used to advance the party's ideological agenda. It is noteworthy that many informants studiously avoided the topic of slavery, a decisive chapter in Seychellois history. References to slavery have largely disappeared in favour of a government discourse which better fits the theme of an egalitarian society, and which was commonly echoed by informants. These historical narratives are created and invoked in order to evoke the notion of national community. The tactics referred to in the work by Charles Keyes (2002) or Liisa Malkki (1995) as discursively policing the boundaries and disciplining the population have been put to good use by the SPPF. It is perhaps its greatest achievement.

Notwithstanding the socialist ideals and rhetoric, during 2004 (coinciding with our arrival in the Seychelles), the spectre of rising crime, child abuse and domestic abuse triggered the launch of a campaign promoting family values (US Department of State, Bureau of Democracy, Human rights and Labor 2004, cf. speech of René February 2004, SPPF website).[17] National radio, television and the newspapers *Nation* and *The People* were filled with images of the traditional family. The year 2004 was to be one of 'Moral Renaissance', celebrating the family as the cornerstone of society. Depending on one's point of view, the campaign was either justified or belied by the fact that most Seychellois have been reared outside the traditional family unit. Benedict and Benedict (1982: 221) report that already in 1976, 56 per cent of the children were registered as 'illegitimate children'. In 2003, this percentage had increased to 76 per cent (see US Department of State, Bureau of Democracy, Human Rights and Labor 2004). A study of the Management and Information Systems Division (2003: 10) further shows that of the 1481 children who were born in the Seychelles in 2002, 364 were born in wedlock and 1117 out of wedlock. Women assist each other in caring for their children. On Sundays they go with their children and female friends to the beach, or attend church. According to our interviews (see Sylvia), fathers play a minor role in the rearing of their children or providing for them. The men circulate in groups, largely keeping to their own company, drinking and playing dominos.

Women often worked at several jobs to make ends meet. In the life histories of women, relationships with men were described as fleeting and unsatisfactory. Janine, 31 years of age, expressed a typical opinion: 'The men here in the Seychelles are good for nothing. All they can do is drink.' Alcoholism is endemic, public drunkenness a common occurrence, and blamed for many of the island's chronic ills. It is viewed as an illness that principally affects men but in fact, in the 1990s consumption by women was on the increase, mostly of home-brewed drink. Twenty-two per cent of the household budget went on alcohol; 33 per cent of male admissions to medical wards and 38 per cent of all admissions to psychiatric wards were alcohol-related (Perdrix et al. 1999).

Existential Security: Fear, Brainwashing and the State's Monopoly on Seychellois History and Culture

There is still a climate of fear prevailing in this country. (*Nouveau Seychelles Weekly* 9 July 2004)

Even in this day and age, when historical truths cannot be suppressed through intimidation and coercion, the SPPF wishes to continue to deny the people of Seychelles their history. (*Nouveau Seychelles Weekly* 27 August 2004)

People gather in a variety of ways, some of which point to a form of community building at the grassroots level (under the long shadow of the Seychellois government's omnipresence as *pater familias*).[18] Meetings of the SPPF party bear the hallmarks of a community: shared ideological framework, boundary marking, insider-outsider configurations, processes of signification based on socialist ideals and symbolic expressions of identifying membership (cf. Cohen 1985). But these meetings are largely orchestrated and ideologically fuelled from the top down. To a lesser extent, other social gatherings at the grassroots level, such as the beach gatherings, contain elements of community building.

Most people interviewed insisted, however, that these were weak bonds. Many were not hesitant to express distrust of acquaintances and family members. The SPPF successfully implements a 'divide and rule' strategy of 'fear and brainwashing' (as one informant put it) that creates a captive audience. Deviations from the party line and from ideal forms of behaviour are punished publicly (lawsuits, imprisonment of dissidents) and, more often, in the backrooms and corridors (arbitrary licensing legislation, blacklists and revocation of licences and permits, requirement of party membership for employment). Finally, no discussion of interference with freedoms is complete without mention of the Copyright Act.

The legal underpinnings for many restrictions on freedom of speech or criticism are contained in the Copyright Act. Pursuant to section 7 of the Act, the government purports to own Seychellois culture or folklore which is vested 'in the Republic' (Copyright Act, section 7). The notion of 'folklore' includes 'all ancient literary, musical or artistic works created in Seychelles, passed from generation to generation and constituting a basic element of the cultural heritage of the Seychelles'. Folklore also encompasses oral history (section 4-1b) and subsists 'without limitation to time'. Section 7(4), which prohibits the assignment of copyright in folklore, effectively meant that the Seychellois had no right to publish their own version of Seychellois history, which would make the grand project of the *Regar* journalist quoted above illusory, unless he submitted his work for pre-vetting by the Republic. The penalty for non-compliance with this provision is 'imprisonment for 5 years and to a fine of R30,000' (section 21-6). Under section 21, the state has a sovereign and unfettered discretion to determine what constitutes a copyright violation. It would also appear that any publication dealing with Seychellois folklore, i.e. its history, risks being deemed an infringement of copyright under the Act. A perhaps unintended, but additional effect of this law would allow the state, under the reversion/escheat provision to claim family letters, love letters and other family documents.

Finally, no matter which side of the ideological divide they stand, every Seychellois is governed by another reality – that of being a geographical speck on the ocean at the midpoint between Nairobi and Mumbai – a full four hours by plane to either destination. Perhaps it is this reality which explains some of the surprising accommodations one witnessed between informants and the government in the day-to-day affairs. Seychellois must constantly deal with the contradictory policies of their government within the reality of their isolation. The national administration wallows in corruption, while promoting morality and family values. Ideologically speaking, the government is locked into a time-space warp, spouting the lexicon of Castro's Cuba, while parachuting tourists into five-star enclaves.

Opposition politicians and newspapers are bullied, but allowed to operate.

The SPPF version of history conditions the school curricula. Liberation day (the date of the coup d'état) is a day of national celebration, deposed former president Mancham continues to collect his salary, and everyone, from former President René right down to the bakery workers, devotes considerable time and energy trying to devise how to get more *forex*, and, if the option is available, how to leave the country entirely. So whereas the horrors of oppression were few in the Seychelles, the government continues to have a stranglehold on the lives of the Seychellois by monitoring social relations and manipulating processes of signification.

CONCLUSION

In terms of human security, the government employs a state-centred approach while assuming a posture as *pater familias*.[19] It instils security concepts to build a nation of comrades by promising physical and social security (free education and health care), food security and even identity security according to the socialist model.

The benefits of 'security' offered by the government prove to be a divisive factor in the Seychelles. Those who adhere to and actively promote party dictates can expect some reward, principally in terms of 'freedom from want'. But it would be misleading to equate this with security as perks and benefits are conditional upon past and future services. People feel policed by the party to the point of censoring themselves, and proving their party loyalty by attendance at party rallies. Some accounts of informing on fellow citizens were reported to us. People who openly disagree with the ruling regime know – but accept – precarity as a fact of life. Their solace lies in the dream of a better Seychelles. Indeed, it might be said that all Seychellois have to devise their own balance between voicing their opinions and taking the risk of provoking state displeasure.

Seychellois who perceive their personal freedoms as suffering infringement, and/or who fall out of grace with the ruling party, express the strongest fears of the 'Big Brother' structures of the state. As stated above, their sense of insecurity and distrust regarding the government extend as far as their fellow citizens. The 'divide-and-rule' politics of the government create a cleavage in the Seychellois nation where one is either 'for' or 'against' the government, and this central reality is internalised by all Seychellois. This Manichean world view naturally propels the government towards devoting disproportionate energy and resources to entrenching its own security (social stability, curtailing 'dangerous' criticism), thus making sure that people are 'for' the ruling party at the expense of citizens' quest for autonomy in determining the sources they deem relevant for their freedom from fear, freedom from want and existential security.

NOTES

1. I wish to acknowledge the invaluable editorial reviews of Thomas Hylland Eriksen, Ellen Bal and Oscar Salemink.
2. During the fieldwork, I was accompanied by my husband and 10-month-old son.
3. This phrase was belied by the shotgun execution of SDP (Social Democratic Party) activist Davidson Chang Him on the police station steps during the coup, the later liquidation of another prominent SDP member, Indian merchant Hassan Ali, and the assassination of Gérard Hoarau, leader of the Seychellois Nationalist Movement, in Middlesex, England, both of whom were suspected of counter-coup activities.
4. James R. Mancham was the first president of the Seychelles after independence. He had not even been in power for a year when Albert René orchestrated the coup.
5. Although an important element of human security, environmental security is beyond the scope of this article on the Seychelles.
6. Most Seychellois are Catholic (89 per cent). Other religions are Anglicanism (6 per cent), Hinduism (2 per cent) and Islam (3 per cent). But these are minorities. Party leaders adhere to the Bahai faith. The adherence of SPPF loyalists to Bahai and their regular attendance at these meetings would appear to indicate that its role is, in addition to being religious, possibly social and political. A deeper analysis of the role of religion will be made in a forthcoming publication.
7. Even though there was little or no information found in the archives that could compromise the SPPF party, I was nevertheless summoned by the Director of the Archives to give back photocopies I tried to make from a children's book in Creole!
8. See: http://www.sppf.sc.=/lepep/index.php?option=com_content&view=articl e&id=138&Itemid=127
9. The *grands blancs* comprised a category of European settlers and/or plantation owners.
10. See: http://www.rsf.org/L-hebdomadaire-d-opposition-Regar.html
11. All names and ages of the informants are fictitious. The cases are excerpts from conversations with informants taken from the fieldwork diary. It should be stressed that all informants granted their explicit permission for publication of their interviews both before and after the meeting took place.
12. An article on the challenges of doing fieldwork in the Seychelles is forthcoming.
13. *Forex* stands for foreign exchange, which plays an inordinately large role in the lives of even ordinary Seychellois, as will be explained in the section 'Freedom from Want'.

14. When shopping in the main supermarket of the SMB in Victoria (the capital), I witnessed physical fights over potatoes and onions which had been out of stock for several weeks. What was offered, however, was of extraordinarily poor quality as people discovered afterwards that most of their take was in fact rotten.
15. See Ellis (1996) on international corruption in the Seychelles.
16. Most tourists are immediately shipped out from the International Airport of Mahé to other islands, where they stay in resorts of various standards and price classes. Tourists therefore have little contact with the local population or awareness of their precarious living conditions.
17. See: http://www.sppf.sc/lepep/index.php?option=com_content&view=article& id=137&Itemid=124
18. Community is meant here as containing both social and symbolic dimensions (see Amit 2002: 1–20). The concept of symbolic community was framed by Anthony Cohen (1985:38, cf. 2002: 165–70), to be viewed as: 'a phenomenon of culture: as one, therefore, which is meaningfully constructed by people through their symbolic prowess and resources'. It is clear that this angle on culture (faithful to Geertz 1975: 5) is quite different from the essentialist form promoted by the Seychellois government (see 'Conclusion' of this chapter).
19. James Scott (1998) analyses the cataclysms of top-down state policies which fail to implement their ideological project on the ground, communist Russia being the most notable recent example, where security concepts of the state were belied by the experience of ordinary citizens.

REFERENCES

Adam, J.L. 1999 [1987]. *Histoires vraies des Seychelles*. Mahé: Printec Press Holdings.
Alcoholism in Seychelles. 1973. Mahé: Union Chrétienne Seychelloise.
Alkire, S. 2003. Concepts of Human Security. In L. Chen, S. Fukuda-Parr and E. Seidensticker (eds) *Human Insecurity in a Global World*. Cambridge, MA: Harvard University Press, 15–40.
Amit, V. 2002. Reconceptualizing Community. In V. Amit (ed.) *Realizing Community: Concepts, Social Relations and Sentiments*. London: Routledge, 1–20.
Benedict, B. 1970. *People of Seychelles*, 3rd edn. London: HMSO.
Benedict, B. and M. Benedict. 1982. *Men, Women, and Money in Seychelles*. Berkeley: University of California Press.
Chow, P. 2004. Albert René – A Dispassionate Look at his Political Career. *Le Nouveau Seychelles Weekly* 23 April.
Cohen, A.P. 1985. *The Symbolic Construction of Community*. Key Ideas Series. London/New York: Routledge.
Cohen, A.P. 2002. Epilogue. In V. Amit (ed.) *Realizing Community: Concepts, Social Relations and Sentiments*. London: Routledge, 165–70.
Department of Social and Cultural Anthropology. 2006. *Annual Report 2005*. Amsterdam: Vrije Universiteit/Free University Amsterdam.
Ducrotoy, A. n.d. *Beautiful Isles, Beautiful People: A Family in Olde Seychelles 1780–1995*. Kent: Rawlings Publications.
Elections in the Seychelles. 2005. Elections around the World, URL (consulted 11 August 2005): http://www.electionworld.org/seychelles.htm

Ellis, S. 1996. Africa and International Corruption: The Strange Case of South Africa and Seychelles. *African Affairs* 95(379): 165–96.

Eriksen, T.H. 2005. *Risking Security: Paradoxes of Social Cohesion* (inaugural lecture). Amsterdam: Vrije Universiteit/Free University Amsterdam.

Geertz, C. 1975. Thick Description: Towards an Interpretive Theory of Culture. In *Interpretation of Cultures*. London: Hutchinson, 3–30.

Keyes, C. 2002. *Cultural Crisis and Social Memory: Modernity and Identity in Thailand and Laos*. (edited with Shigeharu Tanabe). Richmond, Surrey, UK: Routledge Curzon.

Lionnet, G. 1972. *The Seychelles*. Harrisburg, PA: Stackpole Books.

Lionnet, G. 2001. *Par les chemins de la mer: périples aux Séchelles au temps des voyages aux longs cours*. Saint-Denis: Université de la Réunion.

Malkki, L. 1995. *Purity and Exile: Violence, Memory, and National Cosmology among Hutu Refugees in Tanzania*. Chicago: University of Chicago Press.

Management and Information Systems Division (Seychelles). 2003. *Statistical Abstract 2002*. Mahé: MISD.

McAteer, W. 2000. *Hard Times in Paradise: The History of the Seychelles 1827–1919*. Mahé: Pristine Books.

McAteer, W. 2002 [1991]. *Rivals in Eden: The History of Seychelles 1741–1827*. Mahé: Pristine Books.

Perdrix, J., P. Bovet, D. Larue, B. Yersin, B. Burnand and F. Paccaud. 1999. Patterns of Alcohol Consumption in the Seychelles (Indian Ocean). *Alcohol and Alcoholism* 34(5): 773–85.

Reporters without Borders. 2004. Amende abusive après un huis clos judiciaire: les tracasseries continuent par l'hebdomadaire *Regar*, 9 Dec. URL (consulted 11 August 2005) http://www.rsf.org/article.php3?id_article=12052

Scarr, D. 1999. *Seychelles since 1770: History of a Slave and Post-slavery Society*. Asmara: Africa World Press, Inc.

Scott, J.C. 1985. *Weapons of the Weak: Everyday Forms of Peasant Resistance*. New Haven, CT: Yale University Press.

Scott, J.C. 1998. *Seeing Like a State: How Certain Schemes to Improve the Human Condition Have Failed*. New Haven, CT: Yale University Press.

Seychelles General Yearbook/Annuaire Géneral 2004. Mahé: Roma Flash.

Seychelles Chamber of Commerce and Industry (SCCI), July 2000. *The Seychelles Marketing Board: Another Perspective*. Mahé: SCCI.

United Nations Development Programme. 1994. *Human Development Report 1994*. New York: Oxford University Press.

US Library of Congress. 2005. *Country Studies: Seychelles*. URL (consulted 11 August 2005): http://www.country-studies.com

US Department of State, Bureau of Democracy, Human Rights and Labor, 2004. *Country Reports on Human Rights Practices: Seychelles*. URL (consulted 11 August 2005): http://www.state.gov/g/drl/rls/hrrpt/2003/27749.html

World Bank. 2005. *Seychelles Data Profile*. URL (consulted 11 August 2005): http://www.devdata.worldbank.org/external/

World Bank Group (Private Sector Development and Foreign Investment Advisory Service). URL (consulted 11 August 2005): http://www.sidsnet.org/latestarc/trade-newswire/msg00089.html

Newspapers

Nation (published by SPPF)
Regar (published by SNP)
Nouveau Seychelles Weekly (published by DP)
The People (published by SPPF)

Websites

Democratic Party (DP): http://www.dpseychelles.com
Seychelles Marketing Board: http://www.seychelles.net/smb/
Seychelles People's Progressive Front (SPPF): http://www.sppf.sc

11
Harnessing Ceremonial for Political Security: An Indian Princely State on the Verge of Extinction

Dick Kooiman

At the Independence of India and Pakistan (1947), Britain relinquished all the rights and privileges it had obtained in this part of the world since the days of the East India Company. Less known but no less dramatic was the fact that, with the transfer of power, hundreds of Indian princes lost their crowns. These Indian princes had been able to maintain a semi-autonomous existence on the fringe of the British-Indian Empire. The largest princely states levied their own taxes, minted their own money, and sported their own railway or even airline. But when British paramountcy lapsed, their dependence on British protection was glaringly exposed and within one or two years their crowned heads were tumbling in disgrace.

In retrospect, the demise of 'Princely India' seems inevitable. The national movement aimed at the establishment of an independent, all-Indian republic while the colonial government was preparing constitutional arrangements to bring the states into federation with the British provinces. Nevertheless, for a long time the continuing existence of groups of major states remained a possible option at the negotiating table. In some quarters of the British government, not in sympathy with the nationalist movement, that possibility was seriously considered and even encouraged. In vain, as we all know.

Indian novels and travel-stand books have actively furthered an understanding of the states as the real, mysterious India where spiritual values, martial valour and loyalty to the king had remained untouched. Historians and political anthropologists have come to share a less romantic interest in the history of these states and their Hindu and Muslim rulers, the Maharajas and Nawabs. They have started to study the nature of Indian kingship, the system of indirect rule, and the internal social and economic developments as compared with those in the directly ruled British provinces.

This contribution will focus on the increasing insecurity felt by these princely rulers during the approach of Independence. Threatened by the prospect of political extinction, they looked for some kind of political survival, either as part of or in alliance with the emerging independent nation-state. One of the means to strengthen their claims to political importance was an appeal to their repertoire of ceremonial honours. Gun salutes, armorial bearings and seating arrangements at durbars (princely courts or governments) were very prominent among these honours, with gun salutes as the most prestigious of them, as their grant and number determined several other, derivative distinctions. These honours will be the main subject of the following analysis. That analysis is from a historian and is largely based on archival sources covering a past period. But in its attempt to understand the world of princely India from within, its ambition closely resembles that of an anthropologist.

THE STATE OF TRAVANCORE

Central to this analysis will be the state of Travancore, which lay tucked away on the south-western tip of the Indian peninsula. In the eighteenth century it had emerged as a major single power, mainly because of the flourishing pepper trade along this coast. However, by the end of that century it was forced to enter into a military alliance with the East India Company and to recognise the British paramount power. The ruler of the state continued to enjoy some freedom of political manoeuvre, but his powers were rigorously restricted, especially in the field of military defence and foreign policy.

Nevertheless, the British considered the Indian princes like the ruler of Travancore as a powerful aristocracy who held the confidence and respect of their subjects. Therefore, it became part of British policy to secure the complicity of these so-called natural leaders and to use the existing vertical loyalties to strengthen the stability of their own rule. Under the Royal Titles Act of 1876 Queen Victoria was declared *Kaiser-i-Hind* or Empress of India. Her adoption of this title was announced at an Imperial Assemblage in Delhi (1877), which was hosted by Viceroy Lord Lytton. On that occasion, the Indian princes – as the Queen-Empress' most loyal Indian feudatories – were organised in an Indian peerage and received various honours like banners and gun salutes, all based entirely on European conceptions of feudality.

A (Foreign and) Political Department was in charge of all affairs related to the Indian princes. As the Viceroy usually was too much absorbed by his many official obligations to give the states all due attention, it was the secretary to the department who in actual practice exercised the functions of the colonial government. For that purpose, he had at his disposal a number of Residents and Agents who were assigned to the princely courts. These officers held a twofold responsibility: they were servants of the Government of India who at the same time had to watch over the interests of their accredited states. Although known under different titles, in this contribution we will refer to these officers as Residents only.

In the twentieth century, the nationalist movement, operating at an all-India level, was growing in strength and importance. The nationalist vision of an independent India left the states no hope of a continued semi-autonomous existence and decried their rulers as the last remnants of a bygone feudal order. At the same time, the British government was working for a scheme to bring Travancore and the other states into political federation with the directly administered provinces. Under these plans, which were embodied in the 1935 Government of India Act, the states would continue as constituent parts of independent India, but would have to surrender a large part of their remaining powers in revenue, communications and the administration of justice. That was a gloomy prospect for the proud rulers of former kingdoms and the major reason why the majority of the states, including Travancore, refused to accept federation within the terms of the Act.

Earlier, the British had raised a protective umbrella above the princes to shield them against the nationalist fervour that was threatening their borders. Also, they tried to bring all states under the direct charge of the Political Department in New Delhi. Several states used to be supervised through provincial governments as an intermediate level of administration. In 1921 political autonomy was granted to these provinces, but, to prevent nationalist parties from gaining control over princely affairs, this supervision was transferred to a higher level. Thus, in 1923 the involvement of the Government of Madras with Travancore came to an end and the state entered into direct relations with the Government of India. The change was highly appreciated by the Maharaja, as it added to the dignity and prestige of his durbar. The Resident also experienced a rise in status, but remained completely in the dark about his new responsibilities. He could hardly feel set at ease by a letter from the Political Department confiding to him that 'Our knowledge of the Madras States is necessarily limited ...'[1]

Travancore had not only to cope with attacks from outside. Education was spreading rapidly, resulting in a high rate of literacy (29 per cent in 1931) and a vivid social consciousness. Caste associations and political organisations arose, all claiming their rightful share in the expanding state administration, which was heavily dominated by loyal, high-caste Hindus. The Maharaja's throne used to be surrounded by an aura of sanctity, but in successive campaigns several disadvantaged groups openly protested against what they felt to be official neglect at the hands of their ruler.

In 1888 Travancore was the first princely state to institute a legislative council. Though at first purely a deliberative body, its membership and powers gradually increased. In response to a growing agitation for a more adequate political representation and a more responsible government, the Maharaja conceded some constitutional reforms empowering a bicameral legislative to initiate and pass legislation (1932). However, these reforms fell far short of expectations and during the years immediately preceding the Second World War Travancore became the scene of a fierce political struggle between pro- and contra-government forces,[2] thus adding to the insecurity already felt by the ruling family by threats from outside.

SOME THEORETICAL NOTIONS

The recent interest in the subject of human security is often seen as a rational response to the globalisation of international policy (Acharya 2004: 355–6).

The globalisation that Indian princes had to face was the accelerating and irreversible process towards an independent Indian republic, and they felt increasingly uncertain about their own particular place within that larger world. They had grown into the Crown's most loyal subordinate allies, but the impending British withdrawal threatened to leave them without that vital source of support. This chapter focuses on the ways in which these Indian princes, more specifically the princes of Travancore, tried to reconstruct a sense of (political) security in the context of their diminishing, semi-autonomous position and facing an unknown and inauspicious political future. The political security sought by the Indian princes was first of all an attempt to safeguard as much as possible of their remaining power, if need be cast in some modern guise. However, this political security also included cultural, emotional and symbolic dimensions, which may best be summarised in the term *izzat* (honour). The traditional duties of an Indian king included safeguarding his own *izzat* and that of his state, ruler and state being equivalent terms, as they are in this text as well. In the past, ruling families had tried to earn *izzat* by fighting each other on the battlefield, but after the establishment of the *Pax Britannica* they had to compete for honours in less violent ways, for instance by showing themselves useful in the service of the empire. These honours, it will be argued, should not be seen as separate from or secondary to political security, but as contributing to that security as an autonomous factor.

Though it is usual to refer to the Indian princes as a group, they proved unable to close ranks and make a strong common stand. For a long time, the British-Indian government had kept them strictly separated. When, after the First World War, the major rulers met for joint consultation in a Chamber of Princes, the delicate problem of precedence only accentuated existing rivalries. Unwilling to surrender their individual interests to the larger cause of princely India, the states were fighting a lonely, and in the end losing, battle. Travancore was one of the states that declined to take part in the Chamber's activities.[3]

Here, following Bajpai (2004: 360–61), I will define the political security of a princely state as a precarious balance between threats to its honourable survival and its capacities to deal with those threats. The threats can be traced to identifiable human actors, the British government and the nationalist leadership, campaigning both inside and outside princely territory for an end to feudal autocracy. The capacities to resist these threats include the maintenance of law and order, the guarantees under British treaties, and informal, personal connections. To that list I would like to add an increasing and emphatic appeal to ceremonial distinctions as a way to ward off possible threats.

In this discussion of Travancore, I will focus on the ceremonial honour of gun salutes, armorial bearings, and seating arrangements at durbars, all meant to enhance the position of the ruler. Especially in the decades preceding Independence that position required a continuous process of what Winslow and Eriksen (2004: 361–2) have called the construction of symbolic security. A similar process has been analysed by Martin Doornbos (1985) in his study of the last days of Ankole kingship in Uganda. After the mid 1930s,

Ankole kingship suffered from institutional decline and loss of effective power, as it was no longer able to play a prominent role in the overall social and political process. In these circumstances, the Ankole king approached the British district commissioner, requesting the colonial government to kindly provide him with an extensively decorated coronation chair, a royal standard with a coat of arms and other royal attributes. On the strength of this evidence Doornbos (1985) concludes there is an inverse correlation between processes of ceremonialisation and institutionalisation. If a ruling dynasty enjoys undisputed authority, it can afford to remain indifferent to the finer details of ceremonial. But if the institutions that support that authority are weakening, the dynasty may evince a growing passion for honours in order to compensate its loss of power and to increase its feeling of security.[4]

GUN SALUTES

The 1864 table of salutes shows Travancore as entitled to a dynastic salute of 17 guns. Two years later, the Government of Madras, pleased with the modernising zeal of the new Maharaja and his Dewan, advised the Government of India to increase Travancore's dynastic salute to 19 guns. The Viceroy, John Lawrence, adopted this advice and informed the ruler that 'in recognition of Your Highness' excellent administration of the Travancore state', he had directed that his dynastic salute be increased to 19 guns. The revised table of 1867 lists Travancore as a 19-gun state and – what is especially important to note – no particular pressure seems to have been needed to obtain this increase.[5]

The twentieth century, and especially the period after the installation of a new Maharaja in 1924, saw a long and bitter fight over Travancore's gun salutes which reached a climax in 1926. A new Resident had been appointed to Travancore and this officer objected to the programme of a durbar, as the programme mentioned a salute of 21 guns on the arrival of the Maharaja. The Dewan explained this salute in a letter saying that it was his belief 'that within his own state a Ruler is at liberty to order his gunners to blaze away as much powder as he pleased'. The Resident argued in protest that at a durbar attended by the representative of the paramount power, the ruler should not receive more guns than it had pleased the British government to confer on him.[6] Before proceeding with this discussion, it might be useful to give some background to the history of gun salutes.

In Europe, the practice of firing gun salutes was well established by the sixteenth century, and most probably stemmed from naval tradition. Firing all guns would leave a ship, fort or battery virtually defenceless, as guns could not be easily and quickly reloaded. Over time, the practice evolved from an act of submission and peaceful intentions into a mark of respect to honour and rank important guests. It was in this form that it reached India.

Prior to 1855 there was no fixed policy as regards the firing of gun salutes. In 1864 a first table of salutes was published which later on was regularly revised. Though originally assigned on the basis of political importance and cooperation, the criteria governing the allocation of salutes remained vague and inconsistently applied. The table was framed in three parts. First and most important was the dynastic salute, which, when Tupper (1895) wrote his standard work on Indian political practice, was enjoyed by 107 princes. The highest number of salutes – 21 guns – was for three states only, Hyderabad, Baroda and Mysore. There were eight states with 19 dynastic salutes, including Travancore. The number of salute states increased further down the scale with a large number of 9-gun princes at the base (Tupper 1895 III: 234ff.).

Next there were personal salutes, conferred upon ten princes for their lifetime, and not transferrable to a successor. Finally, there were local salutes, which were territorially confined and at that time enjoyed only by four larger states. At the Imperial Assemblage of 1877, Travancore was granted a personal salute of 21 guns or two additional guns for life. The Maharaja died in 1880, but at state functions, jubilees and public durbars 21 guns continued to be fired in honour of his successor, thus creating confusion and controversy about personal and local salutes. The discussion in 1926 was about the local salute.

In 1877, the Secretary of State for India commanded that in India the salute of the sovereign be increased to 101 guns and that for the Viceroy 31 guns. Interestingly, British Governors were assigned 17 guns while British officers in the states received a salute only if they were entitled to a salute in British territory. The Travancore Resident in 1926 obviously had less than 17 guns. The salute list was meant to hierarchise the gun salutes in a linear order and the strict application if its rules was zealously guarded by British political officers.

Even stone could be saluted: in 1934 a limestone statue of Viceroy Lord Irwin was unveiled near the Secretariat Blocks in New Delhi, to the sound of 31 guns. The power to deal with salutes rested with the Crown, although the Viceroy was empowered to provisionally increase, reduce or grant salutes. Yet, his decisions remained invalid: 'until Her Majesty's pleasure in regard to it [should] have been duly taken' (Tupper III 1895: 235).

Information on gun salutes in Travancore for the first half of the nineteenth century is extremely scarce. The Standing Orders of the local military brigade, commanded by British officers, record the salutes fired by its artillery on installation ceremonies, the Raja's birthday or official visits, but not systematically and often without noting the exact number – a matter which later was to assume very great importance. In 1831, 21 guns were fired on the birthday of the ex-Regent Rani, but usually the records refer to the brigade paying 'customary honours', the 'usual salute' or the 'royal salute', without providing further detail.[7] These fragments of information suffice to show that at that time the number of salutes was not considered a very important issue.

In the course of the twentieth century, this indifference was to disappear completely. The 1926 incident mentioned above was just one among many. As the matter could not be solved locally, it was referred to the Political Department in New Delhi. The officer in charge lamented in a private note that it would have been much better if the practice of 21 local guns had been accorded 'the sanction of immemorial custom' and left at that. Feeling compelled to make a statement, the department ruled that the Government of India had no desire to interfere with local practices, with the exception of vice-regal visits.[8] Thus the question of Travancore's local salute was finally settled. The dynastic salute, however, still stood at 19 guns.

During the First World War , a number of princes had contributed men, money and *matériel* to the British war effort. Therefore, even before the end of the war, the Government of India asked provincial governments if they had any suggestions for a revision of the table of salutes. The criteria to be applied in determining the allotment of salutes remained, as usual, delightfully vague, but had to do with population, revenue, the antiquity of the states and the nature of their relations with the British power. Considering these criteria, the Government of Madras found several reasons to recommend that Travancore be given 21 dynastic guns. It had a much larger population than Baroda (21 guns), was the fifth state in terms of revenue, claimed an uninterrupted succession of sovereigns from remote antiquity and had had quite satisfactory relations with the British since 1778. However, what tipped the balance was that

Travancore had contributed very little towards the war effort considering the great wealth of the state. Therefore, a salute of 19 guns was considered commensurate with the position of the state, and the Government of Madras refrained from proposing any change in salute.[9]

A new opportunity presented itself in November 1931, when the young Maharaja was invested with full ruling powers. Immediately after the installation of the Maharaja at a great state durbar, the Government of Travancore forwarded a new memorandum to the Political Department in New Delhi setting forth the claim for a dynastic salute of 21 guns. One of the new arguments put forward was that Gwalior and Kashmir, 19-gun states like Travancore, had been elevated to 21 dynastic guns. The Maharaja submitted that in making this change and leaving out Travancore, the importance of his state had been unjustly ignored. The British Resident supported the request.[10]

The Political Department reasoned again that Gwalior and Kashmir, in contrast with Travancore, had rendered magnificent services duirng the First World War, and that Kashmir held a strategic position as a bulwark between British India and foreign territory. Apart from that, an increased dynastic salute for Travancore would be apt to displease the five members of the circle of 21-gun states and would make it extremely difficult to refuse similar honours to other 19-gun rulers, like Bhopal and Udaipur. Thus, Travancore was informed that the Viceroy, after carefully examining the latest memorandum:

> ... feels that there is little hope at present of any increase in the dynastic salute and considers that His Highness must wait a little longer or until some special occasion arises when the Table of Salutes can be brought under general revision.[11]

That special occasion never arose and the roar of guns at the outbreak of the Second World War finally drowned all further arguments about the Travancore gun salute. To encourage his support for the war effort, the Maharaja was honoured in another way. He was made a Grand Commander of the Order of the Indian Empire (GCIE 1935) and of the Star of India (GCSI 1946), and in 1943 he received his first honorary commission as a Major in the Indian Army (McLeod 1994: 245, 248, 2002: 1–2).

ARMORIAL BEARINGS

As part of the Imperial Assemblage in 1877, the Viceroy, Lord Lytton, acting in the name of the Queen-Empress, was to present 90 ruling princes with large banners upon which were emblazoned their armorial bearings modelled after European patterns. These armorial bearings were virtually imposed on the states, which – as in the case of Travancore – were at best indifferent to, if not reluctant to receive this mark of vice-regal regard. Lord Lytton, however, wanted to honour the Crown's Indian feudatories with banners carrying 'their' arms, and if no arms could be found, they were to be invented.

Discussions about banners and arms for Travancore had begun some time before. As Knight Grand Commander of the Star of India (KGCSI 1866), the Maharaja had received banners with heraldic arms, to be borne before him at an investiture. Therefore, when in 1875 a new investiture was to be held in Calcutta, the (Foreign and) Political Department, enquired through the Resident whether His Highness still had his robes and banner. They seemed to be uncertain about this matter. The Maharaja replied that his robe and banner had newly been made at the suggestion of the secretary of the Order. He submitted the same for the Resident's inspection, and added with hardly concealed indifference that:

> ... if you think the same will do for the present occasion ... I shall take it with me to Calcutta but if you think a new one should be made ... you will be good enough to make the necessary arrangements as you deem expedient in communication with the secretary in the foreign department.[12]

Nevertheless, as the Imperial Assemblage drew nearer, Travancore was again questioned about the existence of any family banners and armorial bearings, this time by the Government of Madras. The Resident referred in his reply to the banner used by the Maharaja as KGCSI and also submitted some hand-made drawings of armorial bearings, 'if they can be called such'. The Dewan, evincing the general ignorance in this matter, suggested that the product of a local historian's fantasy might be what the central government had in mind for the occasion.[13] He informed the Resident that the conch shell was the emblem of the ruling family, adding that His Highness would prefer for the national colour light yellow, a colour denoting prosperity.

In the meantime, Robert Taylor in Calcutta, an amateur heraldist in charge of designing princely arms and banners for the Assemblage, was becoming impatient. In October 1876 he sent a telegram to the Resident urging that he still needed information as to anything remarkable or peculiar in the history of the ruling family, and dismissing the shade of yellow as a suitable colour for Travancore, as it might indicate 'some pretty picture but no heraldic arms'.[14]

As the Maharaja could not keep aloof from this discussion about what was to become his family tradition, he sent the Resident a design for a coat of arms. It is not clear whether the Maharaja had made the design personally or had merely issued the necessary instructions. In any case, the accompanying letter makes it abundantly clear that he approved of the design and considered it good enough for the purpose.

The conch shell, the chief emblem of the state and one of the four emblems held by Vishnu, was in the centre of a banner, which was held by two elephants. These elephants had been introduced, the Maharaja explained, as 'they are the most characteristic and the noblest of the indigenous mammals'. Most probably they were patterned after the two lions in the arms of the colonial government. The elephants held in their uplifted proboscis the chief products of the country, namely the coconut palm and a sheaf of paddy. As at that time the cultivation of coffee was making great progress, the Maharaja commented with a fine understanding of the dynamics of tradition, that '[p]robably in a second edition of the devices a coffee twig will have to be added'. At the bottom, a lotus flower supported the state sword and the feet of Sri Padmanabha, the state's tutelary deity, and the outer circle bore two titles of the Maharaja in Devanagiri characters. The ruler of Travancore concluded that, on the whole, the device was good, and he ended his letter in a rather light-hearted tone by commenting that 'you need not return the design if you can make any use of it'.

This and other letters were forwarded to Calcutta but failed to satisfy Mr Taylor. He rejected the Maharaja's design as absolutely useless and 'like nothing for even a [...?] peer's coat in England'. Also, he was puzzled about the diverse colours.[15] The ruler of Travancore did not attend the Imperial Assemblage in Delhi, but in his absence his colonial masters presented him with royal banners and arms. Taylor had followed his own ideas in designing them, but had made use of much that he had found helpful in earlier correspondence. The two elephants with trunks raised had remained the main heraldic device, but without the trappings the Maharaja had earlier suggested. The silver conch, like the elephants drawn in red outlines, was in the centre and the motto 'Charity our Household Deity' had replaced the titles of the Maharaja (Flicher n.d.).

For a long time, there was no further discussion about the Travancore banners and arms. Then, about 60 years later, the subject was taken up again, this time not by the British government but by the Government of Travancore. By that time, the larger political situation had changed considerably. The Travancore dynasty had come to face serious threats, both from within and from without, and was desperately looking for means to guarantee some kind of political survival.

Leaving the affairs of his family and state in the hands of his Dewan and constitutional adviser, the young Maharaja and his mother, the junior princess, had left for London (1936). There they paid a visit to the College of Arms and requested the College to design two flags with banners, one to serve as 'the national flag of the state' and the other as the personal flag of the Maharaja. As official registration of these flags with arms required a formal application through the Government of India, this initiative opened a new debate on the banners and arms of the Indian princes.

So far, the *Thakore Sahib* of Palitana was the only ruling prince who had registered his armorial bearings with the College in London (1896). In 1914 the India Office (London) had drawn up a memorandum providing rules concerning applications to the College of Arms. This memorandum had never been forwarded to the ruling princes, as the Secretary of State for India was not fully satisfied with its contents. Striking a note radically different from that used at the time of the Imperial Assemblage, the Secretary of State had declared that he saw 'no object in encouraging chiefs or other Indians to take out armorial bearings'. The question was accordingly deferred.

In 1937, the India Office confirmed this official stand and refused either to contest or explicitly admit a claim by Indian princes to the right to devise and bear their own arms. Registration by the College of Arms would be equivalent to recognition of such a right and thus should not be encouraged. In defence of the Indian princes, the Political Department in New Delhi stressed that the princes should be regarded not as subjects of the King of England, but as being in subordinate alliance with the Crown, and thus entitled to bear their own arms. A long and rather technical exchange followed about procedures and forms of application. The India Office wanted an early settlement, as it had been informed that a large number of

Indian rulers, afraid of being outstripped in the rivalry for status, had already applied to the College of Arms for registration. The department in New Delhi welcomed registration, mainly because application offered an opportunity to ensure that no objectionable designs were included in the coats of arms. In the late 1930s, the department had to request several princes to remove symbols of royalty, such as an arched crown or a crest resembling a crown, from their coat of arms.[16]

Travancore had raised the question of the registration of arms. But it seems that, after the long and time-consuming deliberations about formal procedures, the princely states had lost interest. In the course of 1938 the forms of application became available, but two years later the Political Department in Delhi noted that no application had yet been received from the Maharaja of Travancore, who presumably did not wish to pursue the matter for the present. No action was thought necessary, as '[t]he next move, if any is to be made, rest with His Highness'.[17] That move was never made.

SEATING AT DURBARS

An interesting controversy took place about the exact place of the chair of the Resident at durbars. In 1926 a British political officer in Travancore was surprised to discover that the Maharaja was sitting at the head of the table all alone and even on a small dais. On the floor to his right the Resident's chair was placed at the head of a row of guests and to his left stood the chair of the crown prince, also at the head of a row. So the Resident and the heir to the throne sat facing each other. The usual procedure in other states, the officer observed, was that the British representative was seated on the right side of the ruler and level with him, with everybody else sitting at right angles.[18]

Thereupon, the Resident lodged protest to the Dewan against this practice. The Dewan replied that seating arrangements in Travancore might be different from those elsewhere but defended them as a usage peculiar to local tradition and identity. As the Government of India had declared their readiness to consider deviations from standard ceremonial based on past practice, the Dewan first wanted to search all government records relevant to this question. 'Last evening', he wrote to the Resident (19 Sept. 1926), 'I received a large collection of files from 1829 onwards which I am now wading through and there are more papers to come.' Besides, Travancore was then under a Regency and the Maharani-Regent was not prepared to concede anything that might give the impression that she was lowering the prestige of the young Maharaja.

One month later, the Dewan placed the results of his investigations before the Resident. The number of references to public durbars turned out to be small and – what is more important – they gave no particulars about the place and level of the chair of the representative of the paramount power. The most curious piece of evidence put forward by the Dewan was the engraving of a picture in the billiard room of the British residency. That engraving depicted the 1851 durbar that was held for the Maharaja formally to receive a letter from Queen Victoria and made unmistakably clear, in the words of the Dewan, that the throne stood alone and apart, with no seat for the Resident near it. The Resident scribbled in the margin that the engraving showed no chairs at all, and that most probably chairs were lacking, as they were unusual in those days.

Neither did references in the *Travancore Government Gazette Extraordinary* to later durbars throw much light on the position of the Resident's chair or the origin of the existing arrangement. The Dewan referred to several issues of this *Gazette,* but the Resident, who took the trouble to examine the quoted pages, found the information about the question of seating indecisive. Only the more recent issues of the *Gazette* gave some more details. The *Gazette* of 18 June 1880 did not restrict its descriptions to the rich clothing of the Maharaja and the impressive parade of state elephants, but also mentioned that the Resident was seated 'at the top of the right hand row'.[19] Later issues contained the same information.

These findings confirmed the Dewan in his opinion that the seating arrangements as existing in 1926 were justified by past practice. Besides, he thought it inappropriate to place the chair of the Resident too close to that of the Maharaja, as 'a chair European style, however ornate and large, will be dwarfed if drawn up alongside the silver Musnad' (throne). The proposed change would push back the Dewan, who till then had been seated at the right of and slightly drawn back from the throne, and create the impression that his place had been taken by the British representative. The government remained reluctant to introduce any change in the existing practice and the Government of India decided to adjourn a decision in this matter.[20]

After the investiture of the young Maharaja with full powers (1931), the Dewan resumed the initiative with renewed vigour. He had a note written by a local scholar and submitted it to the Resident. That note was elaborate in detail but poor in documentation. It quoted extensively from English publications, like a colourful description of the 1860 durbar by the London missionary Samuel Mateer. What becomes particularly clear from this and other descriptions quoted in the note is that, until recent times, the exact location of the chair of the British representative did not require special attention. The conclusion that the Resident's chair stood to the right of the throne was most probably correct, but does not answer the question whether that chair was in the same line with the throne or at right angles.[21]

The evidence produced by local British officials was also far from convincing. The earliest record traceable in the residency was a collection of notes regarding ceremonials compiled by Major Hayes, who served as Assistant-Resident from 1866 to 1870. In 1895, these notes had been revised and printed by Resident Rees, 'to preserve what is of use in it', as he wrote by hand on the official copy. This collection contains detailed rules on seating, and lays down that at state durbars the Resident sits on the right of the Maharaja, then the Resident's wife, and the staff according to rank, with the Commanding Officer sitting on the left of the Maharaja followed by the other officers of the Travancore Government according to rank. However, these rules did not answer the delicate question of whether or not the chairs stood in the same line or at right angles to the seat of the ruler.[22] Apparently, at the end of the nineteenth century, this was also a question of no great importance for the British. Nevertheless, in the tumultuous conditions of the 1930s on this very issue a conflict was brewing.

The British could not deny that the existing practice had the sanction of custom behind it, but insisted on the need for a change of that practice. First of all, they had a wish to standardise ceremonial rules at princely courts. Besides, Travancore had entered into direct relations with the central government, and the British representative was raised from a local Agent to an Agent of the Governor-General (1923). This enhanced dignity, invalidating any appeal to precedent, should find expression in another position of the Resident's chair. The point at issue, Resident Garstin argued, was not a curtailment of the rights and privileges of His Highness, but an acknowledgement of the increased dignity of the representative of the paramount power. Garstin seems also to have been very much concerned with his own personal dignity, demanding an extension of the mounted guard escorting him to durbars, and a place for his wife on the right of the Maharaja and himself.

The Indian side though, set a high value on the existing practice. After the installation of the young Maharaja, it was actually his mother, the junior Maharani who came to exercise actual power. Louise Ouwerkerk, a teacher at the Maharaja's Women's College and personally acquainted with the palace, described the junior Maharani as an energetic and ambitious woman who was continually frustrated by the restrictions imposed by her sex and age. She was ably assisted in her ambitions by Sir C.P. Ramaswamy Aiyar, constitutional adviser to the throne and from 1936 Dewan of the state. Sir C.P. was an outstanding lawyer and shrewd intriguer, firmly determined to ensure the ruling family had all the honours and dignities he thought them to be entitled to (Ouwerkerk 1994: 74–7).

In November 1935 the Government of Travancore published a fresh note on this question. Acknowledging the increased dignity of the Resident, this note advanced the earlier argument that his promotion to Agent to the Governor-General also enhanced the dignity of the Maharaja, thus keeping existing relations perfectly well-balanced. Further, an adept reference was made to a letter by the Viceroy (1910), exhorting his political officers to scrupulously observe ceremonial 'in accordance with ancient custom', and to the recent discussions in the Committee on Ceremonials (1932), which had acknowledged the importance of local precedents in questions of ceremonial.[23]

As parties in Travancore proved unable to reach an agreement, the question was finally referred to the Political Department in New Delhi. In 1936 the department informed Garstin of its decision. Henceforth at official durbars, like state banquets and garden parties, the Resident's chair:

> … should be placed on the right hand side of the Maharaja in the same line and on the same level and not at the head of the row of chairs on the Maharaja's right hand side at right angles to the masnad.

This change, the department reasoned, implied no loss of dignity to the ruler, as the same ceremonial was observed in large states as Hyderabad and Mysore.

Garstin had his way, but not in all respects. No orders were passed on the Resident's mounted escort and his wife would not be given a place at future official durbars. Garstin was instructed to inform the Government of Travancore of these decisions 'in suitable terms', which he did with great satisfaction. Sir C.P. tried to put up a last resistance with the argument that Travancore had no state banquets and garden parties as such, but Garstin was not in the mood for a fight over definitions. In the beginning of 1937 he explained to the Dewan that the decision of the Government of India was final and did not allow for any further discussion.[24]

CONCLUDING OBSERVATIONS

What is most striking in the discussion about and confusion over princely ceremonial is the paucity of documentary evidence that both British and Travancorean authorities had to cope with, especially for the earlier period. With great difficulty, the governments in Madras and New Delhi could cobble together fragments of evidence. The Travancorean side fared even worse, being thrown back mainly on a few English sources, as the controversy about the Resident's chair clearly shows. For the most recent period more records become available, but the increasing princely concern with honours is not just a function of better documentation. It represents a larger trend also to be noted in the histories of other princely states.

Travancore's dynastic salute was increased to 19 guns in 1866. This enhanced honour seems to have been the result of a one-sided initiative on the part of the government in consideration of the excellent administration of the state. Later, persistent efforts by Travancore to get it further increased to 21 guns were in vain, mainly because the Government of India deemed the state's support during the First World War to have been inadequate in view of its economic potential.[25] In this way, the grant or withholding of salutes was used as a mark of the government's favour or displeasure.

This use of ceremonial honours as a political instrument by the British does not explain Travancore's late eagerness to rise to 21-gun status, or to have its arms formally registered. Here, an interesting argumentation has been put forward by Barbara Ramusack and John McLeod. They acknowledge that most princes came to see ceremonial honours not as hollow gestures, but as precious attributes to their remaining power. No longer free to fight one another on the battlefield, these princes – in the words of Ramusack (1978: 15, 2004: 90) – 'now attempted to best each other in the world of symbols, and here the prime arena was the salute table established by the paramount power'. We may safely add armorial bearings and seating arrangements as part of that contest.

After the First World War, when the British ended the political isolation of the states, gun salutes were eminently suited to mark hierarchical distinctions among the princes (McLeod 1994: 244, 248). However, the pyramid structure of the salute list did not allow for much mobility at the higher levels. In 1895, Tupper's standard work listed 107 princes as enjoying a dynastic salute, and in 1929 the number had risen to 119 only. The few new entrants got stuck at the base of the pyramid and there was not much movement towards the top, except for Gwalior and Kashmir, which reached the capstone, namely 21 dynastic guns. The five states with the maximum number of salutes converted their lack of promotion opportunities into a strong determination to keep their privilege severely restricted. Then, at the end of the 1920s, British interests in the ceremonial of gun salutes began to wane.

A similar, though more recent rivalry among the princely states can be seen in the field of arms and banners. After Travancore had raised the issue of the registration of arms, a number of princely rulers immediately followed suit. Afraid that Travancore's initiative might lower their comparative status, they also applied to the College of Arms to have their arms registered. The bureaucratic barriers created by the British seemed to have discouraged them all.

Personally, I do not think that British manipulation and mutual rivalry among the Indian princes can fully explain the growing passion for ceremonial distinctions that can so clearly be discerned among the Travancore ruling family. Another, maybe more important consideration is the precarious relationship with the British paramount power and the threatening prospect of a withdrawal of British support leaving the states at the mercy of a large and independent Indian republic. Within the state, several movements were fighting for a share of political power, and even though nobody openly questioned the position of the ruling family, the Travancore dynasty was more and more becoming a redundant institution. In this critical, highly uncertain situation, honours that had earlier been treated with a hardly concealed indifference assumed a new and different meaning.

At the time of the Imperial Assemblage, banners with arms were virtually imposed on Travancore and other states, which felt rather embarrassed by their presentation. The poles proved to be of such enormous weight 'as to require two Highlanders to carry this symbol of the Viceroy's regard', and it was not clear to the princely beneficiaries what they should do with them (Burne 1907: 42). The Maharaja of Travancore did not even care to come to New Delhi to receive this distinction from the hands of the Viceroy, Lord Lytton. Much later however, the rulers of the state came to appreciate these honours much more than Lord Lytton could ever have imagined. In the 1930s, the then Maharaja and his mother, the junior-Maharani, travelled all the way to London to have their arms and banners officially registered – though this was not the sole purpose of their visit – and new efforts were being made to have the dynastic salute raised. The placing of the Resident's chair on the right hand side of the Maharaja, absolutely a non-issue in the nineteenth century, was now seen as a serious loss of political prominence, which the state could not afford. The argument of the Government of Travancore that any infringement of the honours of the Maharaja would greatly hurt the feelings of his loyal subjects mainly shows the gradual spread of a democratic idiom. About the real feelings of these subjects, we can only speculate.

The weakening of the institutions upholding the dynasty and the uncertain political future of the state of Travancore are, in my opinion, the main reasons why, on the eve of Independence, the Maharaja and his family so eagerly embraced the ceremonial honours, which earlier had been introduced by the colonial government to mark their subordination. They invoked the power of ceremonial with its gilt and glitter to strengthen their sense of security and to ensure their state a place on the future political map of India. Earlier, the British had granted these honours, as they considered the security of their empire to be intimately connected with the maintenance of a powerful Indian aristocracy. But after the First World War, the British became entangled in a complicated process of transfer of power. They lost their former interest in these ceremonial distinctions and sincerely doubted the wisdom of encouraging tendencies of royalty and autonomy among the princes to which they could give no place in the independent India to come.

NOTES

1. 'Establishment of Direct Relations between Government of India and Indian States in Madras Presidency', R/1/1/1321. Quotation from letter Political Department to Resident Travancore, 7 Nov. 1923.
2. See the Resident's Fortnightly Reports for these years, R/1/1/2338.
3. 'Chamber of Princes, Proceedings', L/P&S/13/287–288.
4. After the 1848 Constitution had drastically curtailed the powers of the king of the Netherlands, forms at court assumed an increasing importance, as can be seen from the recently published private correspondence of a lady at the Dutch royal court, see Hermans and Hooghiemstra (2006).
5. 'Salutes to the Maharaja of Travancore, 1898', R/2/892/274.
6. Letters exchanged between Vernon, Resident, and Watts, Dewan, 3 Aug. 1926 and 4 Aug. 1926, in 'Procedure for the Presentation of Kharitas', R/2/884/160.

7. For instance, enclosure in 'Investiture Maharaja of Travancore with Ruling Powers (1931)', R/2/887/186.
8. All correspondence, including decision Government of India 20 Jan. 1927, R/2/884/160.
9. All correspondence, including letter Government of Madras to Government of India, Foreign and Political Department, 12 April 1917, No. 158, in 'Revised Table of Salutes, 1917', R/2/895/327.
10. Memorandum Maharaja of Travancore, 11 Nov. 1931, and accompanying letter Lt Col. Pritchard, British Resident for the Madras States, in 'Question of Enhancement of the Salute of HH the Maharaja of Travancore', R/1/4/96.
11. All correspondence in R/1/4/96, quotation from letter Charles Watson, Political Department, 11 April 1932, to Pritchard, British Resident.
12. All correspondence, handwritten, 1875, in 'A Banner for the Maharaja of Travancore', R/2/879/4.
13. This suggestion refers to the coat of arms used by Shungoony Menon as frontispiece in his book that was published in 1878.
14. Correspondence in R/2/879/4 and 'Armorial Bearings for Travancore & Cochin', R/2/879/6.
15. Letter from the Maharaja of Travancore, 21 Oct. 1876 and letter from Taylor, Calcutta, 26 Oct. 1876, R/2/879/6.
16. Correspondence in 'Armorial Bearings Travancore', R/1/4/367 and 'Registration of the Armorial Bearings of Travancore State, R/1/4/368.
17. 'Enquiry Registration Coat of Arms 1939', R/1/4/369.
18. Internal hand-written notes Trivandrum Residency, in 'Darbar Ceremonial', R/2/884/162.
19. The extract of the *Travancore Government Gazette Extraordinary* of 18 June 1880 I saw did not have that piece of information, neither had the *Report on the Administration of Travancore for the Year 1055 (1879–1880)*, pp. 84–5.
20. All correspondence on this question in 'Darbar Ceremonial', R/2/884/162.
21. Rao Shib Uloor S. Parameswara Ayyar, 'Note on the Seating of the Agent to the Governor-General in Public Durbars', 1932, R/2/887/205.
22. 'Durbar Etiquette for Cochin and Travancore', 1895, R/2/900/385.
23. Viceroy's letter on 'Strict Observance of Etiquette & Ceremonials in intercourse with Chiefs and Darbars', 1910, R/2/508/166. Letter from Dewan of Travancore, 9 Jan. 1933, with approving comment on discussions in the Committee on Ceremonials, L/P&S/13/1761.
24. All correspondence in 'Ceremonials Travancore State', R/2/887/205 and R/2/888/208.
25. It could also work the other way round with the Maharaja of Morvi claiming an enhancement of his salute in return for the two Spitfires he financed in support of the Second World War, R/2/598/25.

REFERENCES

Archives

Oriental and India Office Collections, British Library, London:
Political and Secret Department, London
L/P&S/13 series, Madras States Agency
Crown Representative's (Viceroy's) Records

R/1/series, Political Department New Delhi
R/2/series, Indian States' Residencies
*Report on the Administration of Travancore for the year 1041–1076
(AD 1865/6–1900/1)*

Acharya, Amitav. 2004. A Holistic Paradigm. *Security Dialogue* 35(3): 354–5.

Bajpai, Kanti. 2004. An Expression of Threats versus Capabilities across Time and Space. *Security Dialogue* 35(3): 360–1.

Burne, Owen Tudor. 1907. *Memories*. London: Edward Arnold.

Doornbos, Martin R. 1985. Institutionalization and Institutional Decline. In Henri J.M. Claessen, Pieter van de Velde and M. Estellie Smith (eds) *Development and Decline: The Evolution of Socio-political Organization*. South Hadley, MA: Bergin and Garvey.

Flicher, Andre. n.d. *Drapeaux et armoires des états princiers de l'Empire des Indes*. Dreux (Kenneth Robbins Collections, Virginia USA).

Hermans, Dorine and Daniela Hooghiemstra. 2006. *Vertel dit toch aan niemand: leven aan het hof*. Amsterdam: Mouria.

McLeod, John, 1994. The English Honours System in Princely India. *Journal of the Royal Asiatic Society* 4(2): 237–49.

McLeod, John. 2002. The New Mansabdars: Honorary Military Rank in Princely India. Unpublished paper, University of Wisconsin.

Ouwerkerk, Louise. 1994. *No Elephants for the* Maharaja: *Social and Political Change in the Princely State of Travancore (1921–1947)*, edited with an introduction by Dick Kooiman. New Delhi: Manohar.

Ramusack, Barbara N. 1978. *The Princes of India in the Twilight of Empire: Dissolution of a Patron–Client System 1914–39*. Columbus: Ohio State University Press.

Ramusack, Barbara N. 2004. *The Indian Princes and their States*. Cambridge: Cambridge University Press.

Tupper, C.L. 1895. *Indian Political Practice: A Collection of the Decisions of the Government of India in Political Cases*, 4 vols. Calcutta: Government Printing.

Winslow, Donna and Thomas Hylland Eriksen. 2004. A Broad Concept that Encourages Interdisciplinary Thinking. *Social Security* 35(3): 361–2.

12
Ritual Efficacy, Spiritual Security and Human Security: Spirit Mediumship In Contemporary Vietnam

Oscar Salemink

After a period of suppression of all things religious by Vietnam's Communist Party-state, a remarkable revival of a wide variety of ritual and religious practices is taking place in contemporary Vietnam. In the words of Australian anthropologist, Philip Taylor:

> An upsurge in fortune-telling, mediumship, spirit worship, and pilgrimages occurred in Vietnam as government policies were pushing the country into unprecedented integration with the capitalist world and as market relations were transforming the face of society. (2004: 83)

Recent discussions about religious developments speak about the *revival* of religious practices in Vietnam. The assumption implied in such words is that traditional religious beliefs and ritual practices have been absent or hidden from view and have re-emerged during the *Đôi mói* period of economic reforms since 1986. In such accounts, this phenomenon is explained in terms of a return to 'tradition' during Vietnam's comprehensive socio-economic reform process, after a period of religious suppression during socialist collectivisation. In my experience the form and scale of activities do not constitute a return to the past, but take place on a much grander scale, assuming novel forms, prompted by old or novel motivations, and in a transnational context. Philip Taylor contextualises this localised insight by referring to the enhanced religious sensibilities in other countries in Asia (Keyes et al. 1994) and to 'new forms of religiosity' in connection with the proliferation of capitalism around the world (Roberts 1995). However, such a crude connection between religiosity and economic system cannot account for the specificities of local practices and the motivations of religious figures and their clients.

In this chapter I take a look at spirit mediumship in Vietnam, which assumes varying forms depending on ethnicity, region and religion. By applying a human security lens, I hope to do justice to the diverse motivations and projects by situating mediumship practices squarely in the present, in connection with contemporary anxieties, uncertainties and insecurities, linking physical and existential dimensions of human security. Provisionally, I distinguish between four forms of insecurity that require spiritual mending: (1) mental and physical health problems (requiring healing); (2) economic insecurity and market risk (seeking good fortune); (3) existential uncertainties related to the dead, e.g. relatives missing during the war (e.g. locating and ritually burying remains); (4) running deliberate risks and their management. Although this list is far from conclusive, I shall argue that the human security lens allows for a holistic approach, which seeks to connect action to motivation in various domains or dimensions of life, without resorting to the simplistic notions that everything can be explained with reference to a quest for security. I shall explore some of these issues in sections on the connections between human security, religious certainty and spiritual security; on healing and security; on economic security; on existential security; and on freedom, risk and security. This will be done in four ethnographic vignettes, designed to illustrate attempts at creating health security, economic security, existential security – or certainty – and risk and security. In the last section I shall draw some tentative conclusions about the usefulness of applying a human security lens when analysing these phenomena.

HUMAN SECURITY, RELIGIOUS CERTAINTY, SOCIAL SAFETY?

Human security is a relatively new concept that usually defines security along economic dimensions ('Freedom from want'), physical and political dimensions ('Freedom from fear') and ecological dimensions ('Freedom for future generations to inherit a sound natural environment'). As a 'people-centred' security concern it constitutes a shift away from the focus on the state as the locus and subject of (military, political) security, towards the individual as the locus and subject of (the right to) 'human' security. In its report *Human Security Now*, the UN Commission on Human Security (chaired by Sadako Ogata and Amartya Sen) speaks of 'security centered on people – not states' whereby 'people' is operationalised as 'individuals and communities' to be protected against threats (Commission on Human Security 2003: 2). It is not only an analytical but a political concept as well, with a largely rhetorical flavour of mobilising political actors into action, i.e. of protecting against threats to security.

An obvious historical analogy can be discerned in the twentieth-century history of human rights. With the establishment of the League of Nations after the First World War the emphasis was on the right to self-determination embodied in nations as the proper locus and subject of such rights (US President Wilson's 'Fourteen Points'). After the Second World War it became clear how this right to self-determination (e.g. of the *Sudetendeutschen* in Czechoslovakia) could easily be manipulated and abused for war-mongering, while the Holocaust served as a reminder of how individual people were victimised in such grand, nationalistic schemes. This prompted the attempt to safeguard individual rights in the Universal Declaration of Human Rights (1948), strongly promoted by US President Roosevelt's wife Eleanor. Interestingly, this individualistic notion of universal human rights was not uncontested at the time of their inception. In 1947 the *American Anthropologist* published a Statement on Human Rights that the Executive Board of the American Anthropological Association (AAA) (1947) had submitted to the UN Commission on Human Rights. The AAA protested against the individualist and absolutist focus, claiming instead that cultures and hence values differ, and that individuals realise their human-ness through culture. Since then, human rights discourse has become a truly global ideology, seemingly becoming more and more 'universal' despite the continued prevalence of 'the national order of things' (Eriksen 2001a, Malkki 1995, Wilson 1997).

Just as the discourse of universal human rights is predicated on the historically contingent construct of the 'individual' as historical agent, so does the discourse of human security constitute an individualisation of the notion of security. Not only does this mirror the capitalist notion of the 'individual' as the primary subject of history (as opposed to, say, Marxist notions about the 'working class'), but this shift also requires methodological individualism if human security is to be operationalised as an analytical concept.[1] Having said that, it would not make sense to strip the 'methodological individual' of her or his human-ness by limiting human security to the economic (material) and political (physical) domains (which is what happens in the late capitalist market economy, where 'individuals' are reduced to producers and consumers). In other words, if the concept of human security is to be meaningful, then those (social, cultural, psychological, existential) dimensions of life that make individuals truly human can only be left out of the equation at great cost. The simplistic example of the 7 July 2005 suicide bombings in London shows that any attempt to analyse this assault on the human security of Londoners without looking at the religious motives of the perpetrators would be misguided.

The research group contributing to this volume expanded the concept of human security to encompass both physical/material dimensions of 'freedom from want' and 'freedom from fear' and existential/cultural dimensions:

> [This] research programme stretches the meaning of human security to include cultural, cognitive, emotional, religious and symbolic dimensions as well, which are here glossed in the concept of 'existential' and which are bound to processes of signification.... The quest for existential security can be linked with and expressed through issues of national, ethnic, gender and religious identity as ways in which people create collective meanings, traditionally within the purview of cultural anthropology. (Department of Social and Cultural Anthropology 2004: 2)

In this manner, we seek to reconnect with the way human security was initially defined in the *Human Development Report 1994* (United Nations Development Programme [UNDP] 1994), namely along the dimensions of economic security, food security, health security, environmental security, personal security, community security and political security. Under the rubric of 'community security', group membership and processes of identification are singled out:

> Most people derive security from their membership in a group – a family, a community, an organisation, a racial or ethnic group that can provide a cultural identity and a reassuring set of values. Such groups all offer practical support. (UNDP 1994: 31)

The report goes on to warn that communities do not necessarily or always foster human security as 'traditional communities can also perpetuate oppressive practices'.

Outside the economic ('Freedom from want'), physical ('Freedom from fear') and ecological ('Freedom for future generations to inherit a sound natural environment') realms, human security is not yet well-theorised (Burgess 2004, Chen et al. 2003, but see Eriksen 2004). For one, because human security is more often defined negatively in terms of threats, risks or violations (cf. Fukuda-Parr 2003) than for what it is supposed to mean in positive terms. Thomas Hylland Eriksen (2004) points to the other possible opposite of (human) security, namely freedom, but freedom and risk are often two sides of the same coin. In his book *Community* Zygmunt Bauman (2001) discerns a tension between the movement toward freedom and the quest for security, against the backdrop of globalisation and 'liquid modernity' which undermine the traditional 'ethical communities' of people with durable face-to-face commitments to each other. Again, a simplistic example will illustrate this tension. Following the US example, more and more collective retirement pension schemes in Europe become individualised in the sense that participants are offered choices as to how and where their contributions should be invested. This freedom of choice often creates new anxieties at individual levels: putting the money 'safely' in the bank might mean that the returns would be so low as to be outstripped by inflation; but investing in stock with potentially higher returns implies that there is a flipside of higher risks at the same time. This new-found neoliberal 'freedom' creates a dilemma involving potentially serious consequences for post-retirement incomes.

So, how to conceptualise human security comprehensively and positively (rather than in negative terms, as 'threats')? This requires us to think about the types of social and cultural needs, anxieties, desires, ambitions and projects to which 'physical security' and 'existential security' would correspond, and what other notions could be used in the same context. For the English language I am thinking about the notions of 'certainty' and 'safety' as bearing a strong family resemblance to security. However, as the meanings and uses of these terms are as much a matter of style and context as of definition, I am not venturing into an abstract discourse on these three related concepts, separate from the specific cultural meanings for people involved. At the same time, given the methodological individualism implied in the concept of human security we shall have to theorise how to relate individual experiences and projects with social and cultural phenomena. Fortunately for us, we do not have to invent the conceptual wheel anew as, already in 1991, Anthony Giddens enriched our sociological thinking in this regard with the concept of 'ontological security' (1991: 183), which he related to 'identity' conceived not as a 'thing' but as a – largely routine – process of identification linking the person with a group or category (Giddens 1991, see also Jenkins 1996).

In anthropology and sociology, a common association of identity is with ethnic and national categories (see Giddens 1991, Jenkins 1997, 2001), linking the self and personal experience with collective categories through processes of (self-) identification and attribution. In the words of Eriksen: 'people's personal experiences are the very raw material of such [ethnic or nationalist] ideologies' (2001b: 68). There is little doubt that 'ethnicity' can have important consequences for human security, as is brought out by its frequent discursive association with 'conflict' (Giddens 1991; Jenkins 1997, 2001). This has raised the question, already implied in the *Human Development Report 1994* (UNDP 1994), why individuals can become so entangled in ethnic projects that they are willing to risk their own or other people's life, health or assets to achieve their aims. Many scholars refer to some form of existential security or certainty in their explanations. Richard Jenkins (1997) borrows Giddens' notion of 'ontological security' as part of people's need for a stable 'self-identity'. In his comparative treatise on the role of culture and ethnicity in contemporary political conflicts, Jack Eller (1999) looks at the way in which the notion of ethnicity creates a 'common past' as a memory that it is worthwhile fighting for. In his book on ethnicity and the state in Southeast Asia, political scientist David Brown (1994) builds on the Weberian notion of ethnicity as the imagining of shared descent – again through narratives about the past – in order to develop a notion of ethnicity as a metaphor for family, and draws on psychoanalytical theories to explain the extraordinary strength of ethnic identifications. In such theories, the assumed security of ethnic belonging would explain the strength of identity politics in that domain. Arjun Appadurai (1999) goes one step further by asserting that violent conflict can be a way for young men to create 'dead certainty' about their identity – both ethnic and gender. Oskar Verkaaik (2003), on the other hand, stresses the 'fun' element in collective violence along ethnic lines. Both Appadurai and Verkaaik seem to imply that young men take risks in order to create ontological security, thereby challenging the physical security of others.

In spite of the anthropological fascination with ethnicity over the past two decades, other forms of identification matter just as much. Whereas nation, region, locality, community and 'race' are often seen as 'variations on the basic ethnic theme of collective identification stressing perceived cultural differentiation' (Jenkins

2001: 8), other identifications may follow class, gender or religious lines. There, too, the distinctions and connections between security, certainty and safety are not always relevant, but it is often assumed that people seek some degree of certainty in their (class, gender, religious) identity, while simultaneously striving to create some measure of security through their notion of belonging to a particular collective (social category, group, 'community'). This is perhaps brought out best in Zygmunt Bauman's (2001) connection of security with his nostalgic notion of the 'ethical community' (*contra* 'aesthetic community') consisting of a 'warm circle' of people having durable responsibilities and commitments to one another against the backdrop of 'liquid modernity'.

The relations of identification between the individual and collective levels, as well as between the various dimensions of identification, are usually extremely complex and entangled. This often results in the paradoxical situation that the striving for or creation of certainty can come at the expense of security in another domain, and vice versa. In the next sections I shall explore how particular religious identifications and practices in Vietnam can be interpreted through a human security lens. I shall offer four vignettes, designed to illustrate attempts at creating health security, economic security, existential security – or certainty – and gender and/or sexual security. In the last section I shall draw some tentative conclusions about the usefulness of applying a human security lens when analysing these phenomena.

HUMAN SECURITY AND HEALING

There is a burgeoning literature on the revival of ritual and religious practices during the *Đôi mói* period, after a period of suppression of 'superstitions' (*mê tín dị đoan*) in the campaign for secularisation and socialist construction. There is a variety of interpretations for the 'new forms of religiosity' (see Roberts 1995) in post-socialist Vietnam. Hy Van Luong (1993) points at more political space for religious and ritual action, at increased wealth, and at a need for spiritual compensation for the economic insecurity inherent in the market. In their village studies in northern Vietnam, both John Kleinen (1999) and Shaun Malarney (2002) draw attention to prestige as a function of economic position through 'conspicuous consumption'. But while these authors speak about religious practice in general, what is striking about spirit mediumship is its highly transactional nature, leading many observers to comment on the 'commercial' character of spirit mediumship. Philip Taylor (2002, 2004) draws attention to new forms of devotion and massive pilgrimage in a modern market context in southern Vietnam. In his book *Goddess on the Rise* (2004) about religious beliefs and ritual practices centred on goddesses in southern Vietnam, Taylor offers the quasi-Marxist interpretation that the transactional nature of people's dealings with deities and spirits is way of 'embodying market relations' (2004: 83–110).

When it comes to the revival of spirit mediumship, most of the contemporary sources draw attention to the practice of *Đạo Mẫu* or Mother Goddess worship which is currently seeing a huge revival in Vietnam. In the course of the last couple of years many temples have been restored and put to renewed use. Spirit mediums and their clients host sessions in their 'own' temples or organise pilgrimages to temple festivals. Some spirit mediums themselves choose to speak of *Đạo Thánh* (worship of saints or spirits, including historical heroes like Trần Hưng Đạo) rather than *Đạo Mẫu*, which may be correct because the Mother Goddess is just one of the many spirits. The *thánh*, then, include the various personas of celestial mandarins, ladies and pages in the pantheon overseen by the Mother Goddess in the 'four palaces' (*tứ phủ*), as well as the various legendary or historical figures who have been immortalised as saints and who possess special faculties that they may use for the benefit of their devout followers. Followers are themselves investing heavily in the possession rituals, with either the master or themselves in the role of medium. One *chầu văn* musician in his 70s told me that he had been travelling around in the Red River Delta as a musician since he was a child, but that at no point in his life had he witnessed so many spirit possession rituals. *Lên đồng* has become a widely accepted, widespread and very popular practice.

In 2002 I visited the Lưu Phái temple complex together with my friend Ngô Đức Thịnh. In a rural area just south of Hanoi, the complex consists of a 'Buddhist' pagoda (*chùa*), a 'Taoist' temple (*đền*) and a 'Confucian' tutelary village shrine (*đình*) next to each other, and all three buildings had been rebuilt or restored in the 1990s following the damage wrought by the wars and the revolution.[2] We went there in order to attend the initiation ritual as spirit medium of Ms Hà, a mother of two and a garment and shoe trader in Hanoi's best-known market, Đồng Xuân, who sought healing for her ailments. For her first, initiatory possession (*ra đồng*), Ms Hà was assisted by Mr Hùng, a professional medium based at a temple in the old quarter of Hanoi, and his own assistants; by the temple master, *thầy* Nghĩa; by an old lady; and by the *chầu văn* ceremonial music band; in the presence of some relatives and friends. Hà had invested a considerable amount of money in the clothes, in the sacrificial objects offered to the deities (and to be returned as heavenly, auspicious gifts – *lộc*), and in the organisation of the ceremony itself. As a first-time medium, she did not know the ritually prescribed acts, and her dancing performance was often quite hesitant and clumsy, to the point that the audience even showed the right moves and finger positions to her. Eventually she grew into her performance as she approached the two final – and most cheerful and exciting – incarnations, of *Cô Chín* (the ninth damsel) and *Cậu Bé* (the youngest page). Suddenly the ritual ended, when the heavenly gifts were distributed among the assistants and the audience. 'Is it over now?', asked Ms Hà. She was exhausted.

I asked Ms Hà why she would want to be possessed by deities and invest so much money and effort to do so. She told me that she had been feeling ill for some time now, but did not get better. Regular doctors could not find the cause of her predicament. The last half year things had taken a turn for the worse, and she 'lost everything', meaning that now not only her health but her livelihood and her family happiness were at stake. Because the cause was allegedly not biomedical, regular physicians could not diagnose her properly. Instead, she was diagnosed by a soothsayer as having *căn* – the spirit root, which means that she is destined (*duyên*) to be entered by spirits and deities (*nhập hồn thánh*). There is no choice, for failing to submit one's body as vessel for spirits to ride means bad luck, first and foremost in the form of bad physical or mental health. In other words, Ms Hà wanted to be initiated as medium in order to placate the spirits that try to enter her body and thus rid herself of the plagues affecting her. In that sense she engaged in an act of healing, thus creating physical and psychological security for herself and her family.

Ms Hà is an 'amateur' spirit medium, but 'professional' mediums often go through near-death experiences. *Thầy đồng* Nam is a professional master medium who practises at various temples in Hanoi and surrounding villages, while also having his own temple and his group of (young male) ritual attendants living with him. Coming from a poor family, Nam showed talent for dance, which is why he was admitted to the *tuồng* traditional opera school in Hanoi. After graduation he worked as artist but became seriously ill, to the point that he almost died. His mother then secretly called for a medium (which was strictly forbidden at the time) who diagnosed Nam as having *căn* – the spirit root. After Nam was initiated into trance possession (*ra đồng*) for the first time, his ailments subsided and he made a career as professional medium. His opera training helped him perfect his performance in this spiritual field characterised by competition between mediums in both ritual efficacy and in aesthetics.[3] A reputation for efficacy is important because many clients come to spirit mediums with prayers for good health.

In other mediumship traditions outside *lên đồng*, sickness and healing are common motivations for people to become a spirit medium. Ms Thi is an idiosyncratic medium who is possessed by the spirits of deceased relatives of clients. Ms Thi was born in a mountainous district in 1956, into a poor, ethnic Dao family. At the age of nine she became very ill. The local health authorities diagnosed leprosy. Then her parents let her go to the provincial ethnic minority school but after two years she became too ill to study. In 1973 she got married but she was still continuously ill until 1982 when the sickness abated. In 1988 the illness seemed to return in the form of a skin disease which crept up from the feet and arms to cover the head and which caused her to have visions of people and creatures wanting to enter her head.[4] One time she saw a snake and a tiger speaking, telling her that she was chosen by the ancestors (*cha cắt mẹ cử*) to have a 'public/meritorious duty' (*việc công*).[5] When she accepted the calling by opening herself to the spirits, she was healed and recovered from her illness. In spite of her own wishes, the spirits will not allow her to do any other work. If she goes to the market she sells nothing, and if she works in the field she becomes crippled. She now lives in Hòa Bình province with her husband and children, with two brothers, their children and their families living in the vicinity. Even though she now lives in a new, concrete house that she built recently, the spirits have not allowed her to move the site of the trance sessions from the old wooden house-temple to the new house closer to the road (see Salemink and Phan Đăng Nhật n.d.).

This observation is confirmed by other scholars. In her analysis of spirit mediums, Nguyễn Thị Hiền (2002) draws attention to the therapeutic function of the initiation and the rituals. If asked what the compelling aspects of *hầu đồng* are in the eyes of the adherents, we can point at two important factors: efficacy and aesthetic pleasure. In her dissertation on nothern *lên đồng*, Nguyễn Thị Hiền mentions both, by focusing on the ritual as drama and performance (2002: 19–20, 73); and as therapeutic practice (2002:

99–124). In terms of therapy or healing, many followers have wishes relating to good fortune and to good health; they hope that their sacrifices and prayers will be rewarded by the Mother Goddess or the spirits. Similarly, in interviews about their life stories, spirit mediums claimed that they had a physical or psychological need to act as medium, and that the occasion for *ra đồng* (mediumship initiation) often was a serious disease. Nguyễn Thị Hiền (2002: 80–91) provides a much more detailed account of such physical and psychological states, and the various strategies of seeking healing – either through institutional biomedical or psychiatric health services, or through informal ritual channels, but usually combining both. But how does this observation relate to human security, we may ask?

In their contributions to the Harvard volume *Human Insecurity in a Global World*, Chen and Narasimhan, in a chapter entitled 'Global Health and Human Security' (2003) and Heymann (2003) in his 'Infectious Disease Threats to National and Global Security', pitch their analyses at the national, regional and international levels. In aiming at international levels of analysis and intervention, they lack specificity and lose sight of the 'people-centred' focus of human security. Their pleas for better coordination between global and national health policies are important, but they lose sight of people as the *subjects* of human security rather than objects ('targets') of policy; and as full human beings rather than bodies without minds and without culture. In this way they deny people's agency as subjects who construe discursively and construct practically their own health security, in connection with other human security dimensions. By keeping their analysis pitched at national and international policy levels, they miss out on the possibilities of universalisation offered by the methodological individualism of the 'human security' concept compared with the narrow definition of security as an exclusively national – and military or police – affair.

In contrast, I would suggest that the vignette above shows us that people employ a variety of culturally specific strategies to ensure their health and well-being. Many mediums and their clients have found ways to cope with and overcome (physical and mental) health problems and other misfortune through mediumship practices. It is easy to speculate that many of the people who found healing this way would have ended up populating hospitals and occasionally mental clinics – as actually happened during the years that spirit mediumship was actively suppressed by the Vietnamese Communist Party-state. Suppressing or ignoring such individual strategies – as the large-scale biomedical approach routinely does – will make us lose sight of the ways such strategies are combined with myriad other strategies that people employ to enhance their human security. After all, in the lives of real people, their health and well-being is entangled with questions of physical safety, livelihood, empowerment and cultural/religious fulfilment.

LIVELIHOOD SECURITY AND THE SPIRITS OF CAPITALISM

'Freedom from want' is one of the core elements in the 'classic' definition of human security. What is meant here is, of course, the absence of poverty (which has both absolute and relative dimensions), because an actual 'absence of want' would make the entire world economy come to grinding halt. After all, the globalised consumerism characteristic of late capitalism and postmodern culture can only make the economy roll if new desires are constantly whetted, if new wants are imagined and if new economic demands are continuously created. So what links freedom from want, consumerism and poverty alleviation to each other? According to statistics offered by the Vietnamese government, by the UNDP and by the World Bank, Vietnam is the latest success story for liberal reforms, with high GDP growth rates and a decline of poor households by 20 per cent from 1993 (55 per cent nationwide) to 1998 (36 per cent nationwide), according to the Vietnam Living Standards Surveys. However, since then economic differentiation has widened and hardened, creating a bottom stratum of inveterately poor people (that includes most of Vietnam's ethnic minority people) facing rising expenses for services (health, education) that were once at least nominally free (Jörgensen 2006). Recently the statistics worsened again when the government decided to raise Vietnam's poverty line to bring it slightly more in line with an internationally applied measure of $1 per day (which again is not so far below the average per capita GDP of $550). Simultaneously, however, poor post-war, post-socialist Vietnam has become a consumer society in its own right, in which entrepreneurs and corrupt cadres can make fortunes and cities witness the rise of a middle class willing and able to spend their wealth on houses and amenities, motorbikes, cars, videos, domestic and foreign tourism, and sumptuous lifestyles. Even for poor people in 'remote areas' it is impossible not to be aware of the lure and promise of consumption, and to be immune from the desire for consumer objects.

Behind the average figures hides a world in which most households are dependent on self-employed livelihoods – as farmers, as traders, in the informal sector – and hence on the caprice of the market. A natural disaster, illness in the household, official corruption, too few or too many children, broken machinery and many other eventualities could make a household lose its land or other assets and push it below the poverty line. But what really contributes to a sense of profound vulnerability and economic insecurity is that volatile market forces or inexplicably wrong business decisions can have the same effect, but without comprehension or predictability. In the words of Philip Taylor:

> Exposure to the market has transformed their lives, causing dislocations, a sense of powerlessness, and a feeling of being controlled by invisible, remote and powerful forces. (2004: 87)

It is this sense of powerlessness that many people seek to overcome in the religious practice that Taylor alludes to, in particular in spirit mediumship.

To a major degree, the efficacy attributed to spirit mediums and related rituals can be connected with wealth. According to Taylor (2002, 2004), this expectation of material wealth can primarily be found in Vietnam's Mekong Delta, which – with the metropolis of Saigon or Ho Chi Minh City – would be the country's most commercialised region. But in my research of various forms of spirit mediumship in the northern and central part of the country I did not notice any significant difference in terms of wishes or prayers (cầu). Many of the wishes of the followers and many of the practices in mediumship rituals revolve around the hope or expectation of gaining material wealth through the intervention of particular spirits, and their blessing of objects or (new, unused) money travelling back and forth to the other world and circulating between spirit medium, attendants and worshippers. Taylor claims that a good proportion of the millions of pilgrims that annually visit the shrine of Bà Chúa Xứ' (Lady of the Realm) in Châu Đốc are market women or people who are otherwise involved in trade. But Nguyễn Thị Hiền (2002: 91–4) found a similar background of spirit mediums and their followers in the northern variant of the ritual. In the area of the former imperial capital of Huế I found a mixed situation in that many of the elderly participants in the pilgrimage on the river were former aristocrats, but many younger participants were urban market traders – usually women (see Salemink 2007). During ceremonies – and especially toward the end – the excitement in the audience usually grows as the amount of 'auspicious' (*lộc*) objects and banknotes distributed by sponsors increases. In an unpublished paper on the rapidly growing popularity of the 'Granary/Treasury Queen' (Bà Chúa Kho) near Bắc Ninh town, Ngô Đức Thịnh relates this phenomenon to Vietnam's transition to a market economy:

> Pilgrims come especially in the beginning of the year to borrow her 'money' so as to make a living or to ask for 'her presents', then at the end of the year they will come back to show their gratitude and repay their debt. (Ngô Đức Thịnh n.d.: 5, see also Lê Hồng Lý 2001)

Completing the ritual engenders enhanced well-being and confidence in the future on the part of participants. In the eyes of the followers, then, the efficacy of the ritual lies in the effects in response to the wishes – whether they be well-being, health or wealth.

It would seem then that the ritual upsurge in Vietnam is not just a compensation for economic insecurity (Luong 1993), or a public expression of new-found cultural liberties (Luong 1993; Malarney 2002), or of new-found wealth (Kleinen 1999, Malarney 2002), but actually takes on the form of a commercial transaction between the deity or spirit in the 'other world' (*thế giới khác*) or 'yin world' (*thế giới âm*) and the client in 'this world' or the 'yang world' (*thế giới dương*). The influential cultural commentator Tòan Ánh invokes the following saying in order to understand the relationship of the living with the underworld:

> We believe that *dương sao âm vậy* [however the yang world is, so is the yin world]: whatever the living need, the dead need the same and however the living lead their lives, the dead do the same. The dead have a 'life' in the underworld, just like the life of people on earth. To put it differently, dead people also need to eat and drink, they need to spend and they need a place to live, just like living people. (1991: 20)

The market becomes a direct metaphor to articulate the transactional relationship between human beings and deities in the other world:

> The intensification of market relations ... since the mid-1980s has given rise to religious subjectivities that relate to the assertion of

personal agency, the quest for predictability, and the management of anxiety. (Taylor 2004: 87)

This assessment of the transactional nature of ritual practice seems to be quite common in Asia, as one is reminded of Asian-style prosperity cults in Thailand, Taiwan, China, Japan. In her essay 'Korean Shamans and the Spirits of Capitalism', Laurel Kendall (1996) offers a view of the quite similar Korean shamans that is very much comparable to the Vietnam case, in that shamans are making a massive 'come-back' in present-day Korea, in connection with the unfolding of capitalism in that country.

Returning to the question of human security as 'freedom from want', it seems clear now that spirit mediumship does play a role in creating economic security in the eye of the beholder – i.e. the clients of the mediums. The clients build up the necessary confidence and trust in order to be successful in their business, and effectively create social capital based on the belief in the auspicious effects of spirit mediums. Clients will use the ritually auspicious goods and money that they 'borrow' from the spirit – or sometimes the Goddess – in order to invest it in their business. If the business is successful, the clients have to pay the spirit back with interest, or else the spirit will get angry and cause harm. This is why so many temples are so rich these days that they are restored, rebuilt, expanded, refurbished and/ or embellished. One famous example is the temple of Bà Chúa Xứ in Châu Đốc, which is stuffed with expensive presents for the Lady (beautiful clothes, gold-engraved plaques, 'meritorious' financial contributions (công đức), etc.). But less well-known mediums, like the ethnic Dao medium Ms Thi in Hoà Bình province, routinely receive presents ranging from clothes to cell phones from satisfied clients as well (but only after the efficacy is 'proven'). I would like to stress that the key word here is ritual efficacy, but that is also the catch. Informants tend to stress that the auspicious effects can only be realised if one believes: 'You just have to believe!' (Mình cần phải tin tưởng thôi). Without belief in the deity and her efficacy, the 'exchange' or transaction cannot work, because the goddess is jealous and will consider this an insult, causing harm rather than good. This often means that if the outcome is not as positive as expected or hoped for, it is the client herself who is to blame for lack of faith.

This reduces the answer to the question of whether spirit mediumship might play a role in creating economic security (i.e. freedom from want – but not freedom from desire for consumer goods or from economic demand) quite literally to a matter of faith. The belief that spirits can help via mediums is important in a situation where people feel disoriented, at the mercy of invisible, remote and powerful market forces, and thus have no signposts to make out whether their business decisions may be right or not. We know from the – often erratic – behaviour of investors and traders in the international stock markets how important rumour, belief and 'intuition' can be in influencing investment decisions and in determining market values of company shares in an economic domain that is supposed to be ruled by rational considerations of profit maximisation by *homines oeconomici*. Groundless optimism can be a reason for soaring stocks, while pessimism is often the cause for disinvestments and hence economic downturns. In Vietnam, the spiritual security sought via mediums not only compensates for the insecurity of the unpredictable market but creates the social capital necessary for investing confidently in new (or old) enterprises, thus enhancing economic security of the traders, their dependents, business partners and clients. This seems a confirmation of Robert Barro's recent thesis of 'spiritual capital' regarding the (positive) correlation between religiosity and economic growth (2004: 64).

IN SEARCH OF EXISTENTIAL SECURITY IN AFTERLIFE – AND THIS LIFE

The ritualised *lên đồng* form of spirit mediumship is certainly not the only form of mediumship, spirit possession, trance and shamanism in Vietnam.[6] There are more individualised forms of mediumship that have also become more popular in the present time. These forms involve special faculties attributed to individual mediums, and their clients usually seek to get in contact with a dead person, with a living person who is missing, or both at the same time. One widespread but contested practice in contemporary Vietnam is the search for remains of people 'missing in action' (MIAs) since the war years. Overseas, MIAs are usually associated with American soldiers missing in action; with the politicised myth of American soldiers still held prisoner in 'North Vietnamese' camps; with Rambo films, and with the political lobbying of right-wing pressure groups opposing normalisation of US relations with present-day, Communist-led Vietnam. But apart from the continuing search for remains of American MIAs, there are also around 300,000 Vietnamese soldiers and militia still missing after the three 'Indochina Wars' (with France, 1945–54; with the US, 1960–75; with Cambodia and China, 1979–89), which is a painful issue for family members of those who are unaccounted for, whose remains have not been located and who have not been buried properly.

In the dominant cosmology in Vietnam, death is a journey rather than a radical departure, which means that the souls of the dead continue to be with us for some time. Across the main religious traditions (Buddhism, Taoism, Confucianism, ancestor worship and spirit worship), death is a transition of the soul from this world to the other world (*thế giới khác*) where the soul lives on as a spirit until s/he is born again. All rituals having to do with ancestor worship both seek to venerate the ancestors out of thankfulness and indebtedness (*nhớ ơn*). Simultaneously, people seek to placate the spirits of ancestors because the spirits can be beneficial as well as potentially harmful, as spirits exert an influence in the affairs of this world as well. Funerary rituals aim to guide the deceased person safely on the voyage to the other world – safely out of reach of humans – while pleasing her/him by showing appropriate grief (see Malarney 1996, 2002). But failing to comply with the ritual prescriptions turns the soul of the dead person into a hungry, revengeful wandering soul (Luu Hung et al. 2003, Malarney 2002). The soul of such a dead person who is not buried with the proper rituals will wander between the two worlds and can exert a harmful influence on the situation of the living. For their relatives or descendants who are getting older, having a family member who has not been buried properly is literally 'unfinished business'.[7]

In order to put the wandering souls of lost loved ones to rest, many Vietnamese are presently looking for remains of lost loved ones in a variety of ways, first of all by consulting the army records. If these offer no clue, many people nowadays resort to the services of a medium, shaman or clairvoyant because they believe that these people have special, supernatural gifts that may help them locate the remains of the MIAs. This belief received a boost when a scientist and former leader in the Communist regime, Mr. Trần Phương, circulated a paper narrating his own experiences which forced him to abandon his scepticism. Many Vietnamese believe in such supernatural phenomena, or at least like to try this avenue when all other avenues have been exhausted, while many others, however, remain sceptical. Yet, over the past five years there has been a remarkable upsurge in the numbers of people seeking the support of mediums, clairvoyants or people with special faculties, as well as public interest in the phenomenon. According to Professor Phan Đăng Nhật who has been studying this phenomenon for some years and who has interviewed hundreds of clients, this upsurge can be attributed to greater wealth among Vietnam's population; better communication and transportation systems; more freedom to travel and more religious liberties than during the era of 'High Socialism'; and the ageing of the clients themselves, who do not wish to leave 'unfinished business' behind that could potentially harm their living descendants or themselves in their afterlives (Phan Đăng Nhật 2003 – personal communication). In an unpublished paper on this topic, Phan Đăng Nhật distinguishes between five different 'special faculties' employed by famous mediums.[8] While some mediums specialise in finding dead bodies, other mediums have a more varied repertoire. What is clear in all of these cases, though, is that the special faculty is highly individual, located within such an individual or in a special relationship of the medium with a spirit, saint or deity. Because of this individual character, rituals around such forms of spirit possession or shamanism are individual, too, and are usually not as scripted as the lên đồng rituals, which go through a prescribed number of stages, each with fixed attributes.

The ethnic Dao medium Ms Thi is someone who is reputed to be able to help find the remains of people who have been lost, being a spirit medium whose body is completely possessed by spirits during the sessions, and whose mind is 'empty' – without consciousness – and who therefore has no recollection afterwards of what goes on during the possession. Take one ordinary day in 2003, when Ms Thi enters the old wooden house which functions as ritual space, and which is already packed with people – some of whom have come from far away – seeking her services. Dressed in normal, everyday clothes, she prays before the altar to ask for permission from the (unnamed) spirits to begin the ceremony. These prayers last for about an hour, while clients continue to prepare the altars and the sacrifices, and burn effigies and votive paper money in the yard outside. All the while, people walk in and out of the room through one of the three doors. After Ms Thi eats a bit, and rests on the mat, she sits down on an upright chair with eyes closed. From there she orders that paper waste be removed from under the altar, and asks whether everybody is ready with their requests. When there is positive response, somebody starts a tape player with music and Buddhist chants. Prayer books from the little table in front of the altar are distributed, and people seated on the mats will chant along with the better-known chants. Prayers are chanted in unison, then Ms Thi asks permission to continue the ceremony from the saints of a multi-ethnic Taoist pantheon.

After sitting upright on the chair for 15 minutes, Ms Thi's head and body start to sway in circular motion, and the audience becomes excited, murmurs chants that ask for 'their' spirit to appear. At 11:45 a.m. Thi suddenly speaks with a clear voice and asks for Hạnh. Ms Hạnh, an elderly lady, comes running in through the main entrance which is the entrance used by the spirits and hence forbidden for the living to use. The spell is broken and Thi opens her eyes, while Ms Hạnh is distraught that she cannot meet her dead child now. She apologises profusely and attempts to mend the relationship with the spirit by renewed praying and offering at the altar. The procedure starts again with chanting to Buddha from the book. Thi begins to sway again but now it is Hạnh herself who goes into a trance while seated on the mat. She shakes her head and entire body, stands up, and speaks, dances and cries. When Ms Hạnh collapses after a few minutes, she does not remember what happened, but the commentary offered by the public holds that she was possessed by the spirit of her paternal grandfather (*ông nội*). After Ms Hạnh recovers, Thi starts to shake her head quickly now. She spreads her hands with palms up, indicating that the spirit is male. Incarnated in the body of Ms Thi, the low voice of her husband calls Ms Nga, and he mentions the names of family members, criticising one family member who has two wives. The spirit laments his fate – why was he alone when he died during the war? Why did she come only now for the first time, after 45 years? Why is fate so hard that he has to wander on the ground of his forefathers? Ms Nga and her daughter Liễu come forward and respectfully offer rice wine, which the spirit (through the body of the medium) accepts and drinks. Why did the other family members not come? Nga whispers that the other children and grandchildren could not come for they are in the south. After some time the spirit leaves Ms Thi's body, and Thi opens her eyes, looks around her as if awaking from a deep sleep.

After a number of other clients have met their dead relatives, the medium does not 'wake up' from her trance and again begins to sway her head and body as the crowd chants the Vietnamese name of the Amitabha Buddha – A di đà Phật. With the palms of her hand stretched out she calls Mô from far-away Nghệ An province, but the crowd answers that Mô went home already. Mô's family had been around for the past couple of days but they went home after waiting for some days without success in meeting with a spirit. Many people do wait, for days or even weeks if necessary, especially those who come from far away. During the next trance the medium puts both hands akimbo, indicating that the body is possessed by an old male spirit, Ông Tạo, who calls his wife Ms Thu, an elderly woman of about 70. From the conversation it becomes clear that she has three brothers killed during the war (*liệt sỹ*), and that she is looking for their graves in Quảng Ngãi province in central Vietnam, below the old demarcation line along the 17th Parallel. The spirit is offered a glass of beer and cigarettes (three at a time), his conversation is very lively, as he is alternately joking and crying with Ms Thu. He encourages her to go look for the graves but his information is not very precise, as far as I can ascertain.

According to some northern Vietnamese, locating graves in this manner would only work for those who had fought on the 'politically correct' revolutionary side of the war, thus becoming war martyrs (*liệt sỹ*) and hence considered to have sacrificed themselves (*hy sinh*) for the nation (see Malarney 2001). However, I have observed that locating graves via spirit mediums is not the exclusive prerogative of politically correct war martyrs. One day at the shrine of Ms Thi, Mr Minh, a middle-aged man, meets the spirit of his younger brother, who had died as a child, and whose grave had been removed in the course of a construction project development. This created great agony for Mr Minh, who did not know where the remains were now and was anxious that his brother might do harm to him or his family for not paying sufficient attention to the grave. When Ms Thi's body is possessed by the spirit of the younger brother, the spirit speaks, moves, laughs and cries like an agitated child, and the conversation ranges over people and topics that are familiar to both brothers, thus visibly moving the audience. Shifting the conversation to the reason for the meeting, the younger brother can put Mr. Minh at ease by giving very precise and detailed information as to where to look for the remains. Sometimes information is checked – five steps from this or from that tree? – but in the end, when the brothers bid goodbye to each other, Mr Minh is satisfied that he will find the remains of his brother, giving him the opportunity to re-bury the bones in a new grave.

For living relatives or descendants who cannot meet the ritual requirements of a proper burial, the continued presence of a family member wandering as a restless, hungry soul between two worlds is not just a source of existential anxiety in terms of not being able to pay the filial debt. It is a source of profound insecurity and uncertainty regarding the present situation. Health, wealth and good fortune are transient, ephemeral and at constant risk of being lost – a risk that will loom large if posed by a malevolent spirit, and which will undermine confidence in the present and the future, and hence self-confidence and decisiveness. On the other hand, bad fortune will be attributed to the hungry souls. The successful search and ritually correct burial of lost remains using the services of a spirit medium will enhance family well-being and self-confidence, which are indispensable components of their sense of human security.

ENGAGING RISK, ADVENTURE AND INSECURITY

If human security is conceptualised as a 'perennial quest' (Department of Social Anthropology 2004), then any analysis that wants to do justice to the richness of human endeavours must come to terms with risk-seeking behaviour, often associated with notions of freedom, adventure, individualism, gambling, risk-taking, etc. In some social practices, such behaviour is more or less institution-alised: for example, in adventure sports, lotteries, some forms of sexual behaviour, criminal behaviour, hooliganism, etc. In Zygmunt Bauman's work (2001: 20), 'security' is nostalgically equated with 'community' (or better: the 'ethical community' which he thinks of as a 'warm circle' of contacts) and seen as opposed to the kind of freedom connected with globalisation and 'liquid modernity'. Needless to say, this is not the freedom of 'freedom *from* want' and 'freedom *from* fear' which defines freedom by the absence of negative phenomena, like 'want' or 'fear'. Rather, this is the positive but inherently risky freedom *to* choose – or to withdraw from the constraints of the community circle if it is not so warm as some cultural critics would claim. Yet this freedom to choose – positively valued in Western culture – can also cause anxieties, even when it comes to deciding what to buy when shopping, as Barry Schwartz argues in 'The Tyranny of Choice' (2004).

Whether positively or negatively valued, in many countries and many domains in life, risk-seeking behaviour is very common, albeit pursued differently by different social categories – as Gerben Nooteboom (2003: 221–45) showed for Java. This is no different for Vietnam. Spend one day in Vietnam's crazy traffic, and the meaning of risk will seem very graphic to the outsider, although it is fair to add that the *emic* assessment must be different from an *etic* assessment of risk by outsiders, and is often balanced against a notion of 'fate'. But fate is to some extent determined in the other world, and can therefore be influenced through ritual and propitiation of the relevant spirits, saints or deities; or it can be navigated through the services of a Tao horoscopist, geomancer (feng shui or *phong thủy*), soothsayer, or *I ching* sticks interpreters. When having to make decisions, when embarking on a risky journey – either real in traffic, or metaphorical – many Vietnamese will seek the services of such mediators.

In March 2005, an informant of anthropologist Malte Stokhof took us to a temple complex just outside of Ho Chi Minh City's Chinese district Chợ Lớn. The man, an ethnic Cham Muslim, owns a café and a longtail boat with which he maintains a ferry service to the temples which from the city can only be reached by water.[9] The temple complex had the usual strangely syncretic array of different religious traditions, including a temple dedicated to the tutelary genie of the village (*đình*), a Buddhist pagoda (*chùa*), a temple dedicated to the five incarnations of the Mother Goddess (*đin*), and an official, political shrine venerating Communist Vietnam's second president after Hồ Chí Minh, president Tôn Đức Thắng. But a bit further away, amid commercial fish ponds alongside the canal, is an inconspicuous site which constitutes a destination of secret nightly pilgrimages. By the river one finds small altars dedicated to the five incarnations of the Mother Goddess, the Lord Tiger and other deities, which are the site of spirit medium practices found elsewhere. A few steps further along a dike one can find two graves – one made of cement, the other a lowly dirt grave – which belong to an orphaned boy and his sister, respectively. The story is that some years ago the boy committed suicide there by hanging himself from a tree, and that some time afterward, the girl did the same thing at the same place. Then somebody came to pray there one day, and she won the big price in the lottery after having communicated with the spirits of the boy and girl. The story about this good fortune, attributed to the spiritual intervention of the souls of both children, quickly spread, attracting many aspiring lottery winners. Now the place is extremely popular with those who seek spiritual intervention or advice regarding lottery games. Clients come secretly by night because the authorities have forbidden the practices as superstitious. Yet the place is slowly being converted to a shrine, with an altar, with one upgraded grave and one grave waiting to be upgraded by a thankful client.

As playing in the lottery is tantamount to taking risks, the argument about seeking spiritual security does not seem to hold here. People do not always seek security, and certainly not by avoiding risk. For many people, playing in the lottery constitutes an obvious gamble and entails consciously running risks in the hope or expectation of making the big hit. But it is not always gambling that involves risk-seeking behaviour. We might think of playing the market, with equally unpredictable outcomes, and with similar inexplicable inequality, thus resembling what Richard Sennett (1997) called a 'winner-takes-all market'. Or we might think of risky sexual behaviour in the age of AIDS (Andersson 2002), engaging in crime (running the risk of being killed or jailed) or extreme sports or extreme adventures (Ortner 1997). Yet, when running risk, people often seek compensation for that risk, for instance by seeking spiritual intervention. This can then be interpreted as a form of compensating for insecurity and reducing anxiety – if not seeking more security – when engaging in risky adventures.

CONCLUSION

In this chapter I have offered a number of ethnographic vignettes in order to show how spirit mediumship practices in contemporary Vietnam are situated within a field characterised by insecurity and risk, but that encompass myriad individual or family projects aimed at seeking either security or freedom. Regarding *healing*, I have argued that people employ a variety of culturally specific strategies to ensure their health and well-being. Many mediums and their clients have found ways to cope with and overcome (physical and mental) health problems and other misfortune through mediumship practices. However, in the lives of real people, their health and well-being is entangled with questions of physical safety, livelihood, empowerment and cultural/religious fulfilment. Regarding *economic security*, the belief that spirits can help via mediums is important in a situation where people feel disoriented, at the mercy of invisible, remote and powerful market forces, and thus have no signposts to make out whether their business decisions may be right or not. In Vietnam, the spiritual security sought via mediums not only compensates for the insecurity of the unpredictable market but also creates the social capital necessary for investing confidently in new (or old) enterprises, thus enhancing economic security of the traders, their dependents, business partners and clients. Regarding *existential* security, spirit mediums cannot, of course, guarantee a life free of anxiety, simply because people get sick and die; fuss and fight; and love and hate. In fact, coming to grips with the inescapable limitations of life seems the stuff of many religious creeds and rituals. But spirit mediumship practices can assuage culturally and historically specific anxieties, for instance concerning the continued presence of a family member wandering as a restless, hungry soul between two worlds, which is not just a source of existential anxiety but also of profound insecurity and uncertainty regarding the present material situation of the living relatives.

But even if we assume that the construction of human security is a socially important motivation – regardless of whether the UN adopts the concept of human security as a political instrument – we cannot presuppose that it is a universal goal. In the fourth vignette, I have described the reverse practice of engaging *risk* in connection with security, as playing in the lottery is tantamount to taking risks. Therefore, the argument about seeking spiritual security does not seem to hold here, implying that spirit mediumship can guide people seeking security as well as those engaging risk. Yet, even then we should be aware of *emic* constructions of the market as being as volatile, unpredictable and opaque as the lottery. Seeking spiritual intervention can then be interpreted as a form of compensating for insecurity and reducing anxiety – if not seeking more security – when engaging in what are, by definition, risky adventures. So where does this discussion of human security as an *emic* construction leave us?

As opposed to the universalising concept of human rights, human security and risk can only make sense if properly contextualised – locally, culturally and historically. In the vignettes presented above, the meaning of security was construed in *emic* rather than *etic* terms. This meaning had a profound local aspect to it in the sense that certain cultural constructions of security – and the attending strategies and projects to pursue them (see Ortner 1997) – would make sense in particular local, cultural and historical contexts, against the backdrop of globalising and transnationalising tendencies, and in connection with *emic* constructions of insecurity, risk and freedom. The anxiety about MIAs, for instance, has to do with the impact of the consecutive Indochina Wars in Vietnam, and the culturally specific meaning attributed to the souls' continued roaming in between this world and the netherworld, turning existential anxiety into a sense of profound (kin-bound social, economic, and health-related) insecurity. While similar forms of spirit mediumship can be found in other countries in East and Southeast Asia, the strategies for assuaging these anxieties and fears – spirit mediumship – are culturally specific for certain parts of Vietnam. Applying a human security lens allows us not only to see where *emic* constructions of and strategies towards security converge with or diverge from *etic* constructions; more importantly, it allows us as social scientists to understand where and how different dimensions of human security – health, economic, political, ecological, gender, religious – are interconnected, and thus how specific projects of attaining human security make sense for people living these insecurities and anxieties.

NOTES

1. 'Methodological individualism' is a Weberian notion that society is the result of the actions of individuals, and that the understanding of individual actions and motivations is important for the understanding of social and historical processes.
2. I place the words Buddhist, Confucianist and Taoist between apostrophes in order to indicate that these distinctions are *etic* rather than *emic* distinctions, and hardly do justice to the many syncretistic cross-overs.
3. Stanley Tambiah (1985: 2) uses the word 'efficacy' in relation to ritual in order to be able to understand ritual from an actor's perspective and to avoid becoming entangled in fruitless discussions about rational causality or in positivist statements as to the truth or falseness of ritual claims.
4. Judging from the description this disease may have been psoriasis, which is known to provoke profound and disturbing hallucinations in some people. This is beautifully represented in Dennis Potter's television series *The Singing Detective* (1986) which has recently (2003) been turned into a Hollywood film by Keith Gordon (see http://www.psoriasis.org/publications/advance/singingdetective.php).
5. Lord Tiger and Lord Snake are mythical animals in the Taoist pantheon. The tiger and snake are venerated as part of the Mother Goddess worship and, in many religious traditions in Vietnam, usually have their own small altar on the ground below the main altar.
6. In spirit mediumship, a spirit take possession of the mind of a living person acting as medium, while in shamanism the spirit or soul of the shaman leaves her or his body in order to commune with the spirits.
7. Vietnamese people often use the word *việc* (lit. 'work') in connection with 'family affairs', including care and rituals.
8. These methods are: (1) complete spirit possession (whereby the medium is no longer conscious); (2) partial possession (whereby the medium is conscious of the spirit possession); (3) translation (of the meaning expressed by spirits); (4) prophesying (whereby the medium is making announcements); and (5) being prophesied (whereby the spirits reveal a prophecy to the medium). According to Prof. Nhâts respondents, many people have been able to locate graves or dead bodies in these ways.
9. The Cham are an Austronesian-speaking ethnic group living in pockets in Vietnam, Cambodia, Malaysia, and scattered around the US and France. They form the remnants of an old Hindu trading kingdom on the coast of present-day Vietnam, but most of the present-day Cham are Muslims.

REFERENCES

American Anthropological Association, Executive Board. 1947. Statement on Human Rights. *American Anthropologist* 49(4): 539–43.
Andersson, Jens A. 2002. Sorcery in the Era of Henry IV: Kinship, Mobility and Mortality in Buhera District, Zimbabwe. *Journal of the Royal Anthropological Institute (incorporating Man)* n.s. 8: 425–49.

Appadurai, Arjun. 1999. Dead Certainty: Ethnic Violence in the Era of Globalization. In Birgit Meyer and Peter Geschiere (eds) *Globalization and Identity*. Oxford: Blackwell, 305–24.

Barro, Robert J. 2004. Spirit of Capitalism: Religion and Economic Development. *Harvard International Review* 25(4): 64–7.

Bauman, Zygmunt. 2001. *Community: Seeking Safety in an Insecure World*. Cambridge: Polity Press.

Brown, David. 1994. Ethnicity and the State. In *The State and Ethnic Politics in South-East Asia*. London: Routledge, 1–32.

Burgess, J. Peter (ed.). 2004. Special Section: What Is 'Human Security'? *Security Dialogue* 35(3): 345–88.

Chen, Lincoln and Vasant Narasimhan. 2003. Global Health and Human Security. In Lincoln Chen, Sakiko Fukuda-Parr and Ellen Seidensticker (eds) *Human Insecurity in a Globalizing World*. Cambridge, MA and London: Harvard University Press, 183–94.

Chen, Lincoln, Sakiko Fukuda-Parr and Ellen Seidensticker (eds). 2003. *Human Insecurity in a Globalizing World*. Cambridge MA and London: Harvard University Press, Global Equity Initiative.

Commission on Human Security. 2003. *Human Security Now: Final Report of the Commission on Human Security*. New York: United Nations. URL: http://www.humansecurity-chs.org/finalreport

Department of Social Anthropology. 2004. *Constructing Human Security in a Globalizing World* (research proposal). Amsterdam: Vrije Universiteit/Free University Amsterdam.

Eller, Jack David. 1999. *From Culture to Ethnicity to Conflict: An Anthropological Perspective on International Ethnic Conflict*. Ann Arbor: University of Michigan Press.

Eriksen, Thomas Hylland. 2001a. Between Universalism and Relativism: A Critique of the UNESCO Concepts of Culture. In Jane K. Cowan, Marie-Bénédicte Dembour and Richard A. Wilson (eds) *Culture and Rights: Anthropological Perspectives*. Cambridge and New York: Cambridge University Press, 127–48.

Eriksen, Thomas Hylland. 2001b. 'Ethnic Identity, National Identity and Intergroup Conflict: The Significance of Personal Experiences. In R.D. Ashmore, L. Jussim, D. Wilder (eds) *Social Identity, Intergroup Conflict, and Conflict Reduction*. Oxford: Oxford University Press, 42–70.

Eriksen, Thomas Hylland. 2004. *Risking Security: Paradoxes of Social Cohesion* (inaugural lecture). Amsterdam: Vrije Universiteit/Free University Amsterdam.

Fukuda-Parr, Sakiko. 2003. New Threats to Human Security in the Era of Globalization. In Lincoln Chen, Sakiko Fukuda-Parr and Ellen Seidensticker (eds) *Human Security in a Global World*. Cambridge, MA and London: Harvard University Press, 1–14.

Giddens, Anthony. 1991. *Modernity and Self-identity*. Cambridge: Polity Press.

Heymann, David. 2003. Infectious Disease Threats to National and Global Security. In Chen, Lincoln, Sakiko Fukuda-Parr and Ellen Seidensticker (eds) *Human Insecurity in a Globalizing World*. Cambridge, MA and London: Harvard University Press, 195–214.

Jenkins, Richard. 1996. *Social Identity*. London: Routledge.

Jenkins, Richard. 1997. *Rethinking Ethnicity: Arguments and Explorations*. London: SAGE.

Jenkins, Richard. 2001. The Limits of Identity: Ethnicity, Conflicts, and Politics. Sheffield University Online Paper 2000, URL (consulted August 2006): http://www.shef.ac.uk/socst/Shop/2jenkins.pdf.

Jörgensen, Bent. 2006. Development and 'The Other Within': The Culturalisation of the Political Economy of Poverty in the Northern Uplands of Viet Nam. PhD thesis, Gothenburg University, Sweden.

Kendall, Laurel. 1996. Korean Shamans and the Spirits of Capitalism. *American Anthropologist* 98(3): 512–27.

Keyes, Charles, Laurel Kendall and Helen Hardacre (eds). 1994. *Asian Visions of Authority: Religion and the Modern States of East and Southeast Asia*. Honolulu: University of Hawai'i Press.

Kleinen, John. 1999. *Facing the Future, Reviving the Past: A Study of Social Change in a Northern Vietnamese Village*. Singapore: ISEAS.

Lê Hồng Lý. 2001. Praying for Profit: The Cult of the Lady of the Treasury. Association for Asian Studies annual meeting, Chicago, 22–25 March, URL (consulted August 2006): http://www.holycross.edu/departments/socant/aleshkow/vnsem/lehongly.htmln

Luong, Hy Van. 1993. Economic Reform and the Intensification of Rituals in Two North Vietnamese Villages, 1980–90. In Börje Ljunggren (ed.) *The Challenge of Reform in Indochina*. Cambridge, MA: Harvard Institute for International Development, 259–91.

Luu Hung, Nguyen Trung Dung, Tran Thi Thu Thuy, Vi Van An and Vo Thi Thuong. 2003. Other Journeys of the Dead. In: Nguyen Van Huy and Laurel Kendall (eds) *Vietnam – Journeys of Body, Mind and Spirit* (Exhibition Book, American Museum of Natural History). Berkeley: University of California Press, 196–215.

Malarney, Shaun. 1996. The Limits of 'State Functionalism' and the Reconstruction of Funerary Ritual in Contemporary Northern Vietnam. *American Ethnologist* 23(3): 540–60.

Malarney, Shaun. 2001. 'The Fatherland Remembers Your Sacrifice': Commemorating War Dead in North Vietnam. In Hue-Tam Ho Tai (ed.) *The Country of Memory: Remaking the Past in Late Socialist Vietnam*. Berkeley: University of California Press, 46–76.

Malarney, Shaun. 2002. *Culture, Ritual and Revolution in Vietnam*. Honolulu: University of Hawai'i Press.

Malkki, Liisa. 1995. *Purity and Exile: Violence, Memory, and National Cosmology among Hutu Refugees in Tanzania*. Chicago and London: University of Chicago Press.

Ngô Đức Thịnh. n.d. The Belief in the Granary Queen and the Transformation of Vietnamese Society. Unpublished paper, Viện nghiên cứu văn hóa dân gian, Hanoi.

Nguyễn Thị Hiền. 2002. The Religion of the Four Palaces: Mediumship and Therapy in Viet Culture. Unpublished doctoral dissertation, Indiana University, Bloomington.

Nooteboom, Gerben. 2003. A Matter of Style: Social Security and Livelihood in Upland East Java. PhD thesis, Katholieke Universiteit, Nijmegen.

Ortner, Sherry. 1997. Thick Resistance: Death and the Cultural Construction of Agency in Himalayan Mountaineering. *Representations* 59: 135–62.

Roberts, Richard (ed.). 1995. *Religion and the Transformation of Capitalism: Comparative Approaches*. London and New York: Routledge.

Salemink, Oscar. 2007. The Emperor's New Clothes: Re-fashioning Ritual in the Huế Festival. *Journal of Southeast Asian Studies* 38(3): 559–82.

Salemink, Oscar and Phan Đăng Nhậ (n.d.). Ritual Transformations around a Spirit Medium in the Northern Highlands of Vietnam. Unpublished paper, Second International Conference on Vietnamese Studies, Ho Chi Minh City, 14–16 July 2004.

Schwartz, Barry. 2004. The Tyranny of Choice. *Scientific American* 290(4): 70–75.

Sennett, Richard. 1997. *The Corrosion of Character*. New York: Norton.

Tambiah, Stanley J. 1985. *Culture, Thought, and Social Action: An Anthropological Perspective*. Cambridge, MA and London: Harvard University Press.

Taylor, Philip. 2002. The Ethnicity of Efficacy: Vietnamese Goddess Worship and the Encoding of Popular Histories. *Asian Ethnicity* 3(1): 85–102.

Taylor, Philip. 2004. *Goddess on the Rise: Pilgrimage and Popular Religion in Vietnam*. Honolulu: University of Hawai'i Press.

Tòan Ánh. 1991. *Phong Tục Việt Nam (Thờ Cúng Tổ Tiên)* [Vietnamese Customs (Ancestor Worship)]. Hanoi: Nhà Xuất Bản Khoa Học Xã Hội.

United Nations Development Programme (UNDP). 1994. *Human Development Report 1994*. New York and Oxford: Oxford University Press.

Verkaaik, Oskar. 2003. Fun and Violence: Ethnocide and the Effervescence of Collective Aggression. *Social Anthropology* 11(1): 3–22.

Wilson, Richard A. (ed.). 1997. *Human Rights, Culture and Context: Anthropological Perspectives*. London: Pluto Press.

Notes on Contributors

Ellen Bal is Lecturer at the Department of Social and Cultural Anthropology, VU University, Amsterdam.

Edien Bartels is Lecturer at the Department of Social and Cultural Anthropology, VU University, Amsterdam.

Lenie Brouwer is Lecturer at the Department of Social and Cultural Anthropology, VU University, Amsterdam.

André Droogers is Emeritus Professor, Department of Social and Cultural Anthropology, VU University, Amsterdam.

Thomas Hylland Eriksen is Professor of Social Anthropology and Research Manager at CULCOM, University of Oslo.

Sandra Evers is Senior Lecturer at the Department of Social and Cultural Anthropology, VU University, Amsterdam.

Kim Knibbe is Post-doctoral Fellow at the Department of Social and Cultural Anthropology, VU University, Amsterdam.

Martijn de Koning is Lecturer Arabic and Islam, Radboud University Nijmegen.

Dick Kooiman is Senior Lecturer (retired), Department of Social and Cultural Anthropology, VU University, Amsterdam.

Oscar Salemink is Professor at the Department of Social and Cultural Anthropology, VU University, Amsterdam.

Ton Salman is Senior Lecturer at the Department of Social and Cultural Anthropology, VU University, Amsterdam.

Kathinka Sinha-Kerkhoff is Director Research at the Institute for Asian Development Research Institute (ADRI) in Ranchi, Jharkhand (India).

Marjo de Theije is Senior Lecturer at the Department of Social and Cultural Anthropology, VU University, Amsterdam.

Marion den Uyl is Lecturer at the Department of Social and Cultural Anthropology, VU University, Amsterdam.

Bernhard Venema is Senior Lecturer (retired), Department of Social and Cultural Anthropology, VU University, Amsterdam.

Index

Compiled by Sue Carlton